D0820872

DRAG RACING

DRAG RACING

THE WORLD'S FASTEST SPORT

Timothy Miller

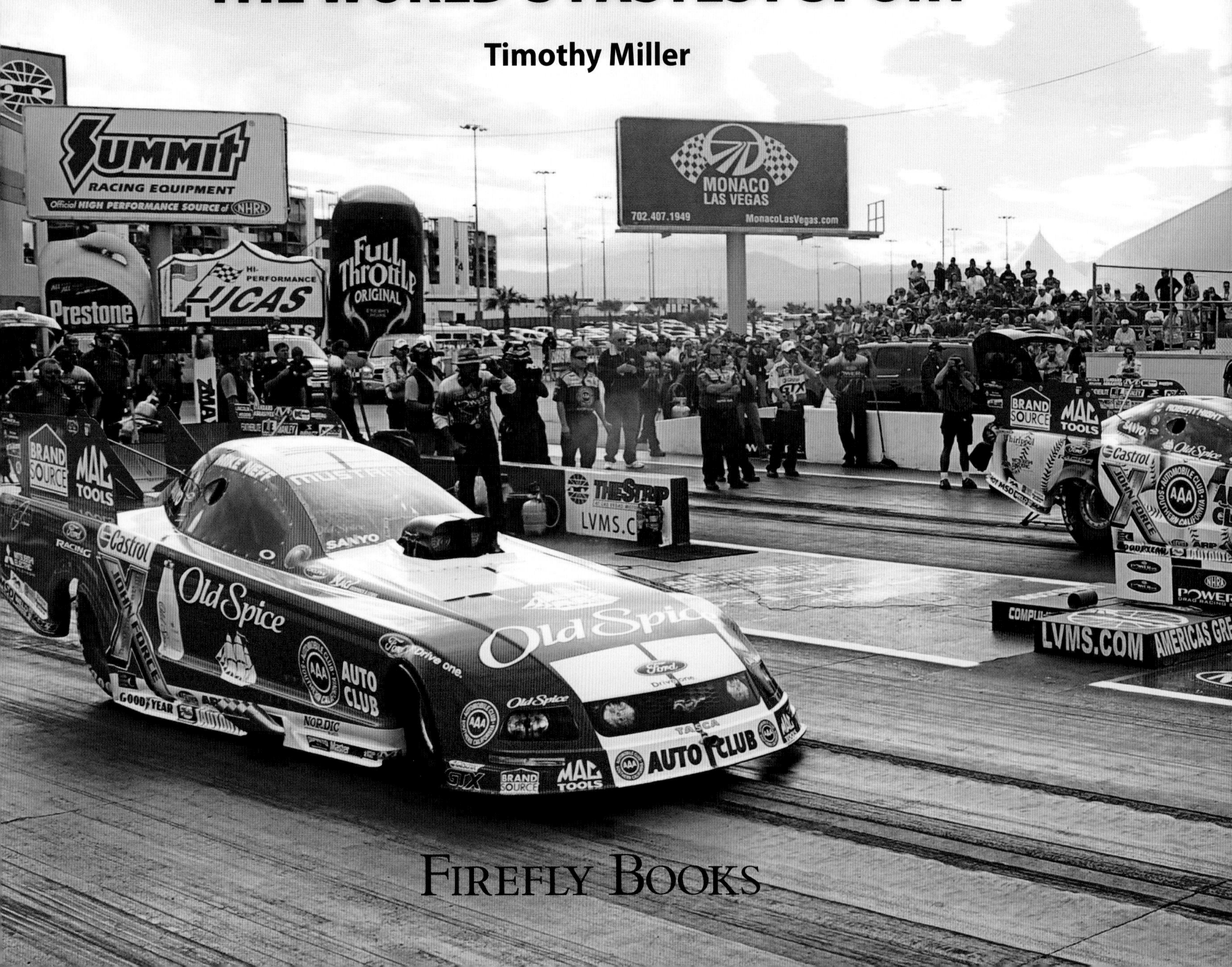

FIREFLY BOOKS

Funny Car drivers Mike Neff (near lane) and Robert Hight get ready for a pass at the November 2008 NHRA ACDelco Nationals at Las Vegas. The drivers are ready, the track is ready, and the fans are ready for the imminent explosion of 15,000 horsepower.

Published by Firefly Books Ltd. 2009

First printing

Publisher Cataloging-in-Publication Data (U.S.)
Miller, Timothy, 1951-
Drag racing : the world's fastest sport / Timothy Miller.
[ ] p. : ill., photos. (some col.) ; cm.
Includes index.
Summary: An illustrated guide to the world of drag racing featuring profiles of top drivers and past legends. Other subjects covered include: history, car classes and rules and regulations.
ISBN-13: 978-1-55407-446-4
ISBN-10: 1-55407-446-0
1. Drag racing. 2. Drag racers – Biography. I. Title.
796.72 dc22 GV1029.3M555 2009

Library and Archives Canada Cataloguing in Publication
Miller, Timothy, 1951-
Drag racing : the world's fastest sport / Timothy Miller.
Includes index.
ISBN-13: 978-1-55407-446-4
ISBN-10: 1-55407-446-0
1. Drag racing. 2. Drag racers--Biography.
3. Automobiles, Racing. I. Title.
GV1029.3.M54 2009 796.72 C2009-900761-4

Published in the United States by
Firefly Books (U.S.) Inc.
P.O. Box 1338, Ellicott Station
Buffalo, New York 14205

Published in Canada by
Firefly Books Ltd.
66 Leek Crescent
Richmond Hill, Ontario L4B 1H1

Cover and interior design: Gareth Lind, LINDdesign
Illustrations: Valerie Potter

Printed in China

The publisher gratefully acknowledges the financial support for our publishing program by the Government of Canada through the Book Publishing Industry Development Program.

Dedication

This book is for Kendall Hebert, a young soul who lost her life doing what she loved best.

Credits

Front Cover: David Allio/Icon SMI
Back Cover: Jeffrey Corder/Icon SMI (Top Left), Tim Defrisco/Getty Images (Top Right), David Allio/Icon SMI (Bottom)
Valerie Potter (Illustration)

A racing icon in his own time, John Force continues to compete and is the biggest name in the sport. He is shown here at Las Vegas in April 2008.

Contents

It doesn't get any better than this. John Force (near lane) and Cruz Pedregon in qualifying runs at Las Vegas in November 2008. Both Funny Cars are running well, as noted by the even, light-yellow flames coming from the headers.

PEDREGON
TOYOTA
Advance Auto Parts
Snap-on
HERZOG
GREAT STUFF
MSD
NATIONALS
JOHN FORCE 7
MUSTANG
Castrol
GTX
HIGH MILEAGE
Old Spice
MAC TOOLS
BRAND SOURCE
Drive one.
AUTO CLUB
AAA
JOHN FORCE
FRAM
NORDIC
Autolite
GOODYEAR
WELD

PONTIAC
GOODYEAR
EAGLE
U.S. ARMY
goarmy.com

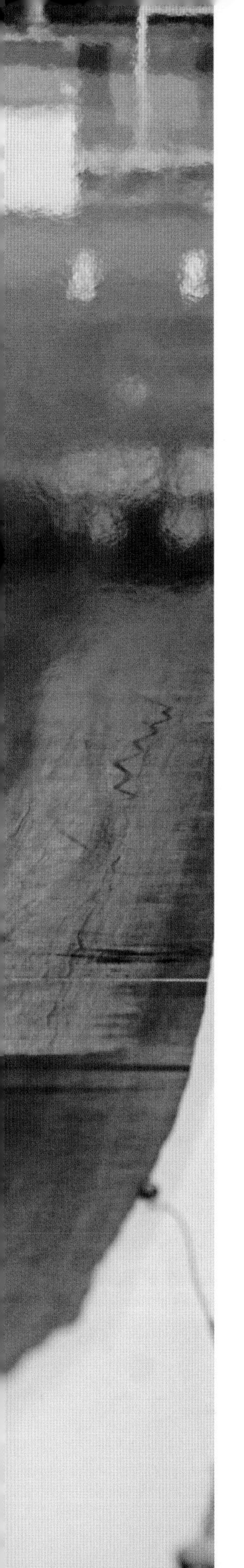

Introduction

Once considered the "bad boy" of motorsport, drag racing has evolved into one of the most technically sophisticated forms of motorized competition. And it produces some of the most exciting racing, based on a simple premise: two drivers race their vehicles, from a standing start, over a measured distance (usually a quarter-mile), competing for the shortest elapsed time.

From its California roots after World War II, drag racing spread throughout North America in the 1950s and 1960s, and today there are close to 400 facilities devoted to straight-line racing. As well, this motorsport has crossed the ocean and established itself in Great Britain, Europe, Australia and New Zealand—something other forms of auto racing can only dream of.

Drag racing has also broken out of the men-only traditional mold when it comes to competitors. It has always welcomed women racers, some of whom have become major players in the sport. It has also embraced youth like no other form of racing, with programs such as Junior Dragsters and Tuner car events where young people can compete.

Fans of drag racing enjoy an atmosphere that allows them to walk through the pits at the track and watch the teams at work on their cars between races, something unheard of in other types of racing. Fans can also, at times, meet their heroes in the pits, and many a child has gone home happy, after getting a hero-card autograph or a chance to sit in a race car.

From the pioneers and their crude homemade cars built with no aftermarket speed equipment and raced on impromptu tracks with virtually no crowd control or fire and safety gear to today's multimillion dollar touring teams and professional racing venues, drag racing stages an assault on the senses like no other form of racing. It entertains in a colorful, loud, fast-paced environment that explodes upon the viewer. Some classes of cars literally shake the ground with the body-thumping vibrations of the loudest mechanical vehicles on the planet. Just watch a person who is witnessing a Top Fuel matchup for the first time. When the tire smoke clears, their jaw is still wide open and their eyes are as big as saucers.

Drag Racing not only talks about where drag racing has been, it also talks about today's racing and the current trends that will help form the future of drag racing. You'll read about the legends of the sport, and how the various sanctioning bodies have shaped drag racing. You'll learn the basics of the sport, and about the makeup of a 7,500-horsepower missile-on-wheels. You'll also get a better understanding about the importance of youth in drag racing, and read about some of the more prominent builders in the sport.

So get staged and watch that Tree!

The air above the track is filled with heat as Top Fuel drivers Brandon Bernstein (left lane) and Tony Schumacher make their qualifying passes at the NHRA Summit Racing Nationals at Las Vegas in April 2008.

A Quarter-mile History

In the vast realm of motorsport, the world of drag racing stands out as a unique form of racing. To the uninitiated, two cars racing side by side down a short length of track seems very simplistic and uncomplicated. And in the beginning, drag racing was simple: It followed the age-old ritual of pitting two individuals against each other in a simple contest of speed. Whoever got to the finish line first was declared the winner.

Since the advent of the automobile over 100 years ago, there has always been the desire to include cars in these competitions. Impromptu, illegal and dangerous contests were held on city streets and country roads. While races of this nature were held in most communities, the seeds of organized drag racing began on the dry lake beds in California before World War II.

Using fenderless, cut-down car bodies, mostly Ford Model Ts and Model As, and powered by Ford's Flathead V8 engines, contestants originally raced against the clock on a measured distance, usually a mile. There was a lot of specially built aftermarket speed equipment developed to make the coupes and roadsters go faster in a variety of classes, depending on weight and engine power.

These "hot rods" ran against the clock on the lake beds; however, the competitive spirit in the racers eventually took on an additional aspect—racing against each other. Sometimes up to five cars were

After his TV and film career, Tommy Ivo had the finances and background to take drag racing to a new level of showmanship. Ivo toured the country with this glass-sided trailer showcasing his two Top Fuelers, while his "around-town" Corvette sat up top.

TOMMY IVO
POWERED
FUEL DRAGSTERS
6.72 E.T.
MEGUIAR
ISKENDERIAN
SUMMERS BROS
KEYSTONE
CYCLONE
TRW
HAYS
DIEST
LAKEWOOD IND
CRAGAR
MALLORY
MILODON
AUTOLITE
VHT
AIRHEART-HURST

After World War II, automotive speed shops offered car enthusiasts a huge variety of performance parts. Here, two racers are checking out multi-carburetion setups. Note the "Don't Speed" sign on the display at right.

lined up in what was known at the time as acceleration races, a dangerous practice on the dusty surfaces. Racers following the leaders would have a difficult time seeing through the dust kicked up from the surface and if a car got out of line or lost a wheel, it could cause a multiple-car pile-up.

After World War II, several things happened that resulted in these acceleration contests becoming the basis of drag racing. Race organizers did away with multiple-car races, pitting only one pair of cars against each other at a time. Servicemen returning from the war had learned a great deal about then state-of-the-art machinery and metallurgy and began applying this knowledge to their race cars: weight-reduction techniques, multiple carburetion and aircraft-inspired aerodynamics.

The introduction of overhead valve V8 engines by Cadillac and Oldsmobile in 1949 also played an important part in the sport's development, providing racers with engines much more powerful than the Ford Flathead, which was approaching its 20th birthday. Across the country, but mostly centered in California, the speed-equipment industry thrived.

All this speed equipment was designed for racing, but before 1950 a lot of that racing took place on the street. The result was a never-ending battle between street racers in their hot rods and law enforcement. People were hurt or killed, and not just the hot

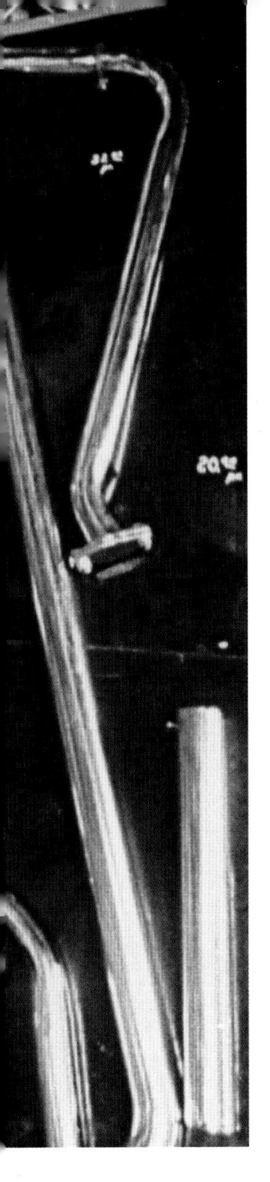

rodders. Many times the road would be lined with spectators, and a car getting out of control could result in tragedy.

By 1950, men with vision started to hold organized drag racing in a controlled environment, and this started on airstrips in Southern California, which offered nice long, smooth, straight runways. Racing at abandoned airstrips mushroomed in California, and it didn't take long to spread to the rest of the U.S. and Canada. While hot rodders and street races remained a couple of steps behind the California fraternity, the longing to compete burned brightly everywhere.

While weekly elimination-based contests were developing on the drag strips, street racing continued in an ugly tug-of-war between law enforcement and rodders. Although most rodders organized into car clubs, and members provided road-friendly services such as cruising highways to help stranded motorists, drag racing still had a negative image.

Wally Parks and His Vision

In 1948, former dry lakes racer Wally Parks co-published, along with Bob Petersen and Bob Lindsay, the first edition of *Hot Rod Magazine*, and Parks became the magazine's first editor. Through the publication, Parks learned there was a large number of enthusiasts who wanted to organize their racing. In May 1951, the National Hot Rod Association (NHRA) was formed with Parks as president, and former racer and Southern California Timing Association president Ak Miller as vice president. Membership in the NHRA could be obtained for two dollars, and within two months there were 350 members.

A large part of the NHRA's mandate was to work with law-enforcement groups in establishing organized and controlled racing events. Car clubs across the nation united with this new sanctioning body, and the clubs worked with their local communities to help get racing off the streets. By 1952, there were 7,000 members in the NHRA. A year later, the NHRA developed rules for car classes, safety guidelines and drag strip layouts. Its first races were held during this time, and spectators in the thousands turned out to watch pioneer racers such as Jack Chrisman and Joaquin Arnett, who raced short-wheelbase front-engined dragsters, and former oval-track racer Don Nicholson, who went on to a great career in Stock and Funny Car racing.

In its quest to not only promote the new sport, but give it legitimacy, the NHRA established its Safety Safari in 1954. This team of drag racing ambassadors

HOT ROD *Magazine*

VOL. 1, NO. 1 PRICE 25c

WORLD'S MOST COMPLETE HOT ROD COVERAGE

JANUARY 1948

HOT ROD OF THE MONTH

Sitting in the driver's seat is Eddie Hulse, who, a few moments after this picture was taken, drove number 668, to set a new SCTA record for Class C roadsters. Hulse, a native Californian, nosed out Randy Shinn, a long-time top honor holder for the RC Class. Shinn's old record was 129.40 in a channeled Mercury T.

Keeping the Car Out Front by George Riley—Page 10

***Hot Rod Magazine*; Vol. 1, No. 1. Started in 1948, *Hot Rod* became the bible for rodders and racers, and it continues to this day with car profiles, race results and how-to articles.**

One of drag racing's true pioneers, Chicago's Chris "The Greek" Karamesines began building and racing dragsters in the 1950s. Now in his 70s, he continues to compete with a Top Fuel dragster.

toured the country to introduce drag racing to potential racers and fans, and show concerned groups that drag racing was a viable, controlled, safe form of auto racing.

The NHRA held its first national meet in Kansas in 1955. During this four day event, Calvin Rice of California won the Top Eliminator title in the fastest of the 30 classes in his dragster with a 10.30 second, 141.95 mph posting. Throughout the remainder of the decade the NHRA continued to grow in size and stature, adding new classes of cars, including the Stock and Super Stock divisions.

Prior to 1957, after experimenting with alcohol and methanol to power their cars, dragster teams had been using nitromethane, an organic compound developed as a cleaning solvent. This super fuel, when mixed with gas, produced unheard of power. But it was expensive, dangerous and could blow a gasoline car's engine up all over the track. In 1958, the NHRA made a decision to ban fuels other than gasoline in cars, citing preferences of California track operators, in the interests of safety concerning volatile fuels and in the interests of competition concerning ever rising costs. (The ban on the use of nitro and other exotic fuels was enforced until 1963.)

A Home for Fuel Cars

While there were dozens of classes in drag racing by 1958, the fastest cars—the dragsters—were the most popular and received the most recognition from the press and fans. After developing engines based on running nitro, these teams were reluctant to return to running straight gasoline. Also the fans wanted to see the fastest cars, and to draw the largest audiences, the track promoters relied on booking the fastest cars. Promoters needed these cars and their drivers, men such as Don Garlits, Chris "The Greek" Karamesines and Emery Cook.

The gas-powered dragsters of the late 1950s were on average 25 mph slower than fuel cars. A good run of 140 mph at 10.5 seconds for a gas dragster was viewed as standing still when compared to a run of 160 mph at 9.5 seconds in a fuel car.

In 1954, the then one-year-old Chicago-based Automobile Timing Association of America (ATAA) staged its World Series of Drag Racing in Illinois, with fuel cars grabbing the spotlight. Soon after, the Kansas City based American Hot Rod Association (AHRA), established in 1956, began racing fuel cars, with former racer Jim Tice overlooking the sanctioning body. The ATAA's World Series of Drag Racing continued for a couple of years, but merged into the NHRA in 1958.

Welcoming and running fuel cars ended up being the AHRA's ace up the sleeve. Even without the NHRA's penchant for publicity and its membership organization, the AHRA grew in scale from its small midwestern beginnings to include national races in Arizona, California and Texas. By 1969 the AHRA boasted 10 national events at places such as

Detroit, New York, Tennessee and Oklahoma. In 1970 the NHRA announced two new events: the Gatornationals in Florida and the Summernationals in Pennsylvania, boosting its national event total to seven, including the World Finals and the NHRA World Championship Series.

Two New Racing Divisions

While fuel dragsters were the mainstay of AHRA competition, the sanction also fostered the development of two classes that have become mainstays in the world of drag racing. Through the evolution of the Super Stock class, the Pro Stock and Funny Car classes emerged.

Super Stock cars became very popular in the 1960s, with strong factory involvement from Ford, General Motors and Chrysler. Running engines of over 400 cubic inches, this semi-professional class with few mechanical limitations evolved into a class called Super Stock Eliminators and led to the formation of today's Pro Stock class. With the 427-cubic-inch Ford Mustangs and Chevy Camaros, and the 426-powered Plymouth Coronets and Barracudas, these 10-second, 130-mph cars were instant hits with the fans in show and match racing. By 1970 the cars were toned down as the class developed, using smaller, non-supercharged engines and returned to more stock-appearing cars. The class of Pro Stock thrives today and is a professional division in NHRA and IHRA competition.

NASCAR Ventures into Drag Racing

In the mid-1950s, stock car giant NASCAR took a sharp turn from its traditional oval track ventures with a solid attempt at sanctioning drag racing. There was some straight-line action as early as 1956 as part of the Daytona Beach Speedweeks.

A major event was held four years later. Wally Parks and NHRA division director Ernie Schorb met with NASCAR vice president Ed Otto and presented the week-long Winternationals at Daytona Beach's Spruce Creek Drag Strip in February 1960. As the NHRA had a ban on fuel cars, dragster teams, such as Don Garlits's, modified their engines to run on gasoline so they could take part in the event.

While Garlits, who was the local hero, accumulated enough points in several races during the week to win the overall Top Eliminator prize, he had a fight with Parks after he turned around on the track and drove back up the strip after the start of a run. Parks disqualified Garlits for the race, and the feud lasted many years. The legendary dragster pilot match-raced across the country and ran with the AHRA before returning to NHRA competition.

After this one-time trial of 1960, NASCAR made a committed foray to drag racing in 1965, and for the next two years, up to 29 strips operated under NASCAR, closely following NHRA rules and car classifications. Ed Witzberger headed up this division from his Pittsburgh, Pennsylvania, base. Most tracks were in Ohio, New Jersey and Virginia, although there were some sanctions farther away, such as Niagara International in Western New York and the Cayuga drag strip in southern Ontario, Canada.

NASCAR believed it was filling a void in drag racing. In the east there were many oval tracks, and the NASCAR name was established in the racing world. It thought it could plant some drag racing roots, as the NHRA was more west-coast oriented, with only a couple of solid footholds in the east.

NASCAR highlighted its early drag racing with match races between some of its Grand National personalities. Fireball Roberts, Fred Lorenzen and Wendell Scott were among Grand National drivers that did some match racing. Richard Petty campaigned a Barracuda while he sat out of Grand National racing over a fight with NASCAR head, Bill France, regarding the use of the powerful Chrysler Hemi engine. Cotton Owens built the Cotton Picker, a crowd-pleasing, rear-engined Dodge Dart station wagon.

The 1966 program ran four national events, and there was a weekly tour package including races with Top Fuel dragsters and Grand Stock (NASCAR's name for Super Stock). The shows had NASCAR's organizational expertise, good crowds and good car counts. But by the end of 1967, car counts began to drop as the NHRA moved into the east. As a result, NASCAR pulled the plug on drag racing and returned to focus on what it did best in the racing world.

In 1964, Jack Chrisman set the stage for today's Funny Cars, as he ran the first supercharged, nitro-powered, flip-top, altered wheelbase car: a supercharged nitro-burning 427-cubic-inch Ford under a Comet body shell.

The other offshoot of the Stock Eliminator—the Funny Car class—went the opposite way. The big engines, exotic fuels and superchargers went into an anything-goes division with production car bodies; but this was soon to change.

Altering a race car's wheelbase for better weight transfer and traction had been applied for many years, but on stock-bodied cars, the appearance of these wheelbase alterations were a caricature of the car's true dimensions, and the term "Funny Car" was applied.

Officially, the cars were classed as Factory Experimental (FX), and several Dodges and Plymouths showed up to race at the 1965 AHRA Winternationals, some with the front wheels moved forward 10 inches and the back wheels 15 inches to the rear, driven by such notables as Sox and Martin, Bill Jenkins and Tommy Grove with his "Melrose Missile."

These cars were not sanctioned by the NHRA, but that did not stop competitors like Don Nicholson or Jack Chrisman or Gene Snow from driving specially built, one-piece fiberglass-bodied replicas of Comets and Darts with supercharged nitro-burning engines. With its one-piece, flip-top body hinged at the rear to enhance engine and cockpit access, the name flop, or flopper, became common, a term still used today to describe the car's classification. At first, the cars were usually booked in races by track promoters as match or exhibition cars, but as the Funnies, which were becoming very popular, developed into a legitimate class they became sanctioned by the NHRA (in 1970).

The Drag Racers' Union

Up to the early 1960s, the two major existing sanctioning bodies with national events throughout the country, the NHRA and the AHRA, had been ruling drag racing with an iron fist, but professional racers and the other competitors began to demand more prize and appearance money. In 1963, racer Tom McEwen and a former drag strip manager, Doug Kruse, formed the United Drag Racers Association (UDRA), not only to promote better events, but to work with racers, car owners and track promoters, and to foster better relationships among all parties involved.

This democratic thinking was compared in the press of the day to the labor union movement in the early 1900s, and how the laborers (racers) did all the work while the management (track owners) reaped the profits. But through the efforts of McEwen and California dry lakes racer and engine builder Lou Baney (Kruse went back to promoting in Southern California and building dragster bodies), the UDRA treated the racers with more respect and larger purses (especially those who raced Top Fuelers — the fastest cars). While the UDRA basically died in California, its original idea was kept alive and it has grown over the decades to become a solid owner/driver motorsports organization based in the Chicago area, with chapters across North America.

In keeping with its mandate of giving the drivers and teams a voice in its operations, the UDRA backed away from the ever-increasing expense of fuel cars, and in the 1970s had a streamlined group of classes on the circuit with alcohol-powered dragsters and Funny Cars, and Unlimited Pro Stockers. Some name racers who came up through the ranks of the UDRA include Dick LaHaie, Warren Johnson and Frank Hawley.

Today, this nonprofit racing organization features three classes at several Midwestern U.S. venues: supercharged Funny Car, supercharged Dragster and Pro Modified.

Match Races and Exhibitionists

In an effort to not only race, but to survive, professional and semiprofessional drag racers would compete in one-on-one matches with similar cars, a practice that continues but on a much smaller scale. These events would be highly publicized by the local track promoter much the way a boxing promoter publicizes the "main event." For many fans, it would be their only chance to see their straight-line heroes in action.

Before she climbed into a Top Fuel Dragster, Shirley Muldowney teamed up with Connie Kalitta and drove her "Bounty Huntress" Funny Car, shown here in the mid-1970s.

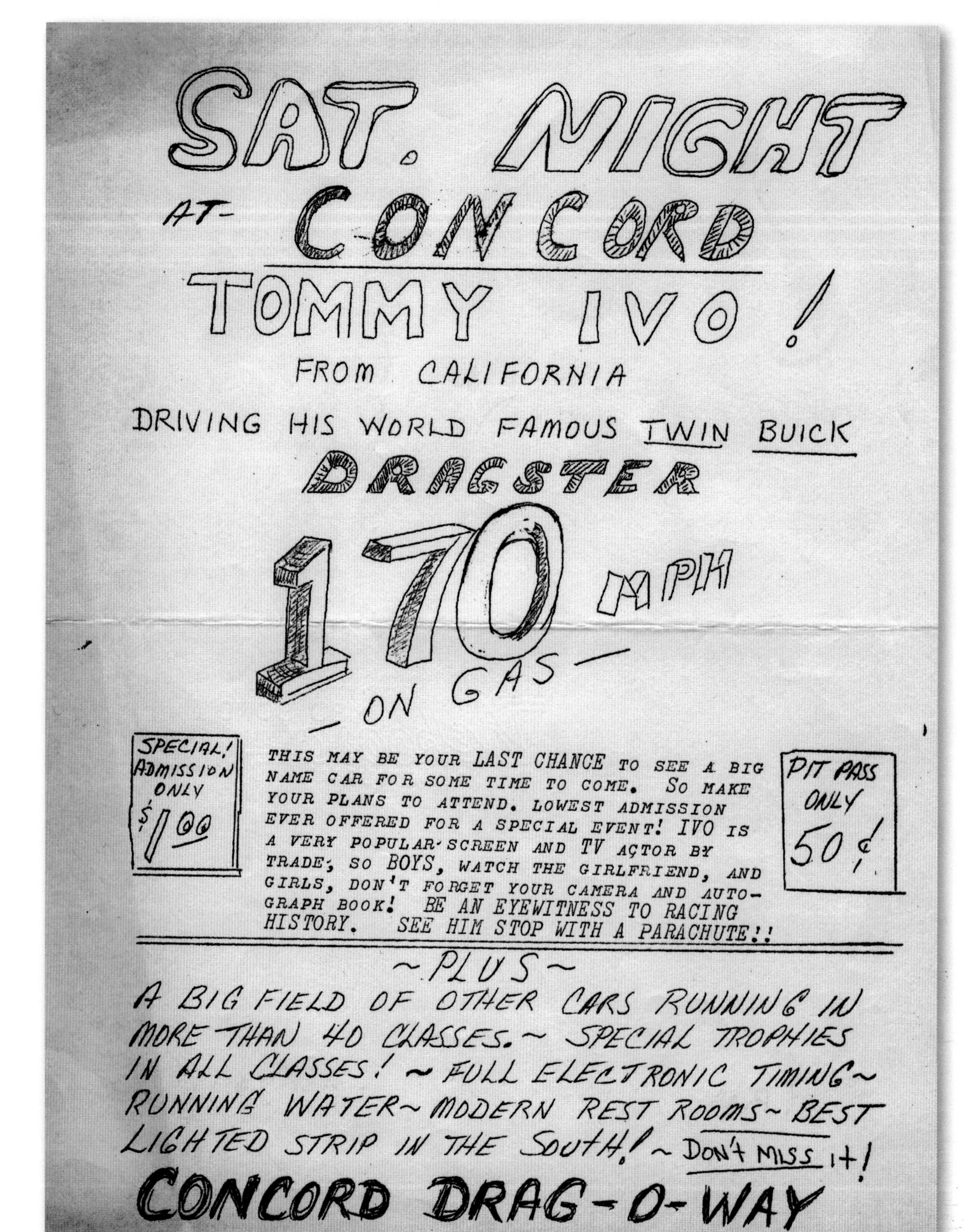
SAT. NIGHT
AT- CONCORD
TOMMY IVO!
FROM CALIFORNIA
DRIVING HIS WORLD FAMOUS TWIN BUICK
DRAGSTER
170 MPH
— ON GAS —
SPECIAL! ADMISSION ONLY $1.00
THIS MAY BE YOUR LAST CHANCE TO SEE A BIG NAME CAR FOR SOME TIME TO COME. SO MAKE YOUR PLANS TO ATTEND. LOWEST ADMISSION EVER OFFERED FOR A SPECIAL EVENT! IVO IS A VERY POPULAR SCREEN AND TV ACTOR BY TRADE, SO BOYS, WATCH THE GIRLFRIEND, AND GIRLS, DON'T FORGET YOUR CAMERA AND AUTOGRAPH BOOK! BE AN EYEWITNESS TO RACING HISTORY. SEE HIM STOP WITH A PARACHUTE!!
PIT PASS ONLY 50¢
~PLUS~
A BIG FIELD OF OTHER CARS RUNNING IN MORE THAN 40 CLASSES.~ SPECIAL TROPHIES IN ALL CLASSES! ~ FULL ELECTRONIC TIMING~ RUNNING WATER~ MODERN REST ROOMS~ BEST LIGHTED STRIP IN THE SOUTH!~ DON'T MISS it!
CONCORD DRAG-O-WAY

The Concord Drag-O-Way operated from the late 1950s through to the mid 1960s on a stretch of pavement 100 feet wide, located one mile outside the city limits of Concord, North Carolina; a far cry from today's state-of-the-art facilities. This poster was made for a special event in 1960.

Match race competition was unique to auto sport. While other car racing, such as oval track, provided weekly shows featuring touring drivers, the competition in drag racing was organized in such a way that racers stuck close to home. For major oval-racing circuits like NASCAR Grand National or USAC Champ Car racing, the schedule was long and arduous, and there was little time for extracurricular auto events or appearances. The prize money offered oval racers was also much greater, as was sponsorship money to help offset costs.

Although oval-track racing had its outlaw drivers and hired guns that would show up at the local dirt track from time to time, match racing seldom occurred in oval racing, despite being a way of life for many drag racers.

Although most drag strips were sanctioned, only the best in terms of driver and fan amenities were selected for the large national events, which guaranteed fast, star-studded lineups. Small-time track operators needed to put fans in the seats, so a cottage industry within the drag racing world was established where the racing "stars" would get booked into smaller facilities. Although at first handled by the teams themselves, eventually drag racing booking firms were established.

Almost all professionals match-raced to help pay their expenses. They traveled like gypsies, racing at one track one night, packing up and then hauling all night and a big chunk of the next day to another match event hundreds of miles away. They had to carry lots of spare parts in case of breakage, and pray the engine in the pickup hauling them, or the race car, would not blow up.

Match racing made a lot of sense for a racer who was not concerned with winning national titles. A name match racer would show up at a track as the headliner, get lots of local publicity, wow the fans with his runs, sign autographs in the pits and pick up his appearance money after the racing was finished. A match racer also did not have to run his equipment into the ground trying to beat his opponent. Usually a match-race event would be the best two wins out of three. Most match racers traveled together, and sometimes worked out a "you win at this track, and I'll win at the next one" system, not unlike deciding the winner in a wresting match, just to keep the fans interested.

Some drag racers made a good living at match racing, and some made a big name for themselves. Drivers such as Tommy Ivo and Jungle Jim Liberman rarely competed in points meets, preferring to wow the fans with their show, and get handsomely paid for their efforts. Don Garlits was match racing steadily in the late 1950s, and was booked into countless shows with the likes of Setto Postoian, Chris "The Greek" Karamesines and, later, Shirley Muldowney.

As Funny Cars became popular, fans flocked to the local strip to see the Floppers match-race, especially the fuel cars. The stands would be jammed when Don Prudhomme went up against Gary Burgin, or when John Force raced Bruce Larson.

Several women drivers were very popular on the Funny Car match-race circuit, including Paula Murphy, Della Woods and Carol Burkett.

Exhibition-type drag racing began in the early 1960s using jet-powered vehicles, and while the purists scoffed at this, it became very popular with the fans. Walt Arfons and Romeo Palamides started the trend, bolting a General Electric or Westinghouse jet engine designed for aircraft to a home-built frame with four wheels. Due to the nature of the jet engine, the thrust would come on gradually, not like an internal combustion engine, which developed all its power at once.

So, while a fuel dragster would leave the starting line in a great hurry, a jet car would take its time with a minimum of excitement. But by half track, the excitement had done an about-face, and while a piston engine would be out of power, the jet would be coming into its own as the thrust built up.

With times and speeds unheard of, and with a showy, smoky entrance to the starting line, jet cars were a track promoter's dream come true. Fans couldn't get enough of the jet-powered cars.

But jet cars were regarded by the sanctions as freaks, and even though the technology for these cars has evolved greatly over the years, there is still no official competition for them with respect to drag racing sanctioning bodies. The jet cars were allowed on AHRA tracks, and eventually by 1975, the NHRA was not banning its member tracks from running them.

So jet cars raced jet cars, putting on a great show for the fans. And then jet cars would race Top Fuel dragsters, which was a great show as the dragster would take off in a flurry and by half track the jet would catch up and the race could then belong to either racer.

The jet cars, called "weenie roasters" by the fans, did have a poor safety record. The cars were very fast at the top end, and had problems slowing down, even with bigger and bigger parachutes. The greatest drawback was when an engine exploded, which could send pieces across a huge area, much larger than when a conventional engine exploded at speed.

But issues were addressed, and jet cars, whether they are in dragster, Funny Car, or truck mode (Les Shockley built a Peterbilt semi truck with three jet engines), are still very popular on the match-race circuit.

The other nontraditional drag racing vehicle that became the mainstay of exhibition racing is the wheelstander. Developed in the mid-1960s, these racers, which rode down the track on their rear wheels only, are some of the best known vehicles in drag racing. The Hurst Barracuda "Hemi Under Glass," Bill Golden's "Little Red Wagon" and Chuck Poole's "Chuckwagon" are very familiar names in drag racing.

Jet-powered vehicles have become a mainstay of drag racing entertainment. Les Shockley's Shockwave, capable of speeds over 250 mph in the quarter mile, is the ultimate in this kerosene-burning class of exhibition vehicles.

Bill "Maverick" Golden's "Little Red Wagon," shown here pitted against Bob Riggle in the Hurst "Hemi Under Glass" do battle at Ohio's Thompson Drag Raceway in 1968.

Considered by drag racing purists to be the "clowns" of the sport, wheelstanders do race down the track, but do it with such a flair for exhibitionism that they cannot be taken seriously.

And these vehicles got wilder and wilder. Used in the early 1960s, the cab-over-engine pickup, such as Ford's Econoline and Dodge D100, gave the driver some view of the track, but for others a hole in the floor was what gave the driver some idea of where he was going. All types of vehicles showed up to do battle, from a wide variety of car-based bodies to the outrageous, such as school buses, fire trucks and military tanks.

Wheelstanders are still very popular, and will be booked in for shows between rounds of drag cars in regular competition.

The AHRA's Star Begins to Fade

During the 1970s, the AHRA continued to expand, and it brought forth ideas in drag racing that are now taken for granted. For example, in 1970 it introduced its Grand American Series of Drag Racing which involved the season-long concept of a points chase. The Grand American Series involved all the big racers who toured the circuit working towards the ultimate goal of amassing enough points in their class to be declared the champion at the end of the season. A lot of premier drag racers got their start, and found their place, in the AHRA world, including Jeb Allen, Richard Tharp and John Force (who won his first Funny Car title in AHRA competition in 1984).

The other major step forward in the drag racing world, at least for the drivers, was the introduction of large payout purses. Most of the professional drivers were not satisfied with hauling all over the country only to race for paltry payouts. Some of the more prominent racers banded together with Jim Tice and in 1972 put on the inaugural "National Challenge" for the professional classes.

From 1961 until 1976, the AHRA held its most prestigious event at Green Valley Race City in Texas, and continued with its other national events across the country.

But the AHRA began to suffer due to low sponsorship and low car counts, especially after 1975 when both the association's old rival, the NHRA, and new rival, the IHRA (the International Hot Rod Association), received major funding from the R.J. Reynolds Tobacco Company (through its Winston brand of cigarettes sponsorship). Both the NHRA and IHRA were solidly entrenched with large payouts, more national events and the ever-important television coverage. The AHRA name is still used in some events in Washington State, but when AHRA president Jim Tice died in 1984, in essence so did the AHRA.

The NHRA Continues to Grow

Under the leadership of Wally Parks, the NHRA established major events throughout the U.S. in the 1960s and 1970s. In 1963, two significant factors boosted the presence of the NHRA. The nitro-burning dragsters returned to regular competition, and the U.S. Nationals, the NHRA's biggest race, was televised nationally.

During this time, participating NHRA track counts began to grow, along with membership, and in 1970, both Pro Stock and Funny Car were introduced as professional categories along with Top Fuel. Three years later, the Alcohol Dragster and Funny Car classes were introduced. Then in 1975, a points system was established, along with the announcement of a $100,000 Winston Drag Racing Series points fund from the tobacco giant R.J. Reynolds, a company that would stay with the NHRA for the next 27 years. In 1983, the points fund was up to $325,000, was double that in 1987, and hit more than $2.2 million in 1995.

By 1975, there were eight national events on the schedule, and the first Winston champs were Don Garlits in Top Fuel, Don Prudhomme in Funny Car and Bob Glidden in Pro Stock.

While originally the NHRA board had been comprised of former racers, car builders and track

Big Money for the Big Classes

Tired of the NHRA's low payouts, some professional racers got together with AHRA president Jim Tice in 1972 to form the Professional Racers Association (PRA). Don Garlits was the main proponent for the PRA, and the new organization's objective was to have a large payout for a Labor Day event going up against the NHRA's Nationals in Indianapolis.

Sanctioned by the AHRA, the 1972 "National Challenge 72" was held at Tulsa with a purse of $150,000, the largest ever posted in drag racing at the time. Prizes for Top Fuel, Funny Car and Pro Stock were to be $25,000 each and, according to Garlits, who was PRA president at the time, many thousands in contingency money had been raised.

In a letter dated July 6, 1972, sent to PRA members from PRA President Don Garlits, he emphasized that no-one who entered the National Challenge 72 should feel they were switching sides and leaving the NHRA Nationals.

"For those of you who have been pressured by the powers that be, let me say this, come Labor Day weekend, it's your right as citizens of a free country to race where you please," Garlits said in his letter. "We of PRA would love to have all the professionals racing at Tulsa for a truly professional purse of $25,000 to Win, plus Contingencies for TOP FUEL, FUNNY CAR and PRO STOCK, instead of peanuts and a trophy, and a lot of supposed 'publicity.' "

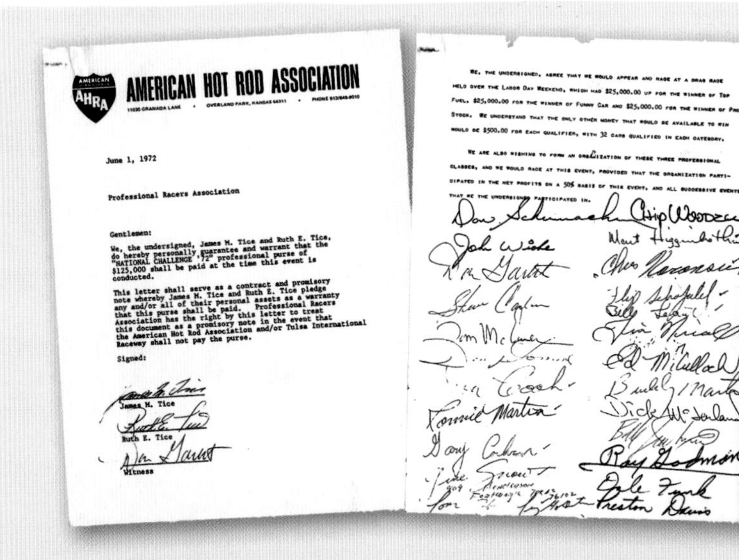

AMERICAN HOT ROD ASSOCIATION

11030 GRANADA LANE • OVERLAND PARK, KANSAS 66211 • PHONE 913/649-8010

June 1, 1972

Professional Racers Association

Gentlemen:

We, the undersigned, James M. Tice and Ruth E. Tice, do hereby personally guarantee and warrant that the "NATIONAL CHALLENGE '72" professional purse of $125,000 shall be paid at the time this event is conducted.

This letter shall serve as a contract and promisory note whereby James M. Tice and Ruth E. Tice pledge any and/or all of their personal assets as a warranty that this purse shall be paid. Professional Racers Association has the right by this letter to treat this document as a promisory note in the event that the American Hot Rod Association and/or Tulsa International Raceway shall not pay the purse.

Signed:

James M. Tice

Ruth E. Tice

Witness

We, the undersigned, agree that we would appear and race at a drag race held over the Labor Day Weekend, which had $25,000.00 up for the winner of Top Fuel, $25,000.00 for the winner of Funny Car and $25,000.00 for the winner of Pro Stock. We understand that the only other money that would be available to win would be $500.00 for each qualifier, with 32 cars qualified in each category.

We are also wishing to form an organization of these three professional classes, and we would race at this event, provided that the organization participated in the net profits on a 50% basis of this event, and all successive events that we the undersigned participated in.

Attached to the letter was a list of 34 pledging sponsors for the event, several (including Keith Black, Champion Spark Plugs and Crane Cams) with $1000 for each of the three classes. Goodyear Tire, Firestone Tire and M&H Tires all pledged $600 each, as did the header firms of Hooker, Hedman, JR and Doug's.

As Garlits and the PRA planned the National Challenge 72, the NHRA had already cautioned its track owners in a letter dated May 11, 1972.

"As some of you are aware, a movement is underway to force higher purses in drag racing," stated the NHRA letter. "It is spearheaded by some of the sport's top

A racer performs a burnout prior to a run at the NHRA World Finals at Pomona in 1995. The sanctioning body long enjoyed the support of tobacco giant R.J. Reynolds and its Winston brand.

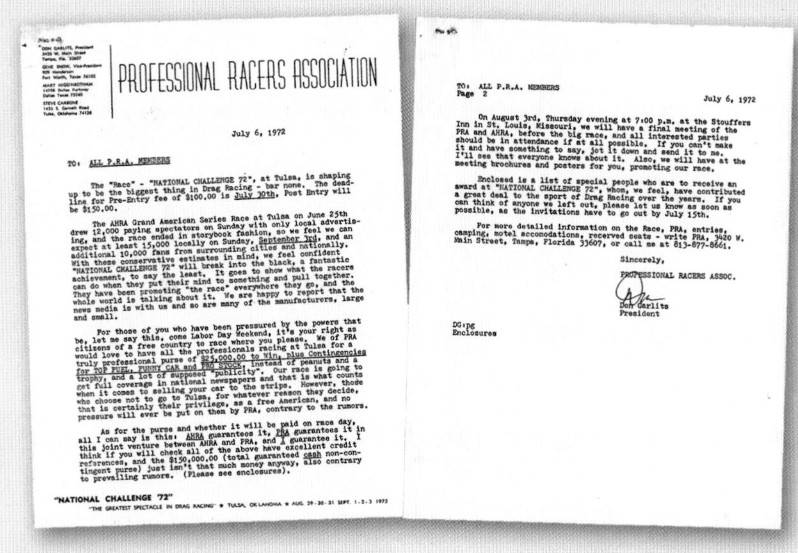

DON GARLITS, President
3420 W. Main Street
Tampa, Fla. 33607
GENE SNOW, Vice-President
909 Henderson
Fort Worth, Texas 76102
MART HIGGINBOTHAM
14700 Dallas Parkway
Dallas Texas 75240
STEVE CARBONE
1433 S. Garnett Road
Tulsa, Oklahoma 74128

PROFESSIONAL RACERS ASSOCIATION

July 6, 1972

TO: ALL P.R.A. MEMBERS

The "Race" - "NATIONAL CHALLENGE 72", at Tulsa, is shaping up to be the biggest thing in Drag Racing - bar none. The deadline for Pre-Entry fee of $100.00 is July 30th, Post Entry will be $150.00.

The AHRA Grand American Series Race at Tulsa on June 25th drew 12,000 paying spectators on Sunday with only local advertising, and the race ended in storybook fashion, so we feel we can expect at least 15,000 locally on Sunday, September 3rd, and an additional 10,000 fans from surrounding cities and nationally. With these conservative estimates in mind, we feel confident "NATIONAL CHALLENGE 72" will break into the black, a fantastic achievement, to say the least. It goes to show what the racers can do when they put their mind to something and pull together. They have been promoting "the race" everywhere they go, and the whole world is talking about it. We are happy to report that the news media is with us and so are many of the manufacturers, large and small.

For those of you who have been pressured by the powers that be, let me say this, come Labor Day Weekend, it's your right as citizens of a free country to race where you please. We of PRA would love to have all the professionals racing at Tulsa for a truly professional purse of $25,000.00 to Win, plus Contingencies for TOP FUEL, FUNNY CAR and PRO STOCK, instead of peanuts and a trophy, and a lot of supposed "publicity". Our race is going to get full coverage in national newspapers and that is what counts when it comes to selling your car to the strips. However, those who choose not to go to Tulsa, for whatever reason they decide, that is certainly their privilege, as a free American, and no pressure will ever be put on them by PRA, contrary to the rumors.

As for the purse and whether it will be paid on race day, all I can say is this: AHRA guarantees it, PRA guarantees it in this joint venture between AHRA and PRA, and I guarantee it. I think if you will check all of the above have excellent credit references, and the $150,000.00 (total guaranteed cash non-contingent purse) just isn't that much money anyway, also contrary to prevailing rumors. (Please see enclosures).

"NATIONAL CHALLENGE '72"
"THE GREATEST SPECTACLE IN DRAG RACING" ★ TULSA, OKLAHOMA ★ AUG. 29-30-31 SEPT. 1-2-3 1972

TO: ALL P.R.A. MEMBERS
Page 2

July 6, 1972

On August 3rd, Thursday evening at 7:00 p.m. at the Stouffers Inn in St. Louis, Missouri, we will have a final meeting of the PRA and AHRA, before the big race, and all interested parties should be in attendance if at all possible. If you can't make it and have something to say, jot it down and send it to me. I'll see that everyone knows about it. Also, we will have at the meeting brochures and posters for you, promoting our race.

Enclosed is a list of special people who are to receive an award at "NATIONAL CHALLENGE 72", whom, we feel, have contributed a great deal to the sport of Drag Racing over the years. If you can think of anyone we left out, please let us know as soon as possible, as the invitations have to go out by July 15th.

For more detailed information on the Race, PRA, entries, camping, motel accomodations, reserved seats - write PRA, 3420 W. Main Street, Tampa, Florida 33607, or call me at 813-877-8661.

Sincerely,

PROFESSIONAL RACERS ASSOC.

Don Garlits
President

DG:pg
Enclosures

names, and the plan is to produce an event that will compete directly against our Nationals on Labor Day weekend."

After mentioning that the NHRA had been providing larger purses for its major events, the letter added the NHRA had been aware of its responsibility to its tracks and the tracks' operating costs.

"We do not, therefore, intend to succumb to pressures that are suggested in this direct competition, by top stars, against the Nationals," the letter continued. "Our purse will be moderately increased, as it has been each year, within what we consider to be practical limits."

This PRA event was to be a pro race only, no stockers or other slower classes—a format similar to the Professional Dragster Association, founded in California in 1967 to stage high-paying dragster-only events.

Tice suffered some financial problems connected with the 1972 event, which was won by Tom McEwen, Don Moody and Bill Jenkins in their respective classes. The teams were paid in full, but the event did not generate as much money as hoped. The race was held again in 1973 in Tulsa, but was moved one week ahead of the NHRA U.S. Nationals in a spirit of cooperation with the NHRA, which had raised its purses after witnessing the success of the 1972 meet. While not a financial success for its principles, the Tulsa meet was highly successful in showcasing the best teams and drivers.

But again in 1973, Tice lost money. For 1974, a new venue was tried, and although it started with lots of publicity and good intentions, the race on New York's Long Island was a disaster, with poor track organization, rules interpretations and inclement weather.

The event was held for two more years, once at Great Lakes near Milwaukee, and finally at Lakeland, Florida, but the purse and the field of cars was a mere shadow of the first year's event.

With the influx of R.J. Reynolds Tobacco's sponsorship money in 1975, and the start of the Winston points championships in both the NHRA and IHRA, racers started to see larger payouts, and so another obstacle in the realization of drag racing as a major sport had been overcome.

While it never did get as big as the NHRA, the upstart IHRA of the 1970s offered racing just as fierce. Here Clare Sanders and crew celebrate their win with motorsport's first lady, Linda Vaughn, at the IHRA Summer Nationals at Ohio's Dragway 42 in 1972.

owners, there was a new generation of business-oriented professionals coming on board. In 1973, Dallas Gardner started at the NHRA as a financial consultant with a background at Ontario Motor Speedway in California. In 1978, he began serving as the NHRA's vice president and general manager, in 1984 was promoted to president, and became chairman of the board in 2000.

Another Sanctioning Body

Founded by Tennessee businessman Larry Carrier in the fall of 1970, the International Hot Rod Association became a small thorn in the side of the NHRA, and eventually a big thorn in the side of the AHRA.

Based in the southeastern U.S., the IHRA acquired some plums of race tracks including Dallas International Motor Speedway and York (now used only for nostalgia events). The IHRA was the first to sign, in 1974, with R.J. Reynolds Tobacco Company for the lucrative title sponsorship for a series of races and season points battles, and were teamed for a decade.

The tobacco sponsorship came at a very opportune time, not only for the IHRA, but for the NHRA a year later. Drag racing was in a bit of a lull as NASCAR became more dominant in the minds of car racing fans and began to not only build from its southern roots, but also started to offer huge payouts to its drivers and teams through the sponsorship of R.J. Reynolds and its Winston brand of cigarettes.

Drag racers looked on in envy at the prize money going into NASCAR, especially the professional drag racing teams who traveled all over the continent trying to make a living running in one-night events. The Winston sponsorships to the IHRA and NHRA provided an influx of money at this time, and gave drag racers some clout when banging on doors for corporate sponsorship. The entire sport started to receive respect and recognition it had not previously experienced and, by the mid-1970s, the perception of its street racing background holding minor-league events disappeared.

The IHRA continued to grow east of the Mississippi River, but was never a threat to the NHRA. It offered a lower-cost product to teams and fans with a mixture of quarter-mile and eighth-mile strips peppered throughout the Southeast.

By 1975, the IHRA was holding eight national events with a format similar to the NHRA, and attracted many major stars of the day, including Don Garlits, Bill Jenkins, Sox and Martin, Billy Meyer and Raymond Beadle.

Top Fuel was dropped in 1984, but returned three years later. Fuel Funny Cars were dropped starting in the 1991 season, returning to the series in 2006. Escalating costs were the reason given.

In 1990, the IHRA introduced its Pro Modified class, a division of very popular full-fendered cars. The Pro Mod class developed as a more powerful extension of Top Sportsman, the IHRA's quickest class in the amateur ranks. With their widely-diverse body styles and supercharged engines, Pro Mods became an important element in the IHRA's makeup, and remain so to this day. While the NHRA has exhibition-type events for Pro Mods at its national events, it has not welcomed the class with the enthusiasm of the IHRA.

After floundering a bit in the 1990s, the IHRA, through the leadership of then-president Bill Bader, acquired prominence in drag racing with the help of the Hooters restaurant chain as title sponsor, and Michigan-based Torco Racing Fuels. The motorsport division of Feld Entertainment, one of the North America's leading entertainment companies, now owns the IHRA.

The IHRA has found a solid audience in Canada,

Al Billes, a former Pro Modified driver, is now the class's top engine guru and tuner. His services are provided to a number of Pro Mod teams.

as two of the association's 10 national events are held across the border. Drag racing has been a mainstay of the Canadian motorsport scene since the early 1950s, and is well represented in both NHRA and IHRA racing. For close to 20 years, the NHRA Grandnationals held at the Sanair Motorsport Complex near Montreal was a constant on the national circuit, but when the NHRA moved the event to Kansas in 1993, there was a need for a major event in Canada. This void was filled when the IHRA held the Mopar Parts Canadian Nationals in 2000 on the shores of Lake Huron at Grand Bend, Ontario. The IHRA's other Canadian event was established in Edmonton, Alberta, in 2003.

Not only do these Canadian events draw large crowds, there are a large number of IHRA competitors that are Canadian. Some prominent Canadians in IHRA racing include Rob Atchison in Funny Car, and Pro Mod drivers Carl Spiering and Tony Pontieri.

The Middle-East Connection

In 2008 drag racing was provided new impetus with the introduction of new Middle-Eastern endeavors.

Alan Johnson, one of the most successful crew chiefs in NHRA Top Fuel racing, partnered with His Highness Sheikh Khalid Bin Hamad Al Thani to form Al-Anabi Racing. This new team two-car NHRA effort

A new chapter in drag racing took place early in 2009 when ace crew chief Alan Johnson (center) and his Al-Anabi team began to compete in the NHRA with well-known drivers Del Worsham (left) in a Funny Car and Larry Dixon (right) in Top Fuel.

has entries in Top Fuel and Funny Car competition. Veteran Funny Car driver Del Worsham was signed to drive the team's Funny Car. Late in 2008 Larry Dixon severed his 20-year association with Don Prudhomme and Snake Racing. Dixon purchased his release from Prudhomme, and now drives the Al-Anabi Top Fueler.

At the forefront of this partnership is Al Thani's goal to promote the domestic and international awareness of motorsports in the nation of Qatar. Johnson is a seven-time NHRA Top Fuel Championship crew chief, including leading the Tony Schumacher-driven U.S. Army Dragster to four consecutive Top Fuel titles.

Along with the new fuel team, Al-Anabi Racing has built a drag race facility in Qatar, and the Al-Anabi team has several Pro Modified cars and drivers competing locally in Qatar, as well as having class aces Mike Castellana and Shannon Jenkins competing under its umbrella in the IHRA and NHRA. The Pro Modified class has also been embraced in Bahrain (an island state in the Persian Gulf between the coasts of Saudi Arabia and Qatar) with the Popeye Racing Team. It too has many local racers, as well as NHRA Top Fuel driver Hillary Will, who debuted the Kingdom of Bahrain KB Racing, LLC Top Fuel dragster at the inaugural NHRA Carolinas Nationals in September of 2008.

The American Drag Racing League

A new kid on the block has taken a unique and successful approach to drag racing.

The ADRL, started in 2004 from its Missouri base with Outlaw Pro Modifieds (cars with performance modifications not allowed in IHRA or NHRA sanctioned events), offers heads-up racing in several doorslammer classes at several eastern and southern U.S. tracks. By keeping admission prices low, and offering non-stop eighth-mile racing, the ADRL has become a fan favorite. The ADRL's Pro Extreme, Pro Nitrous, and Extreme 10.5 classes have been experiencing large car counts for its 16-car fields, and its top two classes have been filled with many Pro Modified teams using both superchargers and nitrous powered cars. Cars in the Pro Extreme class are capable of sub-four-second clockings at speeds of just over 200 mph.

Running at 1000 Feet

Imagine two NFL teams playing on a field 20 yards shorter than the standard length; imagine the Indianapolis 500 shortening its race to 400 miles. Modifications this immense would forever change each spectacle—and in drag racing, a change of this magnitude is taking place.

Prompted by the death of Funny Car driver Scott Kalitta in June of 2008, along with the death of Funny Car driver Eric Medlen in 2007 and the bad crash of legend John Force in the same year, the NHRA decided to take a stand in the interest of safety for the drivers of nitromethane-burning Top Fuel Dragsters and Funny Cars by establishing a new 1,000-foot track length. Racers previously darted down a quarter mile; the new length is 320 feet shorter. The hope is that the new length will keep top speeds down, which will allow engines to run less vigorously and heighten overall safety.

On the traditional quarter-mile track, the speeds of both classes are well over 325 mph at times in the mid-to-high four-second mark. On the new track, the cars are still very quick. Top Fuel Dragsters are posting under four-second times at speeds of over 315 mph, while clockings for Funny Cars have decreased to times just over four seconds at speeds just over 300 mph.

A whole new era in drag racing began in July 2008 at Denver for the running of the 29th annual Mopar Mile-High Nationals. It did not take long for the fuel teams and drivers to adapt to racing on the shorter track.

"We've always been a good ET car not so much a big speed car so I don't expect the shortened track will change how we do things," NHRA 2008 Funny Car champ Cruz Pedregon said going into Denver. "The main thing, and I can say this with certainty because I've competed in a lot of eighth-mile races, is paying attention to where you are on the track. If you're standing there looking at 320 feet, it looks like a long way, but when you're going 300 mph, 320 feet is nothing."

Some drivers, like 2008 NHRA Top Fuel champ Tony Schumacher welcomed the new format.

"I think it's great," said Schumacher about the rule change. "The NHRA needs time to fully evaluate and analyze what happened with Scott's crash. Until there are some clear, definitive findings, we need to do this."

Schumacher also thought the show for the fans would not really be any different.

"No question about it," he added. "In fact, there may be better side-by-side racing. I guarantee you that the sights and sounds of nitro racing will still be there."

And drag racing icon John Force has said the new track length has been a positive move. "NHRA made the right call," said the 14-time Funny Car champion. "The stands are still full, the racing is closer than it's ever been in Funny Car—it's like Pro Stock. There's so many positives to stay at 1,000 feet than to go back to 1,320."

Some of the other positives in the shorter track have been a noticeable reduction in costs. The highly-temperamental fuel engines still pack the same wallop, but are no longer running at maximum output for as long, resulting in less breakage. Tire failure on the rear slicks has also been lessened since the new track length was instituted. Cars that do lose their braking power or suffer a parachute malfunction have more track to slow down on. The NHRA has said it will work with fuel teams to develop new engine combinations to reduce the power in the two classes, and the 1,000-foot track will remain for the 2009 season.

Drag Car History

Not long after the invention of the automobile, the popularity and accessibility of cars led to the sport of auto racing in all shapes and sizes. Before World War II, road and oval track racing were the prominent contests, but some performance-driven individuals started to compete in an organized fashion on the flat dry lake beds of California.

Most cars were cut-down Model T and Model A coupes and roadsters, and Flathead Ford V8 engines were the norm in measured mile top-speed competition, where racers raced the clock to beat previously posted times. But these same cars were also going head-to-head in straight-line match racing. It was a simple premise: the first one to the finish line won the race.

Flatheads were cheap and reliable, and there was a large performance aftermarket industry that catered to the Ford engine introduced in 1932. When the Cadillac and Oldsmobile overhead valve V8 engines were introduced in 1949, hot rodding and racing hot rods went to the next level with these powerful engines.

Racers learned quickly that to go fast, a car had to have maximum power and minimum weight, and by the early 1950s, multi-carbureted V8 engines were wedged between crude, home-built chassis with little regard to safety, braking and aerodynamics.

Men working on a multiple-carb "nailhead" Buick engine with homemade headers mounted in a Ford roadster with whitewall tires—the scene is from Long Island, New York, in the 1950s, but it could have been from any dragstrip of the era.

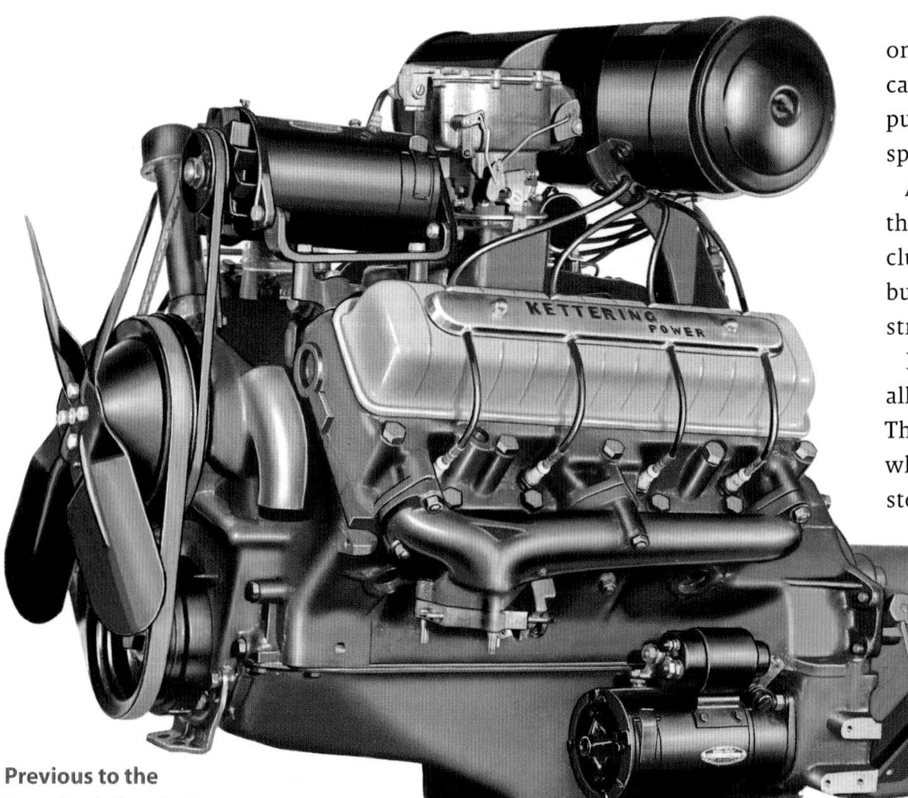

Previous to the launch of Chrysler's Hemi in 1951, the 303-cubic- inch "Rocket" Oldsmobile V8 engine (pictured), along with the new Cadillac V8 from General Motors, became the engine of choice in 1949 for street rods and drag cars, replacing the Ford Flathead V8.

The vehicles and technology of drag racing evolved differently from other racing such as stock cars or the open-wheeled cars of the Indy-style Champ Car circuit. There were some crossovers between the different cars, mostly in the use of weight-saving metals and fuel-management systems, but builders of drag racing cars did not have to worry about sophisticated suspension systems or aerodynamics as did builders of Grand National stockers or Offy-powered roadsters. For the builders of drag cars, their task was simple—in theory, anyway—and that was to produce the most power possible and get this power through the back wheels and onto the drag strip.

There were several other factors to differentiate a drag car from other racing automobiles. Many drag racers used their street cars for racing, and while these cars would have powerful engines, the owners obviously needed their creature comforts and legal items for cruising the boulevards and going to the drive-ins. Drag racing was a sport for the masses, and one could take their non-modified, everyday driving car to the strip to race. Just take off the hubcaps and put on a helmet and go racing—an aspect of the sport that continues to this day.

And while hot rodders could individually race their cars, most were members of car clubs. A car club was able to pool its talent and resources to build an all-out race car that would get towed to the strip each weekend.

During the 1950s, a number of classes evolved, all based on the familiar power-to-weight formula. The groundwork was being developed to cover the whole spectrum, from the quickest dragsters to stock six-cylinder sedans, and it is from this foundation that drag racing matured to its present state.

Dragsters

Racers with the most knowledge and money tried their hand in the sport's top class: the Dragsters. The cars we today refer to as dragsters were also known as "rail-jobs" or "slingshots." These front-engined cars were built of tubular steel, or "rails," and would accelerate so quickly it appeared as if they were "shot out of a cannon" or accelerated like they were "fired from a slingshot." Racers such as Mickey Thompson, Don Garlits and Pete Robinson, along with many others, played trial and error for several years until the formula for a successful dragster was "right."

Robinson, who worked out of Atlanta, was a master builder in the early years and an expert on removing unnecessary weight from a car. He won the 1961 NHRA Nationals with a light dragster and a small (352 cubic inches) Chevy engine with a supercharger. He experimented with aerodynamics on dragsters, along with some unorthodox engines, such as Ford's overhead cam V8. Unfortunately, he died from injuries sustained in a crash in 1971.

Thompson was a California hot rodder who did it all: raced cars, built cars, managed drag strips and produced his own line of aftermarket performance parts.

Before Thompson went off to the Bonneville Salt

Flats in 1958 to compete and set numerous speed records, he raced in the early slingshot dragsters, and knew there had to be a better way to get the power to the track.

In dragster development in the early 1950s, it was thought power was the key to success. Of course power is important, but in those early times, it was discovered the key to success in drag racing was to get the power to the rear wheels for the best straight-line traction. Former dry-lakes cars were either shelved or rebuilt to provide longer wheelbases and better engine placement in the car's frame for better traction over the rear wheels.

There were others who were working on this, but Thompson was instrumental in narrowing the rear axle, which greatly improved the straight-line takeoff of a dragster and directional stability. He also introduced 12-inch slicks to the sport in 1963, another important enhancement, which helped get the ever-increasing power to the back wheels.

Garlits started racing in his native Florida in 1950. By 1955 he had built and was racing (and winning) with his first dragster, a typical for-the-period, home-built creation with a Flathead Ford V8. But over the next three years, the race cars out of his Tampa shop were powered with Chrysler Hemi engines, longer wheelbases, and had streamlined body work. In 1958, he was turning 180 mph and was winning many titles. He became the best dragster driver, at least east of the Mississippi River, although his innovations were scorned by the California racers who believed they were the best.

When Garlits learned that the California racers were junking the carburetors on their engines and using modified versions of the General Motors supercharger designed for diesel engines, he followed suit, and continued to win.

When the NHRA banned the use of the exotic and volatile fuel called nitromethane in 1958, Garlits, along with some other professional racers, continued to compete with their fuel-fed cars in match races and meets with other sanctioning bodies. While his succession of "Swamp Rat" dragsters followed most of the conventional updates, he was able to spearhead the trial-and-error development of running his cars on nitro, and work with the people who designed and built internal parts for these engines. He also learned the volatile characteristics of nitro and had a head-start on blending nitro with other fuels such as gasoline and alcohol when fuel cars returned to the NHRA in 1963 (where gas-fueled dragsters had been the quickest class).

There had been some rear-engined cars in the 1950s and 1960s, but they were not very successful. Multi-engined cars had also been developed during the NHRA fuel ban as a single engine running on gasoline could not develop nearly the horsepower as nitro, so two 1,000-horsepower engines were coupled together, but their success was limited and this area of development was eventually dropped. Drivers such as Texan Eddie Hill and movie and

Top: Mickey Thompson and crew pose with his Challenger I land speed car at Bonneville in 1960. This car made Mickey the first American to break the 400-mile-per-hour barrier.

Bottom: Mickey Thompson poses in 1954 with the first ever "slingshot" dragster.

Tommy Ivo's personal favorite car: Showboat. Built by Ivo, the dragster is powered by four Buick engines. Showboat was the most publicized car of the time, gracing the covers of just about every car magazine during its heyday in the early 1960s.

television personality Tommy Ivo campaigned multi-engined cars with some success, but after the 1963 fuel ban in the NHRA was lifted, almost all dragsters ran single engines.

While there were numerous updates and improvements in all areas of dragster development during this time, the overall premise of the car's design, with the engine in the front of the chassis and the driver hanging right at the rear of the car over the rear axle, continued.

But a driver's vision was hampered in a front-engined dragster as he had to try and see over and around the tall powerplant. There was also a serious safety element for the driver. If an engine or part of its driveline, especially the clutch, blew up under acceleration, a multitude of bad things could take place.

If an engine sprung an oil or fuel leak while racing, the driver would be showered in fluid, restricting his vision or to the point of not seeing where he was going at all. If the belt on the supercharger broke, it became an errant missile which could smack back into the driver, or go sailing off into the crowd. This could also happen when a supercharger blew up. When an entire engine blew up, a trip down the strip could be devastating. A fire could ensue at 200 mph with flames coming right back into the cockpit. A hole punched through the side of the engine would dump oil on the racing surface, right in front of the rear wheels, resulting in the car spinning wildly out of control.

All Top Fuel drivers knew the hazards. Many of them had experienced at least one heart-stopping ride down the quarter-mile. Several had met their death.

But in 1970, a serious accident endured by Don Garlits ushered in the modern era of dragster design.

In the final round of an AHRA meet at Lions Drag Strip in California in 1970, Garlits was paired with Richard Tharp. As the pair left the line, there was an explosion from Garlits's car, and the car broke in two between his cockpit and the engine. It was later established that the transmission in his car had exploded, and parts came through the steel plate and metal safety blanket below Garlits. Garlits was taken to the hospital with a big part of his right foot missing, and while he was recuperating, he vowed he would design and race a rear-engined car.

Garlits enlisted the help of chassis builder Connie Swingle to build his first rear-engined car, with a 215-inch wheelbase, 426 Dodge engine, and no gearbox, just high gear. Noting that rear-engined dragsters of the day would go fast, but developed very unpredictable handling at high speed, initial testing in Florida showed the cars did not handle well, and the new Garlits car was subject to the same handling characteristics.

After some trial and error with the steering gear, Swingle modified the gear to a slower ratio, and the magic combination was discovered.

Don Garlits's front-engined dragster, Swamp Rat 13, exploded at Lions Drag Strip in 1970, and as a result provided the biggest innovation in dragster development. While Garlits recovered in hospital, he designed a car with the engine behind the driver, providing a great increase in driver safety.

Looking naked without the rear wing, Garlits's first rear-engined car, Swamp Rat 14, was scoffed at initially, but when he started winning with it, the rest of the dragster world quickly followed suit.

While Garlits and his crew were subjected to a lot of ridicule when the new car debuted at the end of 1970, Garlits won several major meets and broke track records everywhere in 1971.

As the rest of the teams scrambled to build rear-engined cars, the modern age of the dragster began, and the foundation for present-day Top Fuelers was set.

Although dragsters were deemed the sport's top class, and received the most attention from builders, track promoters and the fans, slower classes were receiving no less attention in design, development and the quest to go faster.

Stockers

Fans loved to see the out-and-out power and noise of the fuel dragsters, but also enjoyed watching cars they could relate to battle on the strip. As with oval-track stock car racing, loyalty between the makes of cars was important in drag racing for the fans. And for competitors, dragging a car in the Stock classes was an inexpensive way to get into the sport.

By the early 1960s, the Stock classes had been established, using an alphabet designation. The quickest and most powerful cars were in the A/S (A-Stock) class, and this system went right through the alphabet, down to W/S. This system, based on a car's power-to-weight ratio, allowed for fair racing that would pit cars of similar power against each other.

A handicapped starting system was developed that allowed a slower car, such as an E/S car, to get the green light at the line just before a faster A/S car. The slower car could be some distance down the track before the faster car started, and tried to catch its opponent before the end of the quarter-mile.

The cars derived the "stock" aspect of their name the same way oval-track stock cars did: the cars are essentially the showroom stock automobiles available for purchase by anyone. Over the years racers have worked on ways to improve the performance of their "stock" autos, but what keeps the class honest is that a Stock class car can't have chassis or body alterations, and the majority of the mechanical parts must retain the car's corporate identity.

The Super Stock classes developed as a higher, or quicker, level of the Stock machines with engine modifications and weight-saving body panels.

In the early 1960s, with the help of factory backing from the automakers, Super Stock classes developed into pure racing machines, with fiberglass and aluminum body panels for weight reduction, and running the carmaker's biggest engines. Ford, General Motors and Chrysler all fielded teams with these factory hot rods—cars that appeared stock but could never be driven on the street.

The Super Stock wars became very popular with the fans, and the competition could be as heated in the stands as on the track, as the fans would cheer on their favorites in the Ford versus Chrysler versus

Shirley Shahan was the first woman to really crack the male domination of drag racing. After winning the Stock class at the 1966 NHRA Winternationals, the "Drag-on-Lady" continued to race for several more years from her California base.

GM battles. An extension of the Stock Eliminator class, Super Stock became a separate NHRA class in 1967, and the big players in the class were Bill Jenkins, Don Nicholson, and Sox and Martin.

And as the full-size, two-door sedans in the early 1960s made way for the smaller and lighter mid-size sedans, carmakers continued to produce a small quantity (sometimes as low as 50) of cars outfitted with their biggest engines, specially-made running gear and driveline components, and hand-built body shells. Running on an index system as the Stock classes, today's Super Stock cars use the same letter system, and obviously get down the track quicker, with nine-second runs approaching 150 mph.

Altereds

Considered by many to be one of the hardest cars to drive in drag racing, these short-wheelbase cars with nitro-burning supercharged engines showed fans some of the wildest rides, and for the drivers, some of the scariest times behind the wheel of a race car.

Officially known as AA/Fuel Altereds, these cars became popular in the early 1960s, and were powered by the same engines as fuel dragsters. But with such a short wheelbase underneath the Fiat or Bantam roadster body, the cars were a real handful for the drivers when they hooked up.

Although there were not many of these cars, they were a big draw by 1965. There were gas-fueled

"Wild Willie" Borsch performing a burnout in his nitro-powered Winged Express at an evening show at Ohio's Thompson Drag Raceway in 1970.

Altereds with smaller engines, but it was the supercharged nitro-burning cars the fans loved. As one of these 1,000-horsepower cars would head out on a seven-second, 200-mph run, the acceleration would push the driver over to the left side of the car as it hooked up, and he would have to fight to keep the car under control.

Men like "Wild Willie" Borsch and Dale Emery routinely entertained the fans with wheelstands and sideways runs while producing speeds close to a dragster on trips down the quarter-mile.

While the Altereds were popular, by the late 1960s they began to take a back seat to a new class that was considered even more outrageous, the Funny Car.

The Altered's heyday was over by 1971. Some were still competing, but many of the teams got into Funny Cars, which had taken over the number two spot behind Dragsters on the fan scale. Some cars did continue racing in Competition Eliminator ranks, with a longer wheelbase and looking more like a Funny Car underneath but, while exciting to watch, they were not in the same wild category of 10 years earlier. In the late 1970s, Altereds were being built on a Funny Car platform, but their popularity continued to wane. Today, there are several nostalgia-based organizations that have brought back these wild and interesting cars, touring in match-race competition.

Gassers

In the early 1960s, another craze hit the drag strips. In their quest to build fast cars, drivers learned the simplest way was to stuff the most powerful engines in the smallest cars. When supercharged engines running on gasoline were set up in a short-wheelbase light car such as a 1941 Willys or an Austin, fans flocked to see these full-bodied cars with their precision wheelstands. Both the NHRA and AHRA ran Gassers in the A/GS, B/GS and C/GS classes, depending on engine size. The class was restricted to a 90-inch (AHRA) or 92-inch (NHRA) wheelbase. While larger cars such as the 1955 Chevrolet were also popular sitting up high with their straight front axles and flip-up fiberglass front ends, the Austins, Anglias and especially the Willys, became the cars of choice. The early 1950s' Henry J was also a popular car in this class. Although the 1940–41 Willys became the more prominent car, there was a strong following with the 1933 Willys coupe, including George Montgomery, who became a prominent eastern U.S. driver with the name of "Ohio George." Other big names in the Gasser class included John Mazmanian, the team of Stone, Woods & Cook and the Kohler Brothers.

Before he became one of the top proponents of today's modern Pro Modified class, Jim Oddy of Buffalo was always a top contender in his blue BB/GS Austin sedan.

Two of the Gasser greats do battle as K.S. Pittman, with the wheels up on his 1933 Willys, races the 1940 Willys of Stone, Woods & Cook in a 1967 match race event.

By the late 1960s, the older body styles were not as common, and smaller foreign makes such as Opel along with Mustang and Camaro bodied cars started to show up. Up to 11 classes of Gassers were offered, from A/Gas with a minimum five pounds per cubic inch weight to K/Gas with a minimum 10 pounds per cubic inch.

Gassers added a lot of color to the 1960s drag racing scene, posting speeds of 150 mph with the front wheels popping up off the track after each shift.

With the advent of Funny Cars, the Gassers lost some of their appeal, although they are very popular in today's nostalgia meets.

Floppers

The Super Stock Eliminator class of the early 1960s led to the formation of two of drag racing's most prominent classes, one, a logical extension of the stock-car format, which became known as Pro Stock, and the other a totally different approach originally intended for speed and showmanship. These big-engined Mustangs, Camaros and Barracudas that posted quarter-miles of 10-seconds, at 130 mph became the basis for the Funny Car, and there was more to come.

In 1964, Jack Chrisman showed up at the NHRA Nationals with a supercharged, fuel-burning Comet with a slightly altered wheelbase. Although the car appeared close to stock, the interior was gutted, most of the Comet's body was fiberglass, and the car could run in the low 10-second range at 150 mph. It wasn't long before the car received a tubular frame and ran as a supercharged exhibition stocker.

Racers the likes of Chrisman, Don Nicholson and Gene Snow continued altering wheelbases for their cars in order to gain better weight transfer and traction. The distorted dimensions, in contrast to the stock appearance were truly something to behold, and the tag "Funny Car" was given to these nitro-burning vehicles. As the class continued to evolve, the Funnies moved further and further away from the stocks they once were. The car body was replaced with a one-piece, flip-top, fiberglass shell,

A Funny Car interior, circa 1970. Bobby Wood is seen here sitting in the driver's seat of his rare Chevy Nova bodied Flopper. Note the crude, but necessary, driving suit and minimal cockpit.

hinged at the back—which gave drivers and teams better access to the cockpit and engine—earning the cars the nickname "Flopper."

The cars were an instant hit, and teams scrambled to build one of these cars as the momentum continued. But with the power of engines normally reserved for Top Fuel Dragsters, teams of these shorter-wheelbase, full-bodied cars had a period of trial and error in getting these cars safely down the track as new technical and aerodynamic principals had to be sorted out and applied.

Eventually Funny Cars became the darlings of drag racing. With speeds close to Top Fuel Dragsters, smoky crowd-pleasing burnouts and colorful paint schemes, track operators couldn't book enough Funnies into their shows.

Drag racing reached a new level of entertainment at this time as the men and women piloting the Funnies could be as colorful as the cars. Each time a pair of Floppers came to the line, the scene was similar to a Wild West duel: the cars staged and then raced down the track, rarely in a straight line, as the cars' rear ends skittered and bobbed and weaved right through to the finish line.

Several big-name drivers took to running Funny Cars, including Danny Ongais, Don Schumacher, Tommy Ivo and Tom McEwen. Kenny Bernstein, Raymond Beadle and Don Prudhomme all excelled in the Funny Car ranks. Future Top Fuel Dragster stars Connie Kalitta and Shirley Muldowney ran Funny Cars early in their careers.

But the stars were aligned for Russell Liberman,

The sport's greatest showman was "Jungle Jim" Liberman. His big trademark burnouts endeared him to legions of fans. Never one to enter serious sanctioned competition, Liberman was drag racing's top match racer for many years.

who campaigned a series of Funny Cars from the late 1960s until his death in 1977. "Jungle Jim" Liberman was perhaps drag racing's all-time showman, promoting himself and his cars across the country.

A native of California, Liberman set up shop in Pennsylvania to be central to the match-race circuit, as he was not particularly concerned with regular competition. He lived to race for the fans, and was a master at burnouts, usually treating the crowd to a half-track display of tire smoke.

A big part of Jungle Jim's show was due to girlfriend and traveling companion Pam Hardy, who would line him up at the start after his burnout. Known as "Jungle Pam," her clothing was somewhat provocative, and the fans loved her running back and forth getting Liberman staged.

By 1970, the AHRA and NHRA were sanctioning the class and, in 1974, the IHRA included the class in its events. To this day it remains one of the most popular divisions.

Since the acceptance of the Funny Car by the sanctions, its overall design has changed little. The engines and drivetrains have followed the technological progression of the Top Fuel Dragster, including the sophisticated data acquisition and fire protection systems. But overall, this class continues to dazzle the fans with its noise, color and driver skill.

A classic Pro Stock matchup in Ohio in 1971: the Sox & Martin Plymouth vs. the Bill "Grumpy" Jenkins Camaro. Herb McCandless was driving the Plymouth while Grumpy was piloting the Camaro.

Multi-time NHRA champion Warren Johnson in his Camaro at Indianapolis in 1975; the year before Johnson made NHRA Pro Stock racing his fulltime pursuit.

Pro Stock

Perhaps the best way to describe the Pro Stock class is a Stocker on steroids. As the Stock and Super Stock classes developed in the early and mid 1960s, the automakers fielded factory-supplied cars with ever-increasing engine sizes, beefed-up powertrain components and weight-saving body panels in an effort to get the best power-to-weight ratio.

This factory participation flourished and was encouraged by the sanctions, but racers, being what they are, felt the class had become restrictive as the technology advanced and elapsed times dropped. Another hindrance was the handicapped starting system in the Stock and Super Stock classes.

Wanting to keep away from the higher costs of building and racing Funny Cars, and avoid potential driver injury with blower explosions and other inherent safety issues associated with a fuel-powered front-engined car, there were builders and drivers, such as Bill Jenkins, Don Nicholson and the team of Ronnie Sox and Buddy Martin, who wanted to continue with faster stock-appearing, gasoline-fueled cars. There was also an element of factory involvement, as the carmakers wanted to continue with their product identity. At first, these ultimate factory hot rods were matched raced, but by 1970, Pro Stock was an official NHRA class and one of the top three (along with Top Fuel and Funny Car) in the pecking order.

Bill Jenkins won a couple of national Pro Stock events in 1970 with Chevy power, and Ronnie Sox, a master at shifting a four-speed, took three events in the seven-race tour that year and won seven of eight events in 1971 in his Chrysler products.

Soon, through political maneuvering and changes to rules so new the ink had not yet dried, tubular chassis were developed for the new class, even though (for a while) the car bodies were still metal.

The Ford versus Chevy versus Chrysler rivalry remained heated in the early Pro Stock days. This rivalry was intense and appeared to favor Ford and Chevy while punishing Chrysler. Teams that

The Johnson legacy has been passed from father Warren to son Kurt, who is a top driver in today's NHRA Pro Stock ranks. Johnson's Cobalt is typical of the present class, with the large air scoop dominating the engine area.

ran Chrysler's big and more powerful Hemi engine (426-cubic-inches and 425 horsepower in street trim) in Darts, Barracudas and the like, were subjected to weight penalties by the governing sanctions. Ironically, the Ford and Chevys were allowed to run lighter-weight cars whose engines could produce as much or more power than the Chrysler Hemi (750 to 800 horsepower). Eventually this discrepancy between manufacturers was dissolved.

In 1980 the IHRA ushered in the big-block engines in Pro Stock, which were initially in the 450-cubic-inch range. Engine sizes quickly blossomed into the 700-plus cubic-inch range and are now over 800 cubic inches. These engines became known as "mountain motors." In 1982, the NHRA followed the IHRA with the introduction of big-block engines. Engine size has settled down a bit with the NHRA Pro Stock cars of today, where teams are limited to engines no bigger than 500 cubic inches.

Since Pro Stock's inception, and due to the nature of the cars, Pro Stock teams have always offered very close racing with its restrictive format. But there have been some that have risen above, due to their superior engine-building skills and trigger-quick reflexes at the starting line.

In the early days of Pro Stock racing, after Jenkins hung up his driving gloves, Bob Glidden was dominant, winning just about every NHRA national meet he entered with his succession of Ford-powered cars. He set many records over his career, which spanned from 1972 to 1997, including the mark for all-time victories at 85, a number not surpassed until 2000 by John Force. The Indiana native Glidden also won 10 NHRA Winston Championships. Another big name in Pro Stock was Texan Lee Shepherd, who, before his death in 1985, dominated the class with four titles, after an illustrious career in Sportsman class racing.

In the 1990s, one man totally dominated Pro Stock racing in the NHRA. Warren Johnson won 81 national events, took five championships, and was the first driver to top 200 mph in this demanding class. The former Modified Eliminator driver from Minnesota took to racing full-time in 1976, raced in the IHRA for a spell, and then settled in Georgia and concentrated on NHRA racing in 1986 with the help of longtime sponsor General Motors.

This winning legacy has been passed to son Kurt, who has become a dominant Pro Stock driver in his own right. He was the first to run a six-second run in the class, in 1994, and has won at least one NHRA national event every season since 1995.

Two of today's top NHRA drivers in the class are Jason Line and Greg Anderson, both from North Carolina.

Pro Stock racing in the IHRA also offers very tight, closely matched events, with engines of up to 820 cubic inches in a domestic two-door sedan with a minimum weight of 2,400 pounds. (NHRA Pro Stockers are limited to 500 cubes and a weight minimum of 2,350 pounds). Top IHRA drivers include Robert Patrick of Virginia, Ohio's Brian Gahm and Pete Berner of Illinois.

Pro Modifieds

One of drag racing's newer professional classes, and one that has developed into one of the sport's most popular, is the Pro Modified class.

With roots in the Top Sportsman division, Pro Mods evolved from this technologically resourceful class in the early 1990s, running large engines on nitrous oxide and, eventually, superchargers.

While the powerplants were similar to engines in other classes, it was the dynamic use of a wide variety of body styles that gave the Pro Mods their unique style of racing. Just about any car body from the early 1930s up to the present can be found on a Pro Mod, and it is not unknown to see a matchup between a 1933 Willys-bodied Pro Mod and a new generation Camaro Pro Mod.

Early proponents of the class, which developed in the eastern half of North America, include Charles Carpenter, who continues to race with a nitrous-fed 1955 Chevy, Johnny Rocca who campaigned a 1949 Mercury, complete with wide whitewall tires and Gary Irving, who ran a 1952 Chevy-bodied Pro Mod.

Another important name in the development of Pro Mod racing is Jim Oddy, a former Gasser racer who helped morph this class with a solid group of cars from his Buffalo, New York, base. Oddy and driver Fred Hahn were a tough combination to beat.

Pro Modified became a recognized class by the IHRA in 1990, and has been one of that sanction's biggest growth divisions. Whether it's powered by a 2,500-horsepower, 526-cubic-inch supercharged engine, or a nitrous-fueled engine of 820 cubic inches, all Pro Mods are self-starting, and entry into the fiberglass or carbon fiber body is through a regular door.

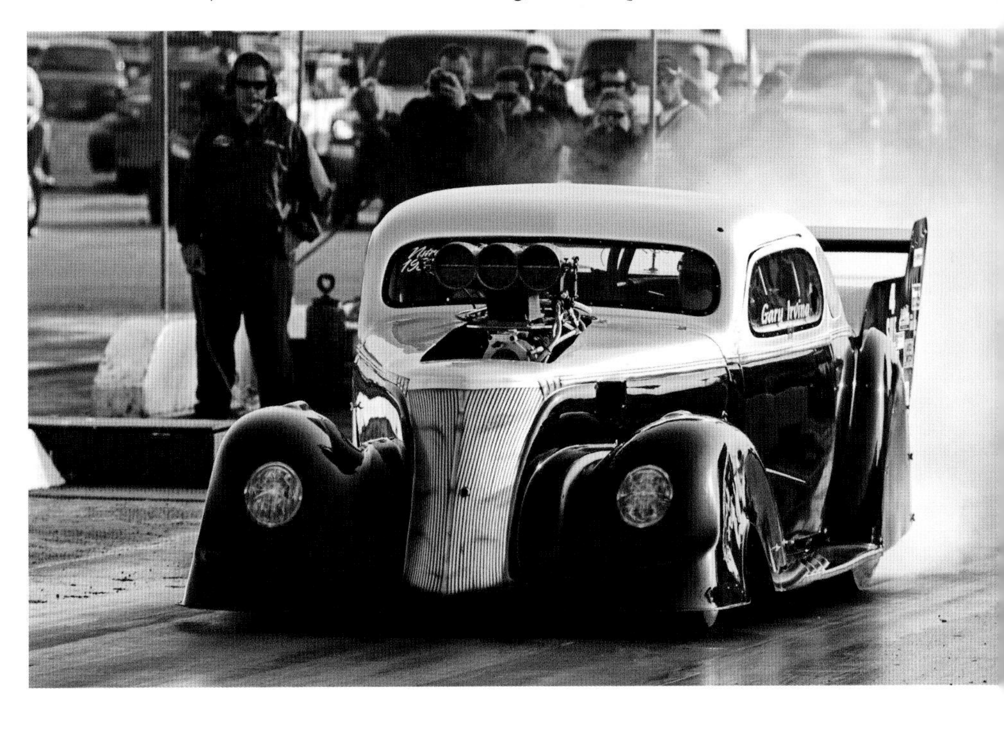

Gary Irving's 1937 Chevy Pro Mod is a great example of the wide variety of crowd-pleasing body styles running in the circuit known for the world's fastest doorslammers.

The NHRA has not embraced the Pro Mod class in regular competition, although it does hold invitational meets at several of its national events.

While there are Pro Mod teams and several series throughout North America, the hottest racing and racers come from the southeast U.S., western New York and southern Ontario, Canada. Some prominent names in Pro Mod today include Scott Cannon of South Carolina, New York's Mike Janis and Shannon Jenkins of Alabama. Several Canadians have been players in the class, both building cars and racing them at the top level, and these include Al Billes, Carl Spiering and Raymond Commisso.

The Builders

The building of drag racing cars has evolved from trial-and-error procedures using parts and materials from many sources in the sport's early years to today's multimillion dollar industry. There are many firms that specialize in systems and parts developed and built solely for quarter-mile racing. There are also firms that build complete turnkey race cars, from the slowest stockers to Top Fuel dragsters.

No matter what the part, system or car being built, there is one common element in this enterprise. For the most part, all builders have been racers themselves, and through their racing experience have devised what they consider to be a better machine in getting down the track. They also work with their customers at the track, taking note of the performance of their product so they can go back to the shop to make improvements.

Of the many builders and innovators, several have become prominent, whether in the building and supplying of race engines, chassis or safety equipment. There have also been builders of the sport itself—men and women with the vision and foresight to provide an organized environment for the sport.

Here are some of the personalities who have helped to make drag racing what it is today.

Ed Donovan in Inglewood, California, in 1960 working on a 392 Chrysler Hemi. Donovan started his own business in 1959 which focused on refining parts for the Hemi that were subject to breakage when applied to drag racing.

DAYTONA INDIANAPOLIS PHOENIX
RIVERSIDE LANGHORNE ATLANTA
CHARLOTTE POMONA HARLINGEN
AUGUSTA BRIDGEHAMPTON ASCOT
YORK HARRISBURG DARLINGTON
CONCORD COVINGTON VINELAND
DETROIT DALLAS MEMPHIS BRISTOL

Where will you see Chrysler Corporation's new hemispherical engine in action?

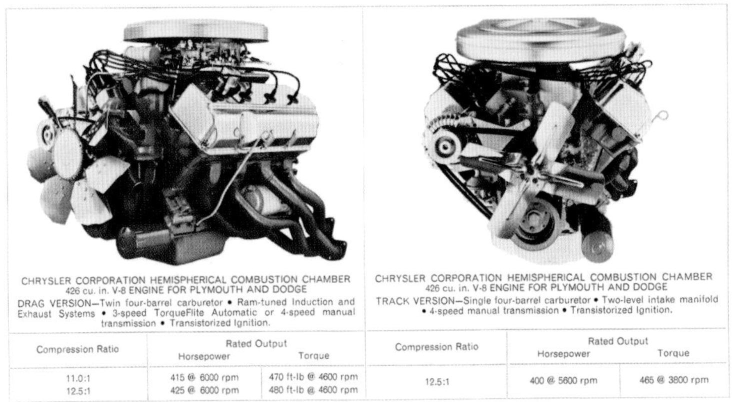

Compression Ratio	Rated Output: Horsepower	Rated Output: Torque
11.0:1	415 @ 6000 rpm	470 ft-lb @ 4600 rpm
12.5:1	425 @ 6000 rpm	480 ft-lb @ 4600 rpm

Compression Ratio	Rated Output: Horsepower	Rated Output: Torque
12.5:1	400 @ 5600 rpm	465 @ 3800 rpm

The very first 5 times out this new engine powered Plymouth and Dodge cars to sweeping victories. A 1-2-3 finish in each of the races—including the Daytona 500! And all in record time! A hemispherical combustion chamber engine is, of course, not new. Chrysler Corporation first introduced one back in 1951. It set quite a few records at the time. Now once again, Chrysler Corporation engineers are capitalizing on a free breathing design that develops greater power per cycle.

Plymouth • Dodge • Chrysler • Imperial

A Chrysler Hemi advertisement from the mid 1960s illustrates the envious racing résumé the engine enjoyed. The 426-cubic-inch engine was used predominately in NASCAR stock car racing and Stock and Super Stock drag racing.

The Big Engines

Racers in the faster classes soon learned the Flathead Ford engine was not the quickest way down the drag strip. While the Oldsmobile and Cadillac V8 engines were a step in the right direction, the engine of choice became the Chrysler Hemi. Introduced in 1951, at 331 cubic inches, this engine with its hemispherical combustion chambers offered superior breathing characteristics and the most power of any of the engines at the time. In 1958, its displacement grew to 392 cubic inches.

During this time, the Hemi was run basically as a stock powerplant, with racers scouring the wrecking yards for a smashed-up Chrysler or Imperial and hauling out the big engine. Multiple carburetors were used initially, usually in a pack of eight sitting on top. Then superchargers were fastened to the front of the engine with the fuel-air mixture traveling along large tubes into the intake manifold. Then the superchargers were bolted directly on top of the engine, driven by a belt from the crankshaft rather than directly off the crankshaft itself, as in the front-blower applications.

It became apparent the Hemi engine was the engine to race, and by 1960 several individuals with racing and engine-building backgrounds went to work on making this engine the strongest and most powerful.

Californian Ed Donovan learned his craft working with the famed engine-building firm of Meyer-Drake. He also learned some ways to increase an engine's horsepower from Ed Winfield. While building the Offenhauser engine of Indianapolis fame in the Meyer-Drake shop, Donovan also spent time and learned from engineering genius Leo Goossen.

Donovan participated in early Bonneville Salt Flats competition with partner Frank Startup, and in the early 1950s built a dragster powered with a supercharged Offy engine running on nitromethane.

It was Donovan's love of drag racing, and what he felt he could contribute to the sport, that enticed him to leave Meyer-Drake and begin his own engineering business with Startup in 1959. He had already begun to make stronger parts for the Hemi drag engine, producing stainless steel valves, which, three years later became part of his focus as he went at it alone developing parts for the 354 and 392 Hemi engines.

Although Donovan developed and built a special clutch known as a "slipper" clutch, a component that helped utilize the immense horsepower of the fuel engines, his focus was on producing parts that were

Ed Donovan ventured outside drag racing and into other forms of auto sport. Here his small block Donovan engine is awarded the fastest stock block qualifier at the 1982 Indianapolis 500. Donavan (far left) celebrates with Bob Stempel, Linda Vaughn, driver Michael Chandler and an unnamed Hurstette.

A former boat racer, Californian Keith Black began to build Chrysler Hemi-based fuel engines for drag racing in the early 1960s. His aluminum "KB" engine became the benchmark for Top Fuel, and is still produced.

subject to breakage and failure on the Hemi engine. He developed titanium valves, forged rocker arms and other valve components, after experimenting with various steel alloys. He built aluminum valve covers to keep gasket leakage to a minimum, and added tall, Offy-inspired breathers for better engine breathing efficiency. His company also built parts for supercharger drives.

Donovan concentrated on engines, but also built some important driveline parts after dragsters featuring his equipment suffered failures in this area. With clutch explosions an all-too-common and devastating occurrence, he devised a one-piece bell housing around the clutch to keep the explosion contained. Donovan also contributed a coupler made to replace the drivetrain u-joint setup used in the powerful cars.

As the junkyard supply of the potent Hemi engines started to dry up, Donovan envisioned the need for a purpose-built drag racing engine in the same manner that the Offy was built for open-wheeled oval track applications. So in 1971, Donovan and his team introduced the 417, an aluminum block based on the 392 Chrysler, but with features designed to withstand the rigors of fuel racing. This engine used chrome-moly cylinder liners incorporating a wet-sleeve design to combat friction heat buildup, and the engine proved to be very strong. Engine number one was successful, powering John Wiebe's front-engined dragster to track records, along with winning several AHRA and NHRA titles.

While Donovan had produced the first true proprietary fuel engine, and competed with it on the track, the timing of the engine's introduction was unfortunate for the company, as builders such as Ed Pink and Keith Black were close to releasing their own versions of a Hemi-based fuel engine. Black's engine, a 426-cubic-inch aluminum version of the Chrysler powerplant, would dominate the market.

After Donovan died in 1989, his wife Kathy Donovan took over the business, continuing to serve the performance market, highlighted with a line of small-block Sprint car engines.

By the mid 1940s, Keith Black had established himself as a top name in boat racing. His exploits on the waves paralleled the emergence of bigger, more powerful engines in drag racing, and two years after he opened up his racing engine shop in 1959, this Californian had amassed nearly 50 national and international records in both boats and cars.

At the request of drag racer Tommy Greer, Black used his boat engine skills to build an engine for a Top Fuel car, and teamed up with Greer and the young Don Prudhomme to campaign the famed Greer-Black-Prudhomme dragster. The combination was a winner right out of the box, as the team won 250 races during 1962 and 1963.

Black continued to build engines during the 1960s while working with some of the top teams, including Roland Leong's series of Hawaiian Top Fuelers. He also continued with the boat side of his business, and was contracted by Chrysler to develop a marine racing engine program in 1965. He continued to improve upon his original engine design, and when he introduced the aluminum 426-cubic-inch, Hemi-based racing engine, the "KB" became the standard in the Fuel class for the next decade, winning all national records in the Top Fuel category between 1975 and 1984. Black's engines dominated the class, and his customers have included names such as Don Garlits, Shirley Muldowney, John Force, Joe Amato and Kenny Bernstein. The engine is still produced, based on the initial design, but with many upgrades and improvements.

Black backed away from his personal involvement in drag racing in the 1970s, working on other projects such as racing applications for Chevrolet and Oldsmobile engines. He died in 1991, but his legacy continues today with the family-operated business.

Although not as big a player as Donovan or Black, another Californian used his hot rod roots and engine-building prowess to build a successful line of fuel racing engines. From his shop in Van Nuys, Ed Pink produced his own line of 426 Chrysler-based powerplants, along with building and assembling Keith Black, Milodon and Donovan 417 engines. Precision assembling and attention to detail of these engines gave Pink a solid reputation and his engines powered many winning cars in the 1960s and 1970s. Today, the firm concentrates on racing venues other than drag racing, such as Ford engines for the USAC (United States Auto Club) Midget division and Chevy V8s for the Silver Crown series in USAC competition.

Early Influences on Engine Building

There were many designers and builders involved with the early development of drag racing engines, and the products of some of them are still produced today.

Fuel injection was, and still is, a powerful way to get fuel into a racing engine. The first practical use of mechanical fuel injection for racing was developed by a former chemist named Stu Hilborn. This transplanted Canadian designed a fuel injection system in 1946 for Midget racers from his California base, a system that became the standard on Offy-powered cars. Applied to drag racing, Hilborn systems sat atop many a gasser and door-slammer, and continue to do so with a wide variety of engine applications.

One of the original speed equipment pioneers, Ed Winfield started in the late 1920s with performance carburetors, and then custom camshaft design and grinding.

Some of the strongest connecting rods were built by Fred Carrillo, starting in the early 1960s, when they earned a reputation not only in Keith Black fuel engines, but were installed in Ford GT40s and Brabham Formula One engines.

Nick Arias Jr. is another Californian who was weaned on racing at Bonneville and the dry lakes, and an early drag racing engine builder. Purchasing Frank Venolia's piston business, Arias developed a line of pistons for many types of racing. He also developed a very powerful big-block Chevrolet engine utilizing hemispherical cylinder heads that has proved capable of holding its own against the Chryslers. Arias continues to this day with high-performance engines and components for a variety of racing applications.

Fueler Chassis Builders

There have not been a lot of successful dragster builders. Most of the early front-engined designs were home-built units, cars known as "slingshots," with the driver tucked in behind the engine and sitting over the rear axle.

Former Bonneville driver Mickey Thompson, who raced, built and promoted just about everything in the racing world at one time or another, made some of the early ideas in dragster building work. With engine builder Ray Brown, Thompson's Hemi-powered car was recognized as the first successful dragster when it debuted in 1955. Not only did the car have good balance, it had a narrowed rear axle, which gave the car a much higher degree of stability and increased traction.

One of the top chassis builders in the 1960s was Connie Swingle. He went to Don Garlits's Tampa shop and started welding up chassis for not only Garlits, but himself, using the light and strong chrome moly for material. As a racer, Swingle teamed up with engine builder Ed Pink in 1965. From their California base, the team was successful with several victories, including the "Mickey Thompson 200 Meet" at the Fontana strip in 1965, winning over Garlits in the final of the dragsters top class, AA/FD. Swingle returned to Florida to work with Garlits, producing some of the most successful cars of the era.

After Garlits's front-engined car exploded in 1970 and he was critically injured, the pair started to work on a rear-engined car. It took a lot of testing to get the Swamp Rat 14 to handle correctly at high speeds, a trait shared by other rear-engined cars at the time. But Swingle made adjustments to the steering ratio to slow it down, which enabled the car to handle correctly.

Garlits got some laughs and funny looks when the new car debuted in 1971, but as he started winning races, it did not take long for his competition to see the new chassis design was a major step in the development of the Top Fuel dragster.

Across the country from Florida, a transplanted Washington State racer, Dave Uyehara, was driving Dick Oswald's AA/Gas dragster in California. In 1969, the team shifted to fuel racing with Uyehara behind the wheel of the powerful cars, including a nitro Funny Car on the weekends.

In 1972, after a few years of experimenting with dragster chassis in his shop, Uyehara developed his first rear-engined dragster, which featured a three-rail front frame design that offered a great deal of stability on the track. His strong, lightweight cars became a big seller for dragster teams. A racer himself until a serious crash in 2002, Uyehara has been totally in tune with the racers, and today's cars owe much to Uyehara's insight.

Another dragster builder who set the stage for

Chassis builder Al Swindahl's contribution to the development of rear-engined Top Fuel dragsters was this longer wheelbase car. The new chassis was built for driver Jerry Ruth in 1979, and the design offered a safe, light, strong, well-balanced package.

the class was Al Swindahl. Asked by racer Jerry Ruth to design a new car, Swindahl went to work in his Washington shop in 1979. Ruth wanted a car with a revamped roll cage to lessen the occurrence of his head slamming into the cage, a 255-inch wheelbase, and the frame rails designed to allow easier starting of the car when the remote starter was hooked up to the engine.

The Swindahl design offered a good balanced car of 1,500 pounds. The design featured enough tubes of the proper diameter in the chassis construction to make it light and strong. The placement of the tubes also helped in protecting the driver more, along with providing high-speed stability. The rear axle drive was built in as an integral part of the car. When drivers such as Joe Amato began winning with the car, other teams began putting in their orders for the chassis. Even after 25 years, the basics of the Swindahl chassis are still in use in today's cars.

Brad Hadman learned his craft working for Swindahl, and today continues to produce dragster chassis based on his former employer's design. One of the major enhancements of the Hadman car debuted in 2003 with the introduction of the one-piece carbon fiber body. Initially used by the Amato team, this new body was stronger and more rigid than the traditional multipanel body, and a few pounds lighter in weight. Today, Hadman is one of a handful of prominent dragster chassis builders.

Another of today's top chassis builders, Murf McKinney, got his start in Funny Cars, both racing them and then building them. McKinney raced fuel floppers in the 1970s and 1980s, but economic reality set in, and rather than get out of the sport, he began to build cars. He has produced some of the top Funny Cars in the past two decades, and continues to construct them in his Indiana shop. He also has become a major builder in dragster chassis, and his cars are prominent in today's Top Fuel racing. He has also been involved with the John Force effort to design and build a safer Funny Car.

The Promoters

Racers just want to race. And the fans just want to watch the racers race. But someone has to bring these two parties together, and operate a racing event. Someone has to coordinate the cars, the series, the fans and the tracks. And try to make a profit.

Organized drag racing has been around almost since the concept of the sport. While there have been, and still are, many organizations big and small that book the racers and promote the races and keep the fans as happy as possible, the focus here will be on the three main sanctioning bodies—the National Hot Rod Association (NHRA), the International Hot Road Association (IHRA) and the American Hot Rod Association (AHRA)—and the men who were the leaders of these three enterprises.

Wally Parks and the NHRA

It is probably safe to say that drag racing would not be where it is today if it was not for Wally Parks.

Parks did not invent drag racing, but he was a racer, and before World War II, a young Parks moved to Southern California from Kansas, where he reported in auto club newsletters on the competitions of the Southern California Timing Association (SCTA). Parks was around for the early SCTA drag racing speed trials, and knew this was an up-and-coming form of automotive competition.

In 1947, he became the SCTA's general manager after working for General Motors for 10 years. In 1948 Parks helped launch *Hot Rod Magazine* with founder Robert E. Petersen. The magazine was part of the Petersen Publishing Company, which became the largest auto-related publishing firm in the world. Parks held the editor position at *Hot Rod Magazine* for several years, which helped in the promotion of drag racing and the NHRA.

Parks started the NHRA in 1951 with several mandates to pursue, such as sanctioning race tracks, standardized track and car safety requirements and membership drives. Formed as a club, the NHRA acquired members from across North America, and these numbers grew immensely during the 1950s. In 1953, the NHRA established rules and guidelines for car classes, safety requirements and drag strips. Also that year it put on its first race, held in April at the Los Angles County Fairgrounds in Pomona. As the regional events grew in number, a national championship program was established, and the

The vision and determination of Wally Parks has made the NHRA the world's largest drag racing sanction. His philosophy of presenting safe, professional racing venues continues to this day.

first Nationals were held on the airport runway in Grand Bend, Kansas, in 1955.

While the racing was an important part of the NHRA, Parks worked hard to ensure the image of drag racing remained positive. He and his staff met with law enforcement and community groups throughout the 1950s to promote the fledgling sport and to give it form and structure. In 1954, the NHRA established its Safety Safari to educate the public about the legitimacy, safety and controlled forums the NHRA provided. The Safari ambassadors helped introduce drag racing in a new light to concerned opposition groups, while it also broadened the NHRA's reach to prospective fans and drivers.

Through its house publication, *National Dragster*, the NHRA provided its members with all the latest racing news, racer profiles and racing tips, and by the late 1950s the NHRA had seven regional divisions, each with its own director.

While the NHRA staff grew in size from its California headquarters, Wally Parks continued to follow his original vision, spearheading the growth of drag racing by having more national meets across North America, acquiring major sponsorships and helping to build what is today the world's largest motorsports governing body.

Parks, along with his wife Barbara, who has been regarded as a strong, behind-the-scenes influence in the NHRA, were a mainstay at the major NHRA races. Before Parks died in 2007 at the age of 94, he had accumulated accolades from dozens of auto- and racing-related groups, highlighted by his induction into both the International Motorsports Hall of Fame in 1992 and the Motorsports Hall of Fame in 1993. Both he and Barbara were inducted into the Don Garlits International Drag Racing Hall of Fame in 1994.

Parks ran the NHRA with a strong, firm hand, and was involved with almost every aspect of the organization. The vision and operation of the NHRA is not unlike the emergence and course of NASCAR. Both were started around the same time (NASCAR took shape in 1949 with Bill France at the helm), and both reflected the philosophy of their founders. The success of the NHRA must be attributed to Parks, whose dedication and perseverance made the NHRA what it is today.

Jim Tice and the AHRA

With roots dating back to 1956, the American Hot Rod Association (AHRA) was a Midwest-based sanction that became prominent in the drag racing world when former racer Jim Tice assumed the presidency of the AHRA in 1959. Shortly after, the sanction decided to allow cars to run nitro, which the NHRA banned in the late 1950s.

Tice, who was in the insurance business in Kansas City, had a vision of how he wanted to see drag racing evolve, but he was more of a promoter and into the business side of the sport than Wally Parks was. He established a strong national series that ran until the early 1980s, but often the series ran a rough

NATIONAL **DRAGSTER**

VOL. 1 — NO. 1 120 1171 N. VERMONT AVE., LOS ANGELES 29, CALIFORNIA FEBRUARY 12, 1960

THIRD ANNUAL CARROT CHAMPIONSHIP

See Page 3

New National Points System

See Page 4

SOLID FOR SAFETY

Not one, but SIX official NHRA record certification teams will be seen in action this year throughout NHRA's vast chain of sanctioned drag strips. They will be easily identified by the new 1960 Plymouth station wagons in which they will carry NHRA's services into all corners of the U. S.

Six division directors of NHRA assembled in Detroit in mid January where they were each assigned one of the new Field Unit vehicles. Their names and the divisions they represent are: Ed Eaton, Northeast; Ernie Schorb, Southeast; Bob Daniels, North Central; Dale Ham, South Central; Jack Merrill, Northwest; and Ed Davis, headquarters, Southwest. The cars were officially turned over to their new handlers by Wally Parks, NHRA president, following a two day NHRA conference and planning session.

The six new vehicles, all Custom 4-door Suburbans, are a part of NHRA's new Field Division. Each car is issued to a division director and is delegated to the furtherance of organized hot rodding everywhere. They're all gleaming white with red interiors. The expert lettering and NHRA emlems were applied in Detroit by sign-painter Joe Fifer, of the South Florida Timing Association, who was flown in from Miami especially to do the job.

NHRA selected Plymouth as the wagon best suited to the particular demands of its Field Divisions; roominess, roadability and ruggedness all being essential requirements — plus "raciness," as they have the big 361 Commando power-plants.

The "Solid for '60" Plymouths will carry an NHRA theme — "Solid for Safety." Look for them soon — they'll be in constant attendance at NHRA drag strips, car shows, conferences, etc., where each will act as a central hub around which its divisional hot rod activities will be orbiting.

FLASH!

WINTERNATIONALS REPORT

CARDEN TURNS 9.88

Daytona Beach, Fla., Feb. 7 — A direct report from the scene of the FIRST ANNUAL WINTERNATIONALS: Lew Carden, NHRA Regional Advisor of Birmingham, Alabama, captured Top Eliminator honors during the night drag races of February 7. Lew turned a low ET of 9.88 in his Chev powered B/Dragster on opening night of the first NHRA NASCAR co-sanctioned week long event.

There will be six nights of trophy drags, with trophies being given in all NHRA classes. The 7th night, Saturday, February 13, will be the event to decide the over all class and eliminator CHAMPIONS for the week. A point system will be used to determine the over all winners. Entries have checked in from all over the south and eastern part of the country to compete in this biggest of winter drag racing events.

Ernie Shorb, NHRA Southeastern Division Director, is serving as event director; assisted by NHRA Division Director, Ed Eaton, the South Florida Timing Association, and other NHRA Advisors.

The WINTERNATIONALS will be featured in the next issue of your DRAGSTER, including a complete report on results.

NATIONAL **DRAGSTER**

1171 North Vermont Avenue • Los Angeles 29, Calif.

BULK RATE
U. S. POSTAGE
PAID
Permit No. 19289
Los Angeles, Calif.

Membership in the NHRA includes a subscription to *National Dragster*, the official publication of the sanction that keeps every racer well informed about the sport. This is the first issue of *Dragster*, February 12, 1960.

course as Tice battled with the NHRA and eventually the IHRA.

The NHRA ban on fuel cars got Tice's foot in the door by presenting the fastest cars of the time at his tracks. Fans wanted to see the loudest and quickest cars, and Tice responded with sanctioned tracks across the U.S., and by 1969 the AHRA had 10 national meets. These big meets were usually a collaboration between the AHRA and a host track, with little or no corporate financial backing. Tice also allowed tracks to run jet cars, something the NHRA did not allow in the early years.

In 1972, the AHRA teamed with many pro racers to run an event with unheard-of (for the time) prize money. For top eliminator in Top Fuel, Funny Car and Pro Stock, $25,000 was awarded. The race was scheduled to be held at Tulsa the same time the NHRA was to run its flagship race, the U.S. Nationals.

While the race was a big success in terms of big-name drivers and a big turnout of fans, it was not a financial success. The event was held again in 1973, once again in Tulsa, but not on the same weekend as the NHRA Nationals. But once again it was a financial flop as too much money was promised (and paid out) to drivers. Tice let Don Garlits (who was instrumental in organizing the event) run the show for the next two years, this time in New York State, and those events were also dismal flops as the big names did not appear, and the attendance was meager due to poor weather at the Long Island facility.

When the IHRA and NHRA acquired the Winston tobacco funding as title sponsor, the AHRA had to do some creative work to keep the fans at their tracks. One way was to continue to bring in the big names in the sport, and in most cases the costs associated with bringing in a Garlits or Prudhomme or Muldowney were split between the AHRA and the host track. Also, an AHRA show would consist of only eight Funnies or Fuelers rather than the usual 16 the other sanctions could afford.

By the late 1970s, the AHRA was getting clobbered by the NHRA and the IHRA. Both the latter sanctions had a much better media presence, including television, and the house publications sent to the memberships were of much better quality in terms of editorial and photo content.

When Tice became ill with terminal cancer in 1980, several AHRA track owners split to form the American Drag Racing Association (ADRA), while Tice's wife Ruth sold the AHRA to Florida businessman Mike Grey. Grey produced several successful AHRA events, but low revenues and some nefarious dealings by the host track in Louisiana at its 1984 World Finals proved to be too much for the AHRA, which never recovered. The ADRA was also a bust, folding up soon after.

Tice was a good businessman who could wear several hats along with keeping his track owners happy. The AHRA survives in name only at Spokane Raceway Park in Washington.

Larry Carrier and the IHRA

Larry Carrier started the IHRA in 1970 because he didn't want to have to play ball with the only two games in town. After building an oval track in 1960, and a quarter-mile strip in 1965, in the northeast corner of Tennessee, outside of his hometown of Bristol, Larry Carrier ran under NHRA sanctioning, holding the sanction's first Spring Nationals. Not wanting to make physical changes to the Bristol facility as per the NHRA's wishes, Carrier's track became an AHRA track in 1969. But he wasn't thrilled with the financial arrangements the AHRA had with its tracks, so he decided to form his own drag racing sanctioning body, going up against two solid sanctions with all the drivers and tracks. It has been noted that AHRA boss Jim Tice was so upset with Carrier that he (Tice) would make sure the AHRA had a major event each time Carrier scheduled a show at either his Bristol or Rockingham, North Carolina, facility.

Not long after its formation in 1970, the IHRA purchased the then state-of-the-art Dallas International Motor Speedway, and by 1972 had amassed about 40 strips, mostly in the southeast U.S., but there were also IHRA strips in Ohio, Indiana, New York, Wisconsin and a couple in Canada.

Carrier and his IHRA followed in the NHRA's footsteps using the formula of staging races with the Pro classes of Top Fuel, Funny Car and Pro Stock. And Carrier one-upped the elder NHRA with a major coup when he signed with the R.J. Reynolds'

Winston brand to sponsor an annual points fund. This agreement took place in 1974 and was the first major corporate sponsorship to hit the drag racing world—one year ahead of the NHRA, which signed with the tobacco company in 1975.

Carrier's IHRA became the main competition for the NHRA and the success of the two sanctions eventually led to the demise of the AHRA. While the AHRA track owners fought among themselves, the IHRA and NHRA secured new tracks and presented better quality racing. The IHRA grew throughout the southern United States, while the NHRA continued to add tracks in the rest of the country and several in Canada.

Aside from drag racing, Carrier, a former contractor and land developer, devoted time to the Bristol Speedway, a main NASCAR venue. He opened the track on a former dairy farm in 1960 and sold it in 1976, only to regain control of operations in 1985 after the owners filed for bankruptcy. Carrier spent considerable time and money to refurbish the track, including the removal of the asphalt racing surface for concrete, and it has since become one of the most popular venues on the NASCAR circuit. The track was sold by Carrier in 1996 to Bruton Smith's Speedway Motorsports Inc. Carrier was also the founder of the World Boxing Federation, which held sanctioned events around the globe. Carrier died in 2005 at age 82.

Carrier sold the IHRA in 1988 to racer Billy Meyer,

Workers are seen in 1960 building Larry Carrier's oval track in the northern Tennessee town of Bristol. Five years later he would add a drag strip. Both would become premier racing facilities and are still in use today.

Carrier, shown here congratulating the great Pat Foster after an IHRA Funny Car victory at Rockingham, built the IHRA from its southeastern U.S. roots to a large sanctioning body that today holds races in the U.S., Canada and the Caribbean.

so that he could concentrate on his Bristol NASCAR effort. The former racer, Meyer, had a tough go of it. He made some poor scheduling and management decisions and did not have the vision of Carrier. A year later he sold the IHRA to a group headed by Ted Jones. With new management the IHRA did expand and was a viable operation, but did not stray much from its southern U.S. roots. By 1998 the IHRA was operated by Norwalk dragstrip track owner Bill Bader and headquartered in Ohio. In 2001 the media giant Clear Channel purchased a majority interest in the IHRA, which then sold its motorsports interests to Feld Entertainment Motorsports in 2008. Feld Entertainment produces shows such as Disney on Ice and the Ringling Bros. and Barnum and Bailey Circus. The IHRA operates tracks primarily in the eastern half of the United States and boasts a strong presence in Canada.

A Door-slamming Legend

For close to 40 years, Jim Oddy built and raced full-bodied cars that were always a threat to the competition. From his Western New York shop came some of the strongest and most innovative Gassers and Pro Modifieds.

Today, Oddy maintains a quieter life since he sold his Elma, New York-based shop, but from the time he got behind the wheel of a 1936 Chevy coupe and

raced it in 1959, he was actively involved in drag racing.

His early years were devoted to competing with a B/G Chevy-powered Anglia, and then an AA/GS 1948 Austin. He won his class at the US Nationals at Indianapolis in 1965 with the Anglia, and did a lot of match racing in the Austin with the likes of K.S. Pitman, Stone, Woods & Cook, and "Ohio George" Montgomery. He won the NHRA Division 1 points championship several times in the 1970s, and the Super Eliminator class at Indy in 1972 with a Hemi-powered Opel GT.

After parking his race car for a few years, starting in 1977, to devote time to his family and set up his shop, Oddy returned to active competition with a Top Sportsman car in 1987. Two years later, Fred Hahn began driving for Oddy, along with Billy Leverentz as crew chief and, for the next 15 years, this combination of talent set the world on fire in IHRA Top Sportsman and Pro Modified competition.

First with a Corvette-bodied car, and then with the familiar 1937 Chevy coupe, this team set records in IHRA Pro Mod racing as well as winning championships on the Super Chevy and United States Super World Circuit tours. With a new 1954 Corvette body, the team finished second in the 1999 IHRA Pro Mod wars, and a year later took the title.

The accolades continued into the 21st century. The

After having a successful career of driving and building Austin and Anglia Gassers, Jim Oddy became a dominant name in the development of the Pro Modified class.

car made a 6.07 pass in 2003, the quickest to date and a number that present Pro Mod teams would like to achieve. In 2004 Hahn retired from driving, and Canadian Al Billes, who had already made a name for himself in the division, took over, driving a new Dodge Stratus in 2005. Steve Bareman replaced an injured Billes not long after, and with a new Corvette-bodied car, set the IHRA speed record with a 236.46-mph run, and then again in 2006, clocking a 238.93.

Meanwhile, Oddy and his crew were always busy in his shop building race cars, along with some of the best Pro Mod engines available.

Before he sold his Western New York State shop and moved to North Carolina in 2006, Oddy was involved in discussions with the NHRA about getting the popular Pro Mods on the NHRA program. Oddy had become frustrated over the IHRA's attitude of favoring nitrous over supercharged Pro Mods in matters such as engine sizes and weight breaks for the non-supercharged cars. The NHRA didn't put the class on the card, but through a sponsorship deal, first with AMS, and then JEGS, the class raced at several NHRA national events each year, but with its own points fund separate from any NHRA competition.

Oddy continued to be involved in Pro Modified racing after 2006, working with his son on the Dave Woods team which competes in the ADRL. Oddy has said that 2009, which will be his 50th year in the sport, will be his last.

"Next year will definitely be my last," Oddy was quoted as saying late in 2008. "I've had a great career. I won the U.S. Nationals as a driver and just about every championship that Pro Mods have ever had. I've gotten to work with my sons Dan and Dave for the last decade and I have had 50 years of fun. Working with my sons has been the happiest time of my racing career. So I've decided to quit while I'm ahead and I won't change my mind no matter what."

Smith and the New Super Stocker

When car manufacturers abandoned rear-drive cars in the mid 1980s, racers of Super Stock cars were left with a dilemma: how to take a front-drive car, stuff in a V8 engine, and build a traditional rear-drive setup without butchering up the car's integrity.

While there were many builders in the class who came up with their own versions, it was from the shop of F.J. Smith that a complete package was developed into a winning combination.

A hot-rodder at heart, Smith built many cars and raced them from his southern Ontario base. In 1976, he built a 1967 Camaro that became a legend in the B/Super Modified ranks, setting records for several years. In 1981, he developed a four-link rear suspension system, which continues to be used to this day.

In the early 1980s, Smith retired from his day job of teaching high school and established Smith Performance Specialties at his shop along the banks of the slow-moving Grand River in Cayuga, Ontario. The activity in the shop, however, was anything but slow as Smith established his engine and chassis business. He knew something had to be done to keep the Super Stock class vibrant in both the NHRA and IHRA, as the domestic car manufacturers stopped building the mid-size autos. Through some opportune meetings with Oldsmobile, he received a 1987 front-drive Cutlass Ciera and went to work.

"I must have hit it off with the Olds people," he said. "They got pumped up and involved. Also at this time Chevy and Olds were feuding over racing, and the Olds people wanted to win."

When he got the Olds home from Detroit, Smith went to work. Building the car as closely as possible to the rule book, he built an SS Olds, which he believed would pass.

"The NHRA realized the project was a good idea," Smith said. "I sat with the division tech directors, and they told me to build a car. Oldsmobile told me all the costs would be covered if the car received the NHRA's blessing."

The car was pronounced legal for NHRA competition.

Built with the original firewall and driveshaft tunnel in place, the car was displayed at the Oldsmobile booth at the 1987 SEMA (Specialty Equipment and Manufacturers Association) show. Then the car went to Gainesville for the real test. It was successful right out of the box, and Smith posted three class runner-ups.

"It was a viable car," Smith has noted in understatement. "It drove fine right off the bat."

For the next few years, the Smith shop was very busy, and he estimated that 150 of the conversion cars were produced, all with the mandated stock floor pan and firewalls, and a small, rear subframe like traditional Super Stock cars.

As an aside, at that time Smith engineered a front-end strut specifically for all Super Stock cars, in cooperation with Strange Engineering, and to this day, it is the only strut allowed in the class in both the NHRA and IHRA.

The shop became a mini-assembly line for Oldsmobile, and then Pontiac Super Stockers. There came many performance awards for his customers and engineering awards for Smith. Oldsmobile won the Manufacturer's Cup several times. Class world champions such as Jeff Taylor and Anthony Bertozzi raced Smith's cars. There are 59 NHRA "Wally" trophies lining the walls of the shop for eliminators, class wins and best engineering awards.

Smith continues to build race cars, but no longer drives. Daughter Victoria, also a strong competitor, is now the test pilot for the new innovations on the Pontiac Sunfire. In 1995, Smith became a pioneer in another sense. He started the Can-Am Stock/Super-Stock Series for racers in Ontario, Quebec, Michigan and New York. This series continues to flourish with larger car counts each year, offering these Sportsman racers a friendly atmosphere in which to compete.

Fred (F.J.) Smith was able to successfully transform the front-drive stock configuration into a viable front-engine, rear-drive traditional format for the Stock and Super Stock classes in the early 1980s. With the backing of Oldsmobile, Smith's cars became the benchmark.

Racing 101

This photo shows a lot more than two racers getting set to stage. Team members, minus the spotters, are behind the cars, along with officials and opponents who are watching, as well as a worker who is cleaning the track. Media members are abuzz on the sidelines and beside the cars.

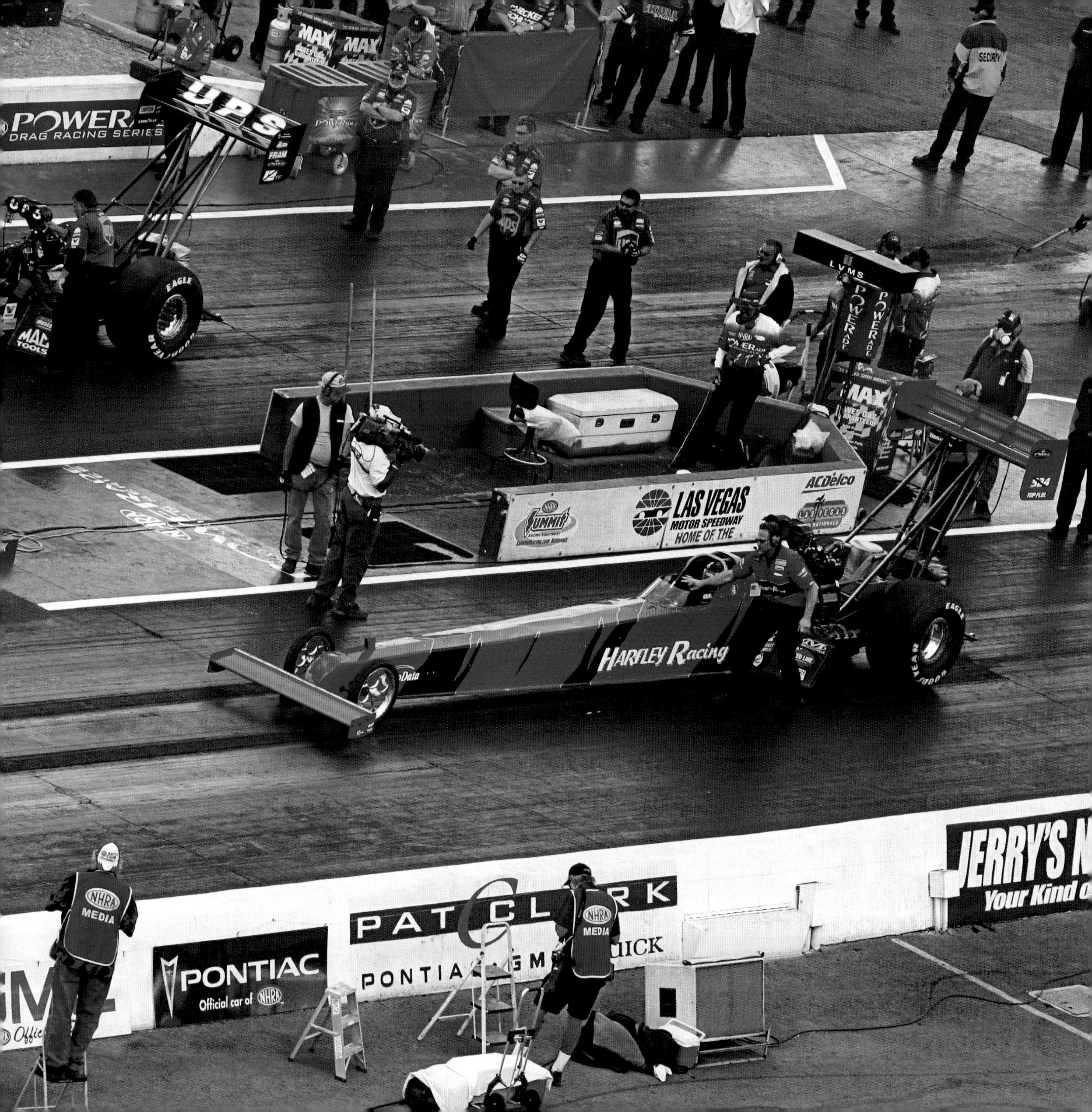
UPS
DRAG RACING SERIES
LAS VEGAS
MOTOR SPEEDWAY
HOME OF THE
ACDelco
LVMS
POWERADE
MAX
TOP FUEL
EAGLE
GOODYEAR
SECURITY
NHRA
MEDIA
PONTIAC
Official car of NHRA

Through the maze of roll cage tubing and fire safety equipment (left), Pro Stock driver Jeg Coughlin sits in a custom-made seat with a five-point harness. The safety net on his door window keeps his arm inside the car in case of a roll-over.

Safety

Safety at a drag strip event basically consists of three elements: safety of the car, safety of the driver and safety of the racing surface.

The Car

Whether it's a 15-second street Bracket racer, or the quickest Top Fueler, all cars that compete are scrutinized by a group of trained officials who ensure every element of the race car is fastened securely and operating properly.

Inspectors use a set of requirements and specifications produced each racing season by sanctioning bodies in conjunction with the SFI Foundation Inc. (originally formed by the Speed Equipment Manufacturers Association (SEMA), in 1963). SFI Foundation Inc. is a nonprofit organization established to issue and administer standards for specialty/performance automotive and racing equipment.

Manufacturers of specialty racing equipment adhere to the SFI specifications, which have been established to promote quality and reliability in the design, manufacture and application of products of the specialty parts industry. These specifications provide seller and purchaser with information to facilitate purchasing and application decisions, and to provide officials of competition events with convenient and reliable references for evaluating products.

However, in many instances, specifications become dated as new technological advances take place, and as a result, the specifications for items such as roll-cage design and clutch assemblies expire each year.

Overall, the faster a car goes down the strip, the more safety equipment it will require. Even the lower levels of the Sportsman class need rollover protection, a fuel cell, and a scatter-shield or heavy metal blanket over the clutch and transmission in case the unit explodes. The driveshaft in the car is also protected with u-shaped loop devices bolted to the car's underside that stop the driveshaft from falling and jamming into the racetrack in the event that it breaks.

Parachutes on faster cars may be a visually stimulating part of drag racing, but they also serve an important purpose. When early dragsters approached the 150-mph-plus speeds, drivers had a hard time after their run slowing their vehicles down with only drum brakes on the rear wheels. Initially, surplus military parachutes were devised to be deployed by the driver, significantly slowing down the car, but soon afterward, purpose-built parachutes were utilized.

Today, cars in Modified and the faster classes (over 150 mph) require a parachute, and for cars that travel over 200 mph, two parachutes are mandated.

Another mandatory item is an engine containment system, commonly called a "diaper." This blanket-type device covers an engine's bottom end to help contain oil and engine parts in the event of an explosion.

Hand-held fire extinguishers are strategically placed at key points along the track surface, such as the start and finish line areas, and inside the autos of the slower Sportsman classes for use in car fires. Elaborate self-contained fire extinguishing systems are required in the Professional class cars, with nozzles pointed at the driver and the engine. The amount of equipment and amount of fire retardant chemical increases in the top classes: A Pro Stock car will use a mandatory five-pound system, while a closed-body Funny Car must have a minimum 20-pound system which, upon use, will direct 15 pounds of flame-retardant chemical into the engine compartment in front of each of the car's eight headers. The remaining five pounds is dispersed into the driver's compartment.

Small windows are built into a Funny Car's firewall near the engine's valve covers to warn the driver of a fire. Another unique safety feature with a Funny Car is the mandatory escape hatch built into the car's roof as an emergency exit for the driver.

Cars with superchargers have presented some safety challenges over the years. When supercharger explosions did occur it was often the result of a bad blower-belt which would then have the potential to whip into the crowd or back at the race car. Today, there are mandatory restraints around the supercharger, including a belt guard, in case of an explosion. Valve-cover restraints, which are wide belts securely fastened around the engine's valve covers, are also mandatory in the Top Fuel and Funny Car classes.

Pro Stock drivers Jason Line and Jim Yates at the end of their runs with parachutes deployed properly. Cars that travel the track at over 150 mph must employ two parachutes for stopping assistance.

Left: Funny Car driver Gary Scelzi waits for his turn to qualify. Drivers in this class must wear additional and stronger fire-resistant clothing (including a head sock). Waiting in a full suit on a hot day can be physically draining.

Right: John Force is filmed as he is getting his HANS (head and neck restraint system) adjusted before climbing into his car.

The Driver

If a race car is made as safe as possible, the driver stands a better chance of getting down the track uninjured, but there's always the possibility of getting into trouble, and things happen fast on a drag strip.

For entry-level Sportsman class cars, a helmet and secure safety belt is needed—usually a four-point harness—but as the speeds get higher the need for driver safety increases. Drivers of front-engined closed cars such Funny Cars and Pro Modifieds are also protected against the chance of fire.

Four- and six-point harnesses offer the maximum in driver restraint, and are made of tightly woven mesh. These belts are pulled very tight across the driver to control body motion and to minimize momentum buildup. Most restraints must be replaced after two years.

Fire-retardant clothing is mandatory in most classes. Drivers of slower cars in the Stock and Super Stock classes must wear a fireproof jacket. For drivers of cars faster than a nine-second quarter-mile, not only are full driving suits required but gloves and footwear also. The clothing is specifically treated with fire-retarding chemicals to lessen the chance of a driver getting burned in a fire.

This clothing comes in various levels of burn rate. The driver of a Super Stock or Pro Stock car will wear clothing with a thermal protective performance rating (TPP) of 19, which will protect for up to 10 seconds before second degree burns are possible. The driver of a Funny Car must wear a fire suit with the maximum TPP rating of 80, which protects up to 40 seconds, and gloves and boots must have a TPP rating of 60, which allows up to 30 seconds.

Funny Car drivers wear head socks with the same flame-retardant characteristics of their suit, and their helmets must also be up to current fire protection specifications.

Open cockpit cars such as dragsters and Altereds will have a full roll cage as an integral part of the car's chassis. Drivers of these cars, along with a full safety harness, will have arm restraints that fasten the driver's arms to the roll cage to help keep his or her arms within the cage in case of a rollover.

Another safety protection device that is now used throughout the auto racing world is the HANS (head and neck restraint system) device.

The HANS device was designed to reduce the chance of injury caused by unrestrained movement of a driver's head during a crash.

Built of carbon fiber and Kevlar, the HANS device is a semi-hard collar held onto the upper body by a harness worn by the driver. The collar weighs 1.5 pounds and has two flexible tethers that attach it to the helmet, which helps prevent the head from snapping forward or sideways. Various lengths of tethers are available to provide the best in comfort and safety.

Developed by engineering professor Dr. Robert Hubbard and sports car racer Jim Downing, the HANS device is widely used in other types of motorsport. While this device is mandatory starting in the Pro Stock class up through to the faster Pro Modified and nitro-powered dragsters and Funny Cars, many drivers of all classes have taken to wearing this safety item.

The Racing Surface

A drag racing strip, much like oval and road racing tracks, must be properly maintained to offer the maximum in safety and performance.

The concrete pad of the staging and start areas on a track, along with the asphalt for the rest of the track, plus the shut-down area, must constantly be kept clean of debris and fluids. Chunks of rubber, small pebbles, or fluid such as oil and engine coolant picked up on the tires of a race car can be extremely dangerous and cause the car to veer or skid out of control. Track workers use brooms, scrapers, blowtorches and mechanical sweepers to ensure the track is clean. Oil and other fluids are removed with an oil-absorbing compound and then dried up with heat. Quite often a small jet-engine, mounted on a custom-built trailer is pulled up and down the entire track to remove any moisture or oil.

When track workers are satisfied that the track is ready, a coating of traction compound (commonly known as "glue") is sprayed on the surface to enhance traction for the cars.

Most drag strips of today belie their airport strip heritage. A double-height metal barrier (two levels of barrier as opposed to the single used on regular roads) or a concrete wall of around three feet in height is now standard at all tracks, which will keep an errant car contained to the racing surface and away from the spectators.

The Safety Crew

At each drag racing event, no matter the size and the class of cars, there is a group of tireless workers who maintain a vigil from the first qualification runs to the final round of eliminations.

Always in constant contact with race officials, the safety crews are with their emergency vehicles for the entire event, and are poised to be at an incident on the track within seconds. Hopefully, the ambulance or fire crews won't be needed, but when they are, they perform their duties as professionals.

At national sanctioning events, two sets of emergency crews are used, one in the starting line area, and another at the top end of the track, to ensure quick response in the event their services are needed.

Despite the best efforts of racing teams, track crew, officials and organizers, accidents do happen. At every racing event there is a crack squad of professional emergency personnel at the ready to assist in any accident, small or large.

Drag racing's biggest moment in 2008 was the premier of the NHRA Carolina Nationals at Concord, North Carolina. The brand new zMAX Dragway was jammed to capacity for the opener, and should be one of the top spots on the tour in years to come.

Business

Drag racing has come a long way since spectators stood and lined both sides of the track to watch the racing.

Unlike early road racing and stock car events, drag racing by its very nature has been held in controlled environments where spectators paid their admission and walked through the gates.

The majority of early drag strip events were held at unused airport facilities, which provided racers wide, flat expanses to compete on and excellent viewing for spectators. Eventually, bleachers were erected for the few fans and families of the drivers, along with a snack bar and crude washroom facilities.

As the tracks joined up with the various sanctioning bodies, standards were established, and not only for the competitors in terms of safety and technical requirements. Track operators started to treat spectators as guests. Smart operators realized they were fighting for entertainment dollars, and would book the best shows possible.

As with other forms of racing, sponsorship has played a key role in establishing the presence and viability of a racetrack in the general community. Initially tracks would get local

businesses to help defray the costs of running a show, but as the cars got faster and the drivers demanded more appearance and prize money, putting on a good show became difficult financially.

In 1970, Jim Tice of the AHRA signed contracts for some of the top drivers of the day who would compete in a yearly series, accruing points, with the top driver taking home the lion's share of the pot at the end of the season.

While the NHRA had its "national" events at this time, there was no points system as such in place, and while costs in the professional categories (Top Fuel, Funny Car, Pro Stock) grew, the purses did not. In 1972, the AHRA and the Professional Racers Association (PRA) held a meet in Tulsa with major prize money: $25,000 for the top driver in the three main classes. This was unheard of money at the time.

This AHRA/PRA event was held for three more years, and each year it lost money. But a savior for drag racing came along late in 1974.

The R.J. Reynolds Tobacco Company, through its Winston brand of cigarettes, pledged money for a series of races with the IHRA. Shortly afterward, the NHRA received major Winston funding with a $100,000 points fund, and drag racing has not looked back since.

The Winston money was just what drag racing needed to go to the next level. It provided the sport with new capabilities, and other sponsors were attracted to the point where today each major NHRA or IHRA national meet has a headline sponsor.

The initial $100,000 from Winston for the NHRA grew to $325,000 in 1983, was double that four years later, and was over $2 million in 1995.

Winston dropped its NHRA sponsorship in 2001 after 27 years in order to concentrate on its NASCAR involvement. That same year, the NHRA signed Coca-Cola and its POWERade products as the series sponsor, and this agreement was renewed in 2005 for another six years. The NHRA, which claimed an attendance figure at its 24 major events in 2007 of two million, currently gets $3.3 million from Coca-Cola. It also has a large contingent of other sponsors, including Budweiser, Caterpillar, Lucas Oil, UPS and Motel 6.

Although smaller in scope, the IHRA has its own national points series, with 10 national events, two of which are in Canada. In 2002 it acquired title sponsorship from the Hooters restaurant chain, and in 2005 Torco Fuels took over as title sponsor. In 2001 the entertainment giant Clear Channel acquired a majority interest in the IHRA, and in 2007, the IHRA Nitro Jam Drag Racing Series purse was increased nearly $7 million from $13 million to almost $20 million. In

This 1991 shot of Top Fuel driver Kenny Bernstein at Pomona abounds in corporate sponsorship: from driver-sponsor Budweiser to the plethora of auto-related advertising on the grandstands. Had it not been for Winston's initial sponsorship in the sport in 1974, drag racing may never have attracted this much advertising.

2008 Clear Channel sold its interest in the IHRA to Feld Entertainment Motorsports, a division of Feld Entertainment, which produces shows such as Disney on Ice and the Ringling Bros. and Barnum and Bailey Circus.

Today's major drag races rival any other sporting events. Most facilities have all the latest in stadium amenities. Bristol Motor Speedway in Tennessee, which seats 25,000, has 35 suites. The Dragway at Lowe's Motor Speedway in Charlotte, North Carolina, is a new facility in the heart of NASCAR country. This new track will host an NHRA meet with seating for 30,000 fans and 40 suites. The oldest venue on the NHRA tour, Pomona, California, had its first event in 1961, and is still going strong with contemporary amenities and seating for 40,000.

Unlike other major sports, which often hold events in the heart of large metropolitan areas, most drag races are held in communities that are usually too small to attract major league football, basketball or baseball. However, communities of any size and any population base can host a drag race of large proportions, and this can have significant financial impact on the community.

Money spent by competitors, fans and event staff can boost a community's economy in accommodation, meals and gas, along with local advertising and promotion, car and airline rentals and souvenirs. A single major race can bring upwards of $30 million to a local economy.

Drag racing is not a cheap sport to compete in at the top levels. Costs to run a Top Fuel dragster or Funny Car are very high, and a team can spend at least $4,000 per run each time the car makes a full pass. And that's if nothing breaks. This figure includes all associated costs, such as crew payments, hauler and travel expenses, along with the value of the race car itself. Many items, such as rear tires, clutches and engine parts must be constantly replaced to remain competitive, an expense that runs into the thousands of dollars. Cars now have state-of-the-art data retrieval systems and fire-suppression equipment, which add to this high figure. In 1966, about $175 worth of nitromethane was consumed during a Top Fuel quarter-mile run. Today, a Top Fueler will consume an average of 20 gallons of fuel, at over $20 per gallon, which is over $400 spent for about five seconds of racing. A set of slicks will cost about $1,000, and are only good for a few passes. Fuel cars go through spark plugs at an alarming rate and need to be replaced for each run down the track.

A competitive Pro Stock car will cost at least $100,000 to build, and a top-running Pro Modified can climb up to over $200,000. Car costs are one thing, but it's racing the car that can consume the contents of a fat wallet in a hurry.

Payouts in both the NHRA and IHRA come nowhere near paying for campaigning a car. The biggest points fund across all classes in the NHRA, awarded to the team claiming the season title, is $500,000 in the Top Fuel and Funny Car classes, and this includes the $100,000 bonus for the NHRA's "Countdown" championship. In the IHRA the same fund is $150,000. These numbers demonstrate that to compete on a regular basis, especially in the quicker classes, sponsorship must be obtained—sponsorship that runs into the millions of dollars.

Historically, sponsorship in drag racing was limited to small local businesses until the mid 1970s, when television coverage put the sport into the mainstream media. The sponsorship involvement of Winston gave the sport a big financial shot in the arm.

Many top racers used to supplement their income with match racing and personal appearances, and this still occurs today, but not as frequently. Drivers like Jungle Jim Liberman and Tommy Ivo made a good living in match racing, and would be booked solid for the racing season, with guaranteed appearance money. A Garlits-Muldowney show, during their reign as king and queen of Top Fuel in the mid to late 1970s, would cost a track owner or promoter $10,000 to $15,000, depending on number of runs made, track location, and potential fans the track could house. This money would go directly to the drivers after the event.

Today, if a track was able to book drivers of the same caliber, such as Tony Schumacher or John Force, for some special runs and autograph sessions, payment would run from $40,000 to $70,000.

There are many touring groups that book into tracks. Touring groups are groups of cars that compete as their own entites, without any formal sanctioning. They have their own rules, purses, and points funds. These include Stock and Super Stock classes, which can cost the track $10,000 to $15,000. Pro Mods and nitro-powered Altereds also tour and can cost a track $15,000 to $25,000. As with any tour, the more cars that race, the higher the purse. These shows happen two ways: most often tours are booked in by the race tracks, usually with a series or race sponsor that helps defray the costs of prize money for the competitors; the other, less often method is having a touring group rent an entire facility for an event. In this case the tour brings in its own sponsorship and technical and support staff.

Exhibition cars such as jets and wheelstanders are always in demand, and offer a lot of excitement. The drivers of these cars, who work through booking agents, usually charge the race track a fee of about $3,000 each. These cars are usually booked in pairs to offer the fans some side-by-side competition, and race in a best-of-three format.

John Force, the biggest name in drag racing, regales his fans at his merchandise tent, located conveniently in the side of his hauler. Racers, like rock stars, have tapped into fan demand for memorabilia and wearables.

Tony Schumacher takes the U.S.Army dragster on another trip down the track. The Sarge was unstoppable in 2008, winning 15 NHRA events in the 24-race season. He was the number one qualifier nine times and was at the top of the points' race the entire season.

Points

In all organized drag racing, racers compete not only for money, but amass points in seasonal championships as is the case with other sports. The more points collected, the better the chances of becoming the champ at the end of the season.

Sanctioning bodies on a national (or international) scale, such as the NHRA and IHRA, offer points structures at different levels. This is also true for sanctions in Europe, Great Britain and Australia. Racers compete for points at a regional level and can compete for points at a national level.

Smaller drag racing organizations, of which there are many, sanction events of their own and are totally removed from any participation in other sanctions. For example, there are organizations comprised of only one class of cars, such as Pro Modifieds or Super Stock cars, and these groups race together in their own sanction with their own rules, points structure and payouts. These groups are also known as a Touring Series. The series will usually travel to tracks within a short distance of its "home" track for several events per season. The series director will arrange, or book, race dates with track owners, draw up a schedule, and the series will then compete at the tracks as its own entity or race package. The tour is totally separate from other racing activities at the track. Sometimes the series will be fully sponsored for these events, other times the series and the track owners work out a payment arrangement involving percentages of the admission price.

While there are many different classes in drag racing, there are two main divisions, the Professional classes and the amateur classes (or Sportsman as it is often called). The Professional classes are the fastest and most expensive cars fielded by highly sponsored teams that compete at a national level. Professional teams operate themselves as a business—for these teams, their livelihood is racing. Pro classes include the nitro-burning Top Fuel Dragster and Funny Car, Pro Stock, and some Pro Modified cars.

The Sportsman classes are everything else in the drag racing world. The quicker and more expensive Sportsman cars, such as the Alcohol Dragster and Funny Car, are expensive to race, and are considered a semi-professional endeavor.

There is one exception to the professional/amateur rule. Pro Modified cars in the IHRA compete in the sanction's Pro ranks, and even though Pro Modifieds are considered a Professional class in the NHRA, they do not compete regularly in the sanction and their racing is not a part of official NHRA competition. The Pro Mods competing at NHRA events operate like a touring series with its own sponsorship: The series will compete at selected NHRA national events with its own points and payout structure, but is totally separate from the main body of NHRA racing.

Local Racing

Local tracks have a weekly points system for its regular classes, where racers collect points on a sliding scale, similar or identical to the IHRA or NHRA. The amount of points given can vary, depending on several factors, including the number of cars in the class and the number of times racing is held. Sometimes a pair of classes will be grouped together if the car count is low. Points may also be awarded for attendance and qualifying. The racer or team that collects the most points at the "home" track during the season will be declared the track champion in that class.

Divisional or Regional Events

Racing at a divisional level is similar. The stakes are higher, but so is the cost and competition.

The IHRA and NHRA are set up in regional sections, or divisions, throughout North America. The IHRA presently has six regional divisions throughout its domain. In the NHRA, there are seven divisions. Both sanctions have sanctioned tracks within each division and regional programs for these tracks.

The regional programs allow teams to compete on a larger scale by giving a competitor that competes at a local sanctioned track the opportunity to race in a regional or divisional event. This event will be comprised of Sportsman classes, as the national touring Pro teams must concentrate on the major national events.

A driver cannot just show up at a regional event. The competitor must have competed successfully in several events at a local track to be eligible to race at a regional event. In some cases, the team with the highest number of points obtained in local-track racing will be the team to represent the local track at the regional event.

Drivers from participating tracks throughout the division or region will compete in all Sportsman classes for purses and points, and the class winners are rewarded with a divisional title and contingency money.

National Events

Teams competing on a national event level are at the top of their game. The cost, travel, and time involved are great, but so are the rewards and recognition.

While national events in both the IHRA and NHRA focus on the Professional classes, Sportsman racers do compete at national events, and make up the majority of cars at a national event. With more prize money and more recognition for a Sportsman class win at a national event, car counts in most classes will be high, and the competition fierce. Although their cars may not go as fast, or be worth as much money, a win for a Sportsman class driver is just as prestigious as a win in a Professional category.

Sportsman class drivers do have the opportunity to accumulate points at a national meet to add to their regional or divisional points, and, as with a Professional category team, the one with the most points at the end of the season is the ultimate champion in that class.

The Pro teams are totally occupied with national events, and rarely race elsewhere. Racing at this level is a demanding, hectic, fulltime business with huge amounts of travel, and requires a substantial amount of manpower, money, and logistics; teams competing at this level race for points, money, and prestige.

Each Pro team starts the year with zero points and accumulates points on its performance at each national event. The team with the most points at the end of the season in its class is declared the class champion.

The NHRA holds 24 national events across the U.S. yearly. The IHRA has 10 major events in the U.S. and Canada per year. There are no events of this stature outside of North America.

NHRA Points

Winning points in the Pro classes at national events works on a small ladder scale. In the three NHRA Pro car classes (Top Fuel, Funny Car and Pro Stock), the event winner gets 100 points, runner-up 80 points, third-round loser 60 points, second-round loser 40 points and first-round loser 20 points. All contestants will receive 10 points with a required one qualifying run. For establishing an official ET (elapsed time) record, the team gets 20 points.

Points are also earned for qualifying, with the number-one qualifier getting eight points, number-two seven points, number-three six points and the fourth-place qualifier receives five points. Four points are given for the fifth and sixth qualifiers and three points for seventh and eighth qualifiers. Racers qualifying ninth through 12th receive two points, and those making up spots 13 through 16 receive one point.

Sportsman class drivers are allowed to compete in both national and divisional meets to accumulate points for their class title whereas Pro classes may only accrue points in national events. The ratio between national and divisional races differs depending on the class, but points are awarded in the same manner.

The points scale for Sportsman racing is somewhat complicated and is dependent on the number of cars in any given class, which can be from four or less cars to 129 and over. For example, a winner in an NHRA Sportsman class, such as Top Alcohol Dragster or Super Stock, will pick up 85 points if the qualifying field has up to 16 cars. For a field between 17 and 32 cars, 95 points are awarded the winner. A class win in fields up to 128 cars is 105 points and in a field greater than 128 cars, 115 points is awarded the winner.

With more cars to race in a given class, obviously the competition is tougher, and there are more rounds to run. Consider a driver who wins in a 128-car field, as he or she must race seven rounds as the field goes from 128 cars to 64 cars to 32 cars to 16 cars to 8 cars to 4 cars to 2 cars for the final. Not only is that a lot of racing, it's a lot of wear on a race car.

There are no qualifying points awarded in NHRA Sportsman racing, but a minimum of 10 points are given to all competitors upon completion of technical inspection and registration.

IHRA Sportsman Points

Field Size	Points Awarded							
	1st Round Exit	2nd Round Exit	3rd Round Exit	4th Round Exit	5th Round Exit	6th Round Exit	7th Round Exit	Runner Up	Winner
4 or less	40							72	95
5 to 8	40	50						72	95
9 to 16	40	50	60					72	95
17 to 32	40	50	60	70				82	105
33 to 64	40	50	60	70	80			92	115
65 to 128	40	50	60	70	80	90		102	115
129 and up	40	50	60	70	80	90	100	112	125

NHRA Sportsman Points

Field Size	Points Awarded								
	1st Round Exit	2nd Round Exit	3rd Round Exit	4th Round Exit	5th Round Exit	6th Round Exit	7th Round Exit	Runner Up	Winner
4 or less	33							64	85
5 to 8	32	43						64	85
9 to 16	31	42	53					64	85
17 to 32	30	41	52	63				74	95
33 to 64	30	40	51	62	73			84	105
65 to 128	30	40	50	61	72	83		94	105
129 and up	30	40	50	60	71	82	93	104	115

The "Countdown"

In a move to provide more year-end interest, the NHRA altered its points system for its four Professional classes, and presented its "Countdown to the Championship" in 2007 to ensure closer finishes as the year draws to a close.

The NHRA season consists of an 18-race regular series, followed by a six-race countdown for the racers in each class who finished the first 18 races in the top 10 in points.

After the first 18 events, the top 10 in each of the Pro classes will have their points adjusted and separated by 10 points, with 20 additional points going to each class leader. With these changes, first place in the standings will have 2,090 points, second 2,060 points, third 2,050 points, fourth 2,040 points, down to 1,980 points for 10th spot.

This creates an atmosphere very similar to playoffs in other sports, and comparable to NASCAR's "Chase to the Cup," where the 12 top teams are seeded after the first 26 races for the final 10 races of the season.

The NHRA believes this new scoring format provides a stronger opportunity for any of the top 10 class teams in the Countdown to win the championship, as it does not allow for any domination by a team throughout the year. This format puts teams in a two-level chase during the year: the first being the 18-race chase to the Countdown and the second being the Countdown itself. Those outside the top ten still continue to race, and can be especially dangerous to those who are in the Countdown. A non-Countdown participant can still hand a loss to a racer vying for the championship.

Left: NHRA Pro Stock driver Dave Connolly, shown here with his Wally trophy after winning the 2006 NHRA Southern Nationals at Atlanta. The trophy is named after NHRA founder Wally Parks.

Right: Retiring late in 2008, Ohio's Mark Thomas has had a great career in IHRA Alcohol Funny Car competition, winning the championship seven times. Here he proudly displays one of his many IHRA "Ironman" event trophies. R.S. Owens, the same company that designed the Oscar, redesigned the Ironman for the 2008 season.

IHRA Points

Accumulating points in the IHRA's Pro class (Top Fuel, Pro Modified and Pro Stock) is similar to the NHRA system. A class winner gets 90 points, the runner-up gets 70 points, a semi-finalist gets 50 points, a quarter-finalist gets 30 points, and racers finishing nine through 16 get 10 points. For attending the event, racers will receive 10 points. The IHRA awards 41 bonus points if a Pro racer enters all of its national events, and, like the NHRA, a world record in either elapsed time or top speed gets 20 points.

The number-one qualifier in a Pro class gets 16 points, second gets 15 points, third gets 14 points, and so on down to the number-16 qualifier who receives one point.

The Sportsman classes in the IHRA compete at both the national and division level, and points are awarded based on a competitor's best five finishes in eight events at the racer's local track.

Points are accrued in three ways, and are a combination of a driver's entry points, qualifying points and competition points at both the national and regional level. These points are pro-rated, taking into account the field size (number of cars) that determines how many rounds must be held.

If a Sportsman driver wins a divisional meet in a field of up to 16 cars, the driver gets 95 points. In a field of 17 to 32 cars, 105 points are awarded to the winning finalist. In a field of 32 to 128 cars, 115 points are awarded the winner and for a field of 129-plus cars, 125 points are awarded to the top driver. The points structure for round-losers does not change throughout the chart: a second-round loser gets 50 points in an eight-car field right up to a 129-car field. The points the event runner-up receives does change depending on the number of entries, not unlike the points structure of the event winner.

Timing Equipment

While they were colorful in their day, the flag-waving starters of drag racing's early years did not offer anywhere near the precision of today's electronic starting and timing systems.

At first, someone stood at the end of the quarter-mile, and watched as the cars came down the track. Whoever crossed first was declared the winner, which led to a lot of judgment calls, and the official at that end of the track was about as popular as a baseball umpire. Drivers who were familiar with their local starter would, after time, be able to "read" his body language, and could get a "hole-shot" (a quicker start, getting out of the "hole" faster) on an opponent not familiar with the flag-waver.

The early timing setups were devised by modifying timing devices used at the Bonneville Salt Flats and other dry lakes top-speed trials. They were comprised of photocells placed across the start line and across the finish line, which were hooked up with clocks that recorded the speed and elapsed time of each car.

Another early, and somewhat unreliable, method of timing the cars was the use of a pressure-activated hose across the finish line. It was the same setup used at gasoline stations that sounded a bell telling the station attendant that someone was waiting for service at the pumps.

In the early 1960s, the starting line system that became known as the "Christmas Tree" took form. It was a

Originally, a drag race began with an individual waving a flag. By the early 1960s a far superior electronic lighting system put flag wavers out of the job.

pole with two sets of lights, one for each driver, with five amber lights, a green light and then a red light, in that order from top to bottom, on each side. The cars would pull up to the start line, and at the push of a button from the starter, the amber lights would flash sequentially down the pole until the green light came on, signaling the start of the race. If a car jumped the green light before it was activated, the bottom red light would come on, signifying a foul and the driver would be eliminated.

By 1963 a California-based company, Corvonics, became the leader in the development and building of the Chrondek Christmas Tree. The first two, smaller, amber lights at the top of the Tree, labeled "pre-stage" and "stage," were hooked up with the two light beams (now built into the starting line). The two beams were, and still are, seven inches apart, and when both cars cross both beams, placing themselves into the "staged" position, the starter begins the light sequence.

In actual operation, the basics of the Tree have changed little since 1963. Today there is a "Pro" Tree which flashes all amber lights simultaneously before the green, and the "Sportsman" or "full" tree, which is used for all non-pro, handicap classes and flashes all the amber lights sequentially before the green.

There is a 0.4-second difference between the flash of the amber and the flash of the green with a Pro Tree, while on the full Tree, used for handicap racing, there is a 0.5-second difference between the last amber and the green.

Today's computer-based systems time the competition within thousandths of a second, and aside from supplying the car's speed and elapsed time at the end of the track, provide incremental times and speeds at various distances between the starting and finish lines.

Each competitor receives a slip from track officials at the end of his or her run with all this information. This information is also recorded through proprietary computer software packages by track officials in the track's control tower, usually situated near the starting line and offering a panoramic view of the entire race track.

In the last few years the incandescent Christmas Tree lights have been replaced with LED (light-emitting diode) systems, solid-state units that harness a semiconductor chip to turn electric energy into visible light, offering enhanced visibility and reliability.

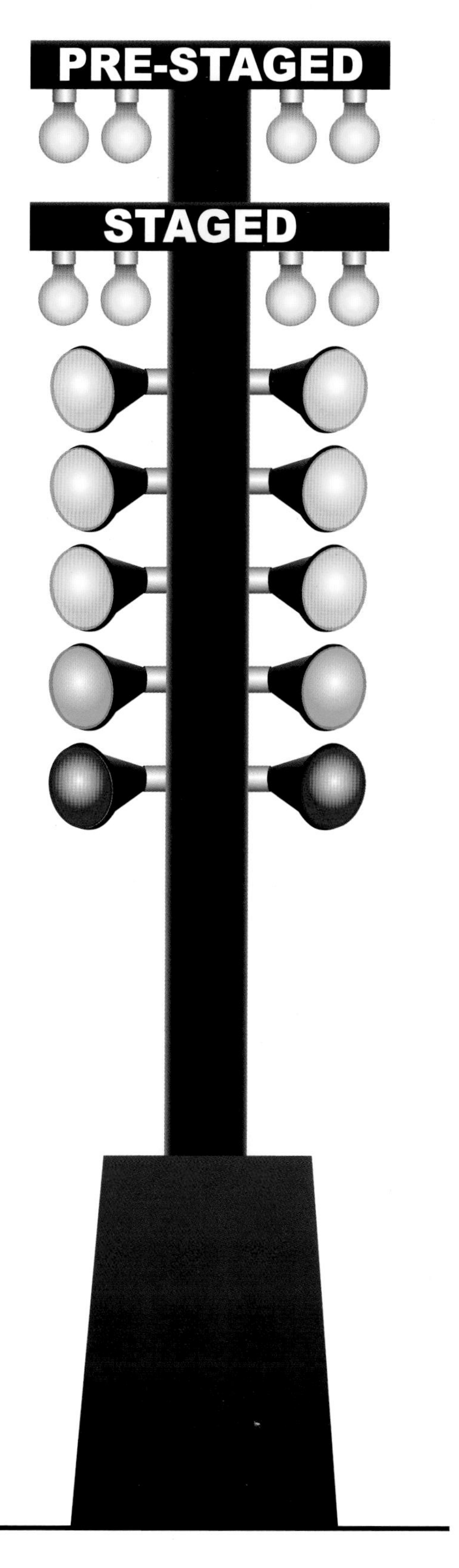

Drag racing's iconic Christmas Tree. No matter how hard you try, you can't beat the Tree to get a jump on your competitor—doing so will result in a red light, in other words, disqualification.

The Race

In simple terms, a drag race is a tournament-style competition that pits two competitors against each other. The competitors accelerate their vehicles from a standing start over a measured distance, either a quarter-mile, or an eighth-mile.

The quarter-mile broken down into the most important segments for racers. After the staging is set and the cars start their runs, elapsed times are recorded at the intervals shown here, which the team then uses to asses the car's performance. Along with the total time of the run recorded at the finish line, the speed in miles per hour (MPH) is also recorded.

Each race is a round of eliminations. The competitor who loses the elimination is finished for the remainder of the event. The winner goes on to compete in the next elimination round.

Competing machines are divided into a variety of classes, and these classes are regulated by sanctioning-body limitations of engine size, car weight, modifications and type of fuel.

Qualifying

Cars must qualify through a time-trial procedure. Contestants post a qualifying time that is pitted against the times of other contestants. The top times from all racers are then chosen to advance to the elimination stage. As an example, if there are 23 cars vying for a starting spot in a 16-car field, the slowest seven cars will not make the eliminations, and their race is finished. Depending on the number of entrants, the group of cars attempting to qualify will be set up in multiples of two. If there is an odd number of cars a contestant will receive a "bye" run, or make a qualifying attempt with a solo pass.

There are usually three sets of qualifying rounds to enable a contestant to make the field. A contestant will be allowed choice of lane for qualifying, and must make two attempts at qualifying for an event. Quite often prizes will be awarded to the top qualifier of a class.

Eliminations

Qualified vehicles are matched up by times posted during the time trials and set up by race officials for the eliminations. This setup is commonly known as the "ladder," which can be anywhere from four to 16 cars. No matter how many cars qualify, the number-one qualifier (the contestant who recorded the lowest elapsed time) will be matched up with the qualifier with the highest elapsed time. The next pairing of cars will continue in this fashion of low vs. high for the remainder of the field.

The winners of the first round will then be paired up for the second round. Once again the fastest car is pitted with the slowest car for the round and the second-fastest with

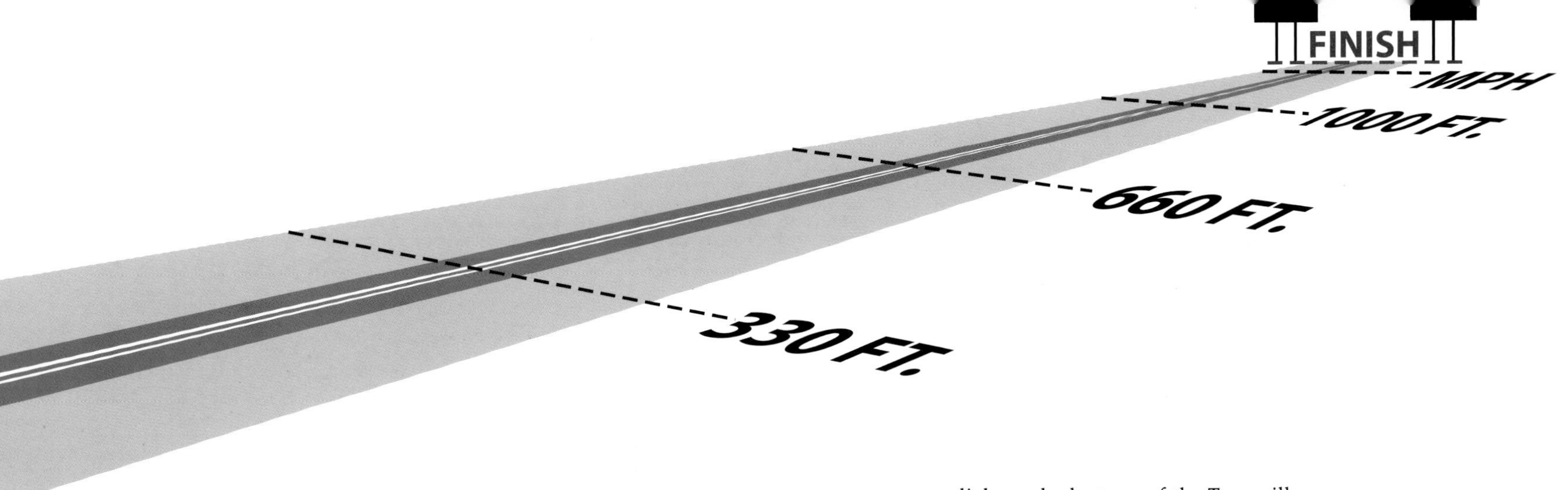

the second-slowest. The fastest car of each pairing is given lane choice before racing. There are no free rides once the eliminations begin. Even if a contestant is scheduled in a "bye" run (a solo run due to an uneven number of cars in the field) or a competitor's opponent cannot make it to the starting line in a round of eliminations, the contestant will still have to race and will usually try to post a good time in order to have a chance to win lane choice for the next round.

As the fields of cars diminish during eliminations, the last three rounds are also known as the "quarter-final," "semi-final" and "final." The final round is between the only two cars not eliminated. The winner is declared the champion of the event.

The Race

The first two cars perform their burnouts (to clean their tires), and then stage at the starting line. There are two sets of light beams across the track for each lane. These photocells are linked electronically to the timing devices and to the Christmas Tree.

When a car's tires break the first light beam, the car is "pre-staged," and this is noted on the Christmas Tree with the top yellow bulb. The car then proceeds seven inches farther ahead, breaking the beam and lighting the "Staged" light on the Tree. When both sets of the staging lights are activated, the cars are ready to race.

When the starter is satisfied that the cars are ready, he activates the sequential lighting system on the Tree, and when the green light flashes, the cars are on their way down the track.

Drivers in the Professional classes see only one amber bulb before the green is activated, while the Sportsman drivers watch three amber bulbs that light sequentially before the green light. If a driver gets on the throttle before the green light flashes, a red light at the bottom of the Tree will shine, indicating the driver started too soon, and he or she will lose the round. Otherwise, the car that gets to the finish line first is declared the winner.

The system used to time the race monitors three performances of each vehicle: the speed in miles per hour, the time it takes to break the beam at the finish line—also known as the "speed trap," and the driver's reaction time. This third element is measured by the length of time it takes the driver to break the beam at the starting line after the flash of the green light. This is timed in thousandths of a second, and the closer this time is to .000, the quicker the driver has reacted to the green light. This practice is called "cutting a light," and can play a significant part in winning a round, as a driver who has a quick reaction time can get a jump on his competitor.

Handicap Racing

Eliminations in classes of Sportsman cars, along with Bracket racers, are essentially the same as the Pro classes except for starting line procedures that follow a handicapped system, allowing slower cars to compete with faster cars, as explained on pages 108–109.

Top: The rear slick on this Top Fuel car is twisted on launch by the car's power, demonstrating the "wrinkle" effect.

Unique Features

Drag racing has developed and progressed technologically, as have other forms of motorsport, but there are several aspects of the mechanics of drag racing that are unique in the racing world. The three main areas where drag racing remains distinctive are the use of slicks for rear tires and cleaning these tires, engine superchargers and parachutes for slowing down.

Bottom: The skinny front wheel/tire is only used to hold up the car and steer it. The back slick is all-important and racers use the fattest tires allowed for maximum traction.

Getting Traction

Even in the sport's early years, drag cars had lots of power. The problem was getting this power to the back wheels quickly and efficiently. It didn't take racers long to figure that a treadless tire with low air pressure offered the best traction. By eliminating any tread, or grooves, on a tire, the largest possible contact patch or amount of actual rubber was available for maximum traction.

Early drag slicks were basically recapped wide car tires of six or seven inches in width. This helped, but it was a frustrating experience as the back wheels would usually just sit and smoke on the line as the clutch was dumped and the throttle was mashed to the floorboards.

The tire of choice was made of butyl rubber, as this synthetic rubber offered good adhesion and heat resistance, but tire technology had still not developed softer compounds that would offer better traction. As car speeds increased, tires blowing up or separating was an all-too-common occurrence. There were tires built for racing, but racing for Indianapolis-style cars and some stock car applications, not drag. A serious bottleneck in the progression of drag racing was due to tire technology, until 1957.

Marvin and Harry Rifchin, who built Midget and stock car racing tires in their Massachusetts shop, developed and built a narrow (six and a half inches) drag-racing specific tire of a softer compound at the request of a South Carolina drag strip owner. When drivers such as Don Garlits used them successfully, M&H Tires began producing a line of several "Dragmaster" slicks, which dominated the market. Goodyear Tire got involved with the making of slicks in 1964, but M&H continued building their slicks, and today is one of the leaders in the market.

Other prominent drag slick manufacturers include Mickey Thompson, Firestone and Hoosier.

Slicks utilize very low pressures to maximize the tread contact area; as such, these tires are constructed to allow the sidewall to be twisted by the torque applied during the car's launch, producing the typical sidewall appearance which leads

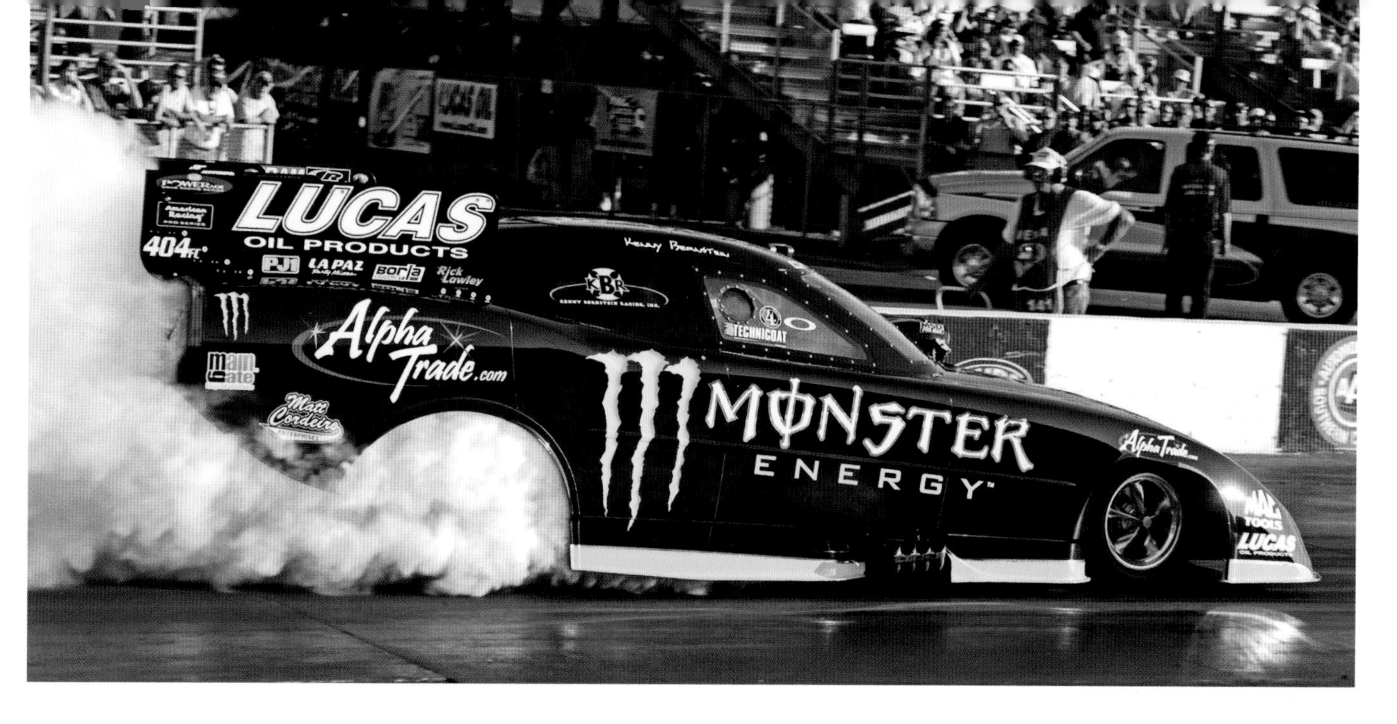

When Funny Cars first incorporated burnouts in order to clean their rear tires, a whole new era in drag racing was born. Using only about half the car's power, fans are awe-struck by the smoke a burnout typically generates. A healthy burnout is shown here by the legendary Kenny Bernstein in 2008.

to their being termed "wrinklewall" slicks. Inner tubes are typically used to ensure that the air does not suddenly leak as the tire deforms under the stress of launching. This softening at the launch reduces the chances of breaking traction. As speed builds, the centrifugal force generated by the tires' rotation "unwraps" the sidewalls, returning the stored energy to the car's acceleration. Additionally, this force causes the tires to expand radially, increasing their diameter and effectively creating a taller gear ratio, allowing a higher top speed with the same transmission gearing.

Cleaning the Tires

"Cleaning the tires" before a race is a common ritual in all types of racing. Formula and stock cars veer sharply from side to side to scrub up their tires and get heat in them during their pace laps.

Drag racers also clean their tires before they race, but in a ritual quite unique in the racing world.

Each racer drives into an area on the track just before the staging area which has been soaked with water. As the car's rear tires enter this area, the driver accelerates in the water to spin the slicks, which not only gets rid of any pebbles and debris picked up on them, but it also can create a lot of tire smoke.

This is known as the "burnout," and it is one of the most prominent features in the world of drag racing.

In the sport's early years, resin, then bleach, was thrown down on the track, and many still refer to this area of the strip as the "bleach box." As the rubber compounds of the slicks improved for better traction, bleach was replaced with water.

This preliminary activity was devised to get better traction. Faster cars such as fuel dragsters were literally spinning their wheels all the way down the track in an effort to hook up and keep the rear tires from spinning.

While burnouts enhance starting-line traction, they have become an exhibition of sorts, as the faster cars will disappear in a wall of smoke.

Top Fuelers provide some burnout action, but Funny Cars and Pro Mods can put on a real show as they smoke their way out of the box and halfway down the strip to the delight of the fans. A big part of the pre-race show for match racers is to come out of the box and really light up the slicks, taking their cars way down the strip in a big burnout.

Superchargers/Blowers

A mechanical device known as a supercharger was developed and in use on a variety of automotive, aircraft and stationary engine applications by the 1920s.

Running off the engine itself, a supercharger, in simple terms, pushes a large air/fuel mixture into the engine, much more than carburetors or mechanical fuel injection. Two large vanes inside the supercharger run at speeds higher than the engine, forcing the mixture into the cylinders.

For drag racers, this meant more power and, more importantly, this power was produced more quickly in the engine.

There are two types of superchargers used in drag racing, the older "Roots-style," and the "screw-style," developed about 20 years ago.

The Roots supercharger is named after the Indiana brothers who patented the device in 1860. This supercharger pulls the air through the housing case with a pair of meshing lobes.

A fuel engine supercharger in the Budweiser pits. Note the long snout at the front of the unit, the protective blanket around the main body of the blower and the large air scoop.

Using the Roots-type supercharger from the General Motors two-cycle diesel engine, racers experimented and rebuilt these early blowers for racing applications. At first the blower was attached to the front of the car's engine, and the fuel/air mixture was pushed into the engine's manifold through large tubes.

As supercharger technology evolved, racers found they could make more power and faster if the unit was sitting on top of the engine, feeding the fuel/air mixture right into the engine, rather than pushing it through the tubes of a front-blower setup.

Soon, aftermarket companies began producing superchargers for racing applications, casting them of lighter materials such as aluminum. The unit was fabricated to sit directly on top of the engine, driven by a wide belt off the crankshaft. At first carburetors fed the blower, then fuel injectors, a system that is used to this day.

Based on the old GMC 71 Series diesels such as the 4-71 (four cylinders, 71 cubic inches per cylinder), 6-71 (six cylinders, 71 cubic inches per cylinder) and so on, aftermarket superchargers grew in rotor and case length to today's 14-71, which is the limit of most supercharger applications today, as mandated by the sanctioning bodies.

These longer cases can hold rotors up to 19 inches long, but with a shorter rotor in the smaller case, the air going into the engine is more efficiently cooled. Builders of superchargers learned quickly that the way to success was how the air enters and exits the blower, and needing less engine power to run the supercharger.

The helix, or angle of twist on the rotor's vanes, can provide more power, especially at higher engine speeds. In most applications, a 60-degree twist is common, and a 120-degree twist to the vanes can reduce the air temperature up to 200 degrees Fahrenheit. And this means more power.

Superchargers also function in an overdrive mode through gearing and pulleys to enhance flow from the supercharger into the engine. These overdrive ratios, which vary depending on the car class, are controlled by the sanctioning bodies for reliability and costs.

In the late 1980s, mechanical engineer Norm Drazy developed a screw-type supercharger based on an 1870s Swedish design that was originaly utilized as a source of oil-free air in many applications. This blower design has a pair of meshing screws inside the housing which compress (cool) the air as it moves through the blower. Known in the drag racing world as a PSI blower, this unit is more efficient than the traditional Roots blower, not only in building power but in keeping internal temperatures lower.

Initially developed for nitromethane-burning fuel engines, the screw blower was banned by the NHRA and IHRA for fuel cars, as the sanctions felt that costs would greatly escalate for the racers. It is currently used in other classes such as Alcohol Funny Car and Pro Modified.

Slowing Down

As the speeds of drag cars increased, drivers had problems slowing them down. The early cars were built to accelerate, and little thought was given to slowing down. Dragsters, especially, with only drum brakes on the rear wheels, would quite often end up off the end of the track shutdown area as the car's crude brakes would heat up and become useless.

By 1958, men such as Jim Deist and Bill Simpson were experimenting with parachutes that would be opened by the driver of a dragster at the end of a run. Simpson, who had broken both his arms in a drag racing crash, went to an army surplus store, and through trial and error successfully developed a parachute that would deploy on demand and slow down the car significantly. Deist, meanwhile, was

applying his aircraft safety experience to the drag racing world, and started to market a parachute around the same time.

As car speeds increased, so did parachute technology. Both canopy design and mounting technology have made huge inroads, as has driver protection from negative acceleration. The ring-slot parachute, today built by Stroud, is a large, circular parachute using a smaller parachute, or bag, that opens first to take slack out of the main parachute, which helps cushion the negative acceleration impact on both the car and the driver.

The other main parachute design is the cross form style, which looks like a large "X" when opened. To help minimize the shock of slowing down, this type of parachute employs a smaller, pilot parachute which is spring-loaded and opens first before the main parachute. Chutes are deployed in various ways, mechanical, pneumatic, or through compressed air.

Sanctioning bodies mandate cars that reach speeds of 150 mph must use a parachute. For speeds of 200 mph and over, two parachutes are mandatory.

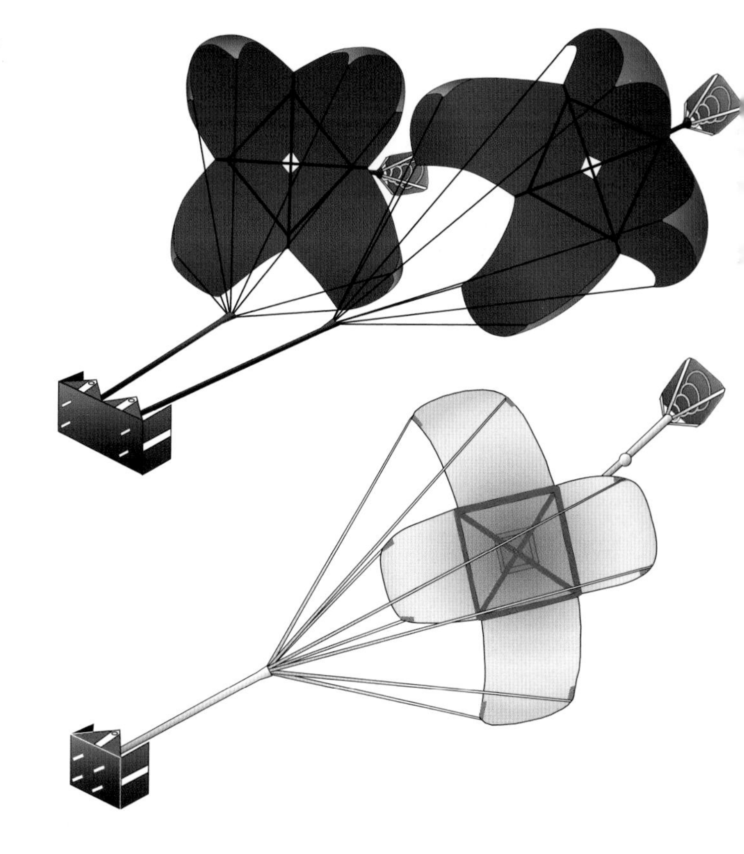

Top: Slowing down a fuel car provides almost as much force on the body as does the acceleration. Even though the driver is strapped in so tightly they can hardly breathe, the forward strain on the body when the parachutes deploy can leave the chest area bruised.

Bottom: Unique to drag racing in the motorsport world, parachutes are used to stop vehicles that travel 150 mph or faster. Most parachutes use a small pilot parachute which opens first and helps to open the main parachute.

Walking the pits is a special part of drag racing. Most fans will never get this close to a fuel dragster. You can bet that many eyes are searing from the nitro fumes and many ears are throbbing from the 7,500 horsepower engine.

Day at the Track

Whether it is for a racing fan or a racing team, a day at the track is an event that requires much planning and stamina to get through. A lot happens over the course of a single day of racing, and with events lasting several hours, both fans and teams need to be prepared for the long haul.

Fan's Day

You can watch drag racing on television, and you can read about the sport in magazines, newspapers and online, but nothing compares to attending an event in person. Witnessing two nitromethane-burning cars with 7,500 horsepower each at full throttle is an experience that can numb the senses. It is the most powerful performance in motorsport.

Gone are the days when spectators lined both sides of the drag strip on spindly wooden bleachers, tried to listen to sound systems drowned out by the race cars, and argued over who won a race as there were no displays to signify the winners, speeds or times.

When attending an event today, fans are able to not only see all the track action, but also large, state-of-the-art displays that instantly project who won the race, along with drivers' speeds, elapsed times and reaction times. A fan can witness an entire drag race from starting line to finish line, something not possible with road racing events. Some oval track races for stock cars and Indy type cars are so large in length that spectators do not see all the racing.

Getting Up Close

Another unique aspect of attending a major event is that all the action does not take place on the track. Fans are welcomed and encouraged to stroll through the pit areas, something that cannot be done in other types of racing.

In the pits fans will see a flurry of activity between rounds. Although the working areas are barricaded, fans can get within easy viewing distance to watch teams work on their cars.

Fans also have little trouble getting autographed hero cards of their favorite drivers, and depending on time constraints may be able to speak with the drivers.

Quite often fans will be in the pits before the cars go to the staging lanes. This is the time when teams have finished working on their cars, and will fire up the engines to determine that all is in order.

Fans flock to the pit area of a Funny Car or Top Fueler when an engine is fired up, as this is the closest they will get to the thunder of thousands of horsepower and the pungent, eye-burning characteristics of nitromethane. With the car sitting on stands, the crew will tune the engine, check the gauges, and blip the throttle, while the fans cover their ears for the roar and shield their eyes from the exhaust fumes. And while this may sound a little dangerous and nerve-wracking, this ritual provides the fans with a lot of excitement and a better appreciation of the technology of these cars.

Three Big Days

There are hundreds of drag strips throughout North America, Great Britain, Europe and Australia. While regular meets are held, usually weekly, at all tracks, the major sanctioning bodies have developed sizeable, multi-day events that offer large purses and bring in the best teams to compete.

A typical national meet will be held on a weekend. There will be qualifying for Sportsman and Pro classes on the Friday and Saturday of the weekend. Eliminations will take place in Sportsman classes on the Saturday, and on Sunday the elimination rounds for the Pro classes take place.

A Variety of Venues

So where to sit?

Most major facilities feature high, permanent stands along both sides of the track, along with suites of several sizes similar to private boxes at other sporting events. Many fans prefer to be as close to the starting line as possible, to capture the noise and excitement of burnouts and launches. Others like to sit midway down the track, so they get a view of the race as it unfolds, and can quite often determine who will win the race, something harder to do when sitting at the starting line due to the angle of view.

And there are fans who prefer to sit right at the finish line where their view offers several angles not available elsewhere. Unless the cars are running extremely close, a fan can tell who won the race without viewing the scoreboard. A fan can also watch the parachutes open when the faster cars are running. And it is here that a fan can see the cars going their fastest.

But there is one constant no matter where a person sits. Whether it's at the starting line, half-track, or at the end of the measured distance, be it a quarter-mile, eighth-mile, or the new 1000-foot distance instituted by the NHRA for fuel cars in 2008, the noise remains constant as engines are pushed to their limits.

What to Wear

Drag racing is obviously an outdoor sport, and one must dress according to the weather. Events are held during optimum weather conditions, which mean sun and heat. Skin must be protected with sunscreen if necessary. Light clothing is usually the norm, but heavier clothing may be necessary at a race depending on geographic location and the season. It is advisable to check the upcoming weather forecast before heading out to a race.

Take lots of liquids with you, especially water. Not only will you need the water intake during the day in the stands, you can always splash some on yourself to cool down. A water-soaked towel is also useful to keep refreshed as the day wears on.

In all of motorsport, drag racing is the loudest. The top classes of cars produce sound ratings that rival a jet plane at takeoff, and ear protection is highly recommended. Smart fans realize that listening to full-throttle assaults of cars for hours is also a full-throttle assault on ears and without protection hearing can be damaged.

Fans have a choice of a wide variety of ear plugs and exterior ear protection. Some fans will use both plugs and protectors, which go a long way to minimizing the ringing in the ears after a day at the track.

Professional racers such as the Bernstein Funny Car team set up shop for the better part of a week in a makeshift pit, which would rival any garage. For the team, this is their office during a national event.

Team's Day

Whether it's competing in a single-day event, or preparing for a major national meet, a large portion of racing for teams both big and small is getting to the track and getting set up.

As a rule of thumb, teams involved with the faster classes of cars spend the most time setting up at the track,

and they will get to the race facility a couple of days before the qualifying begins. The eight to ten team members with a professional team first get the semi-truck hauler parked. Then some members begin to unload the tools and equipment needed for the event, while others assemble and install the overhead canopy, which is fastened to the side of the hauler trailer. The race car is then pushed out of the trailer, and positioned front and center under the canopy, but not before a carpet is placed on the pavement underneath the car.

Inside the hauler, the computers are turned on. Team members read printouts and data acquisitions from past performances, and decide what and how to change the car in order to win more races.

Parts or systems for the race car that need attention will be addressed during this down time while it is relatively quiet.

As team members get organized and gather together all that is needed to work on the car, perimeter barriers are placed around the whole working area. These do not hinder the fans' view of the pit activity, but are necessary for the team to work on the car with no interference from fans.

Another team member readies the food preparation and eating area for the team, which will stay with the hauler and race car throughout the event. For the next several days, this small area of asphalt has become not only the team's workplace, but its home.

Also at this time, drivers and team members will visit with their fellow competitors, not only to bench race, but to socialize. Many teams are on the road for months, constantly traveling, away from home, friends and family. In many cases, this social aspect is most important to the traveling pros, and there is camaraderie between the teams, not unlike the circus troupes which years ago traveled by train from show to show.

Two Very Busy Days

Depending on the class of car, the number of entries and qualifying attempts, a racer will run down the track at least six times (three qualifying, three eliminations) at a major event.

Before the initial qualifying begins, the car's engine and drivetrain are thoroughly checked, inspected and worked on for maximum performance. Team members will adjust and set up the clutch depending on weather factors such as moisture

Professional racing teams just don't sit around between rounds at a national meet. Constant attention must be paid to the car. Here a team works on a Funny Car with the engine half taken apart.

and heat in the air. Aspects of the racing surface are also noted and the car modified to meet optimum performance for the environment, such as the stickiness of the track and the altitude of the facility. Once these nuances are noted, the team will have benchmarks on which to determine the car's set up, and can make adjustments after the initial pass.

When the team believes it is ready, the car is driven, pulled or pushed into the staging lanes. The team may sit with the car for up to 60 minutes, longer if there is a mishap on the track that needs attention. It is at this time that crew members can be found making last-minute adjustments.

When the class is called to prepare to race, the team will ensure the driver is strapped in the car properly, get the car fired up, check all is in order, and watch as the driver does the burnout.

But the team members don't just sit and watch the racing.

The faster classes of cars are allowed to perform burnouts past the Christmas tree, and these cars must be guided back, which means a crew member runs down the track to where the car stops, and working with another crew member behind the starting line, the pair guide the driver back up the lane and into the launching area to get staged. When the car has reversed and is now ready to get staged, a team member will check the temperature of the back tires with a small hand-held unit. It is also at this time that if a car has a parachute, it is readied for use by a crew member who will pull out the safety pin so the driver can engage it during the shutdown procedure. The wheelie bar is also given a final check.

Once the car is pre-staged, the race is now in the driver's hands. The crew members will go off to the side of the track to watch intently in their push vehicle or golf cart.

The amount of work needed at the far end of the track after the race is the same for the crew, whether it's a win or a loss. The only difference is that the team doesn't mind the work as much when it wins and knows it is going to the next round.

For the faster race cars, the crew members travel down to the shutoff area in a support vehicle and by the time they get there the driver is usually out of the car, or at least taking off his helmet. The car is visually inspected, the parachute is folded up and the car towed or pushed back to the team's pits.

This is when the work starts for the crew. Before the next round the amount of work that takes place depends on the class of car. The faster the car, the more work involved, but even the slowest stockers get their sparkplugs inspected, carburetors tweaked and fluids checked. Tire pressures are noted. Often the valves are checked for tolerances, as is the ignition timing.

For the Pro teams, the engine comes apart, even if it ran perfectly. The on-board data collectors tell the crew what went on inside the engine, and the crew can go to work right away on any area not up to standards. To maintain the competitive edge, Pro teams will rebuild as much of the engine as they think necessary to win the next round, and this means working with every internal piece inside the powerplant.

Pro teams have crews of specialists. Each member of the team is a fine mechanic in his or her own right, but each has developed specialties in engine or powertrain management for which he or she is responsible. Several crew members work on the engine, but one will work solely on the valve train while another's forte is the bottom end with the pistons, crankshaft and engine sump containing the heavyweight racing oil. Another team member will be responsible for the supercharger, and making sure it is performing. Another will work with the clutch and driveline. And heading up this effort is the crew chief, often the most important member of the whole racing effort. He or she is ultimately responsible for the car's preparedness.

The crew will thrash at the car at a fevered, but controlled pace, to make sure the car is ready for the call to the next round. The turnaround window can be as little as an hour from round to round, so a team cannot afford to waste any time.

Depending on the situation, and the needed repairs, a crew can hustle constantly between rounds, the only letup coming as the car sits in the staging lanes waiting to race.

This pace continues throughout the event.

Finally, when the racing day is done and nothing major has broken on the race car, it's packed up in the hauler, along with all the tools and equipment that have been outside for the past several days. Then the carpet the car sat on is rolled up and stored, and the awning on the side of the trailer is rolled up and stored, the team has a final meal together, there is usually some social time spent with the other teams, and then it's on the road again to the next event.

Left: After a burnout, the slicks of faster cars are wiped of stones and other debris. This keeps the rubber clean creating the optimum conditions to achieve the maximum amount of traction.

Bottom:
A professional racing team is working long before and after any racing takes place. Here a Top Fueler is being taken out of a hauler to be put in the pit enclosure set up against the side of the hauler's trailer.

Car Classes

Legend

 Fuel Type

 Speeds and Times

 Tranny

 Tires (width)

 Engine Size/HP

 Weight

All figures are based on quarter-mile racing for comparison purposes.

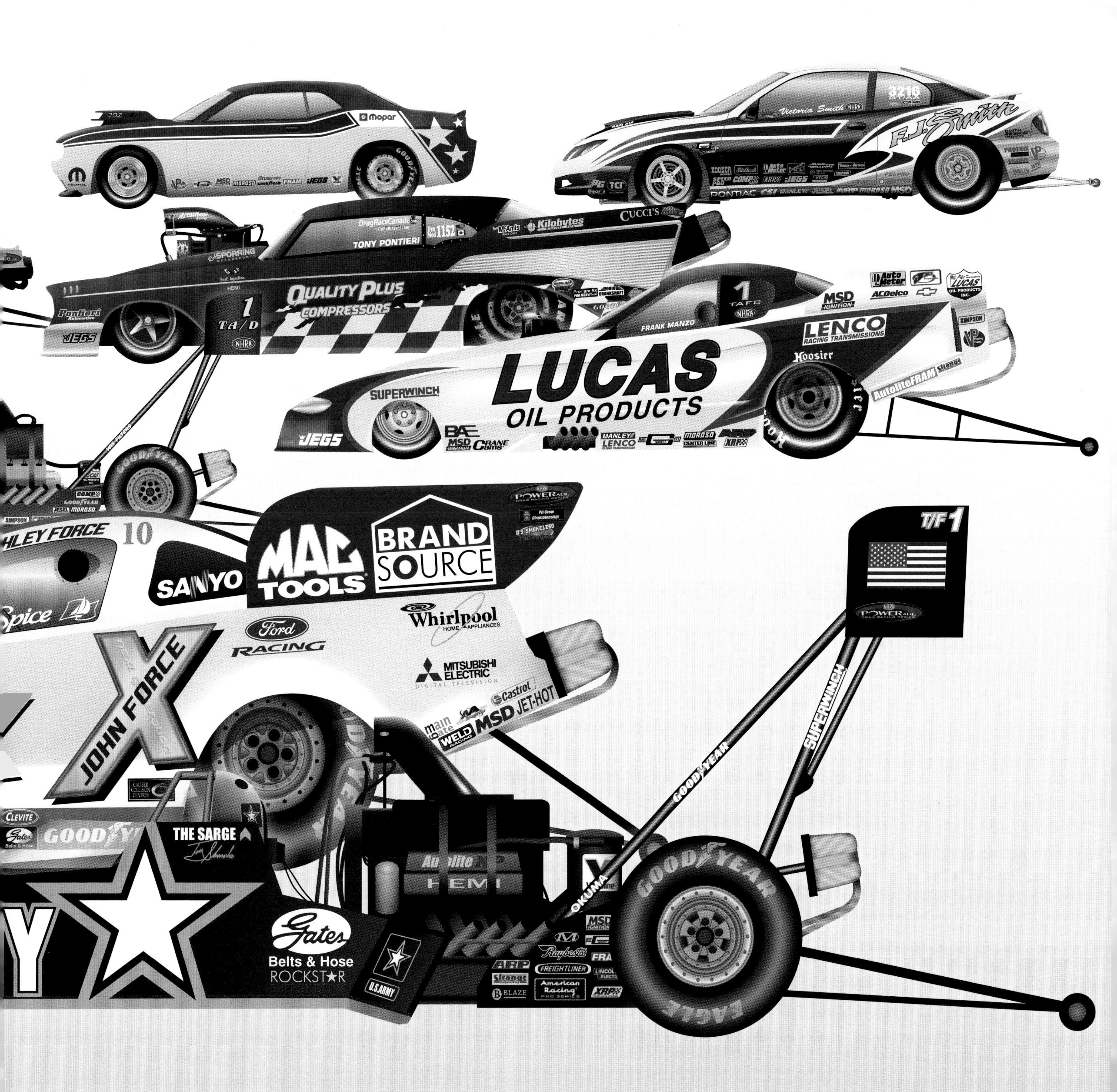
Mopar
Snap-on
GOODYEAR
FRAM
JEGS
Victoria Smith
3216
F.J. Smith
PONTIAC
MANLEY
JESEL
ARP
MOROSO
MSD
DragRaceCanada.com
TONY PONTIERI
Pro Mod 1152
Kilobytes
CUCCI'S
SPORRING
QUALITY PLUS
COMPRESSORS
Pontieri Automotive
JEGS
1
TA/D
NHRA
1
TAFC
NHRA
FRANK MANZO
MSD IGNITION
LENCO
RACING TRANSMISSIONS
ACDelco
LUCAS OIL PRODUCTS
Hoosier
SUPERWINCH
JEGS
CRANE CAMS
MANLEY
LENCO
MOROSO
CENTER LINE
XRP
SIMPSON
GOODYEAR
MOROSO
SIMPSON
ASHLEY FORCE
10
SANYO
MAC TOOLS
BRAND SOURCE
Whirlpool
HOME APPLIANCES
Ford
RACING
MITSUBISHI ELECTRIC
DIGITAL TELEVISION
Castrol
MSD
JET-HOT
WELD
JOHN FORCE
CALIBER COLLISION CENTRES
CLEVITE
Gates
GOODYEAR
THE SARGE
Autolite
HEMI
Gates
Belts & Hose
ROCKSTAR
U.S.ARMY
ARP
FREIGHTLINER
American Racing
BLAZE
XRP
OKUMA
GOODYEAR
EAGLE
SUPERWINCH
T/F 1
POWERADE

Fuel Cars

The top ranks of professional drag racing are Top Fuel and Funny Car. While these two automobiles are quite different in appearance and handling, they do share one common denominator: the ultimate fuel.

It's known as nitro. Pop. Liquid horsepower. Harnessing its capabilities is a science and sometimes a black art. But when fed into a Top Fueler or Funny Car engine, nitromethane has no equal in producing prodigious amounts of power.

No-one who experiences two fuel cars leaving the line will forget the sight, sound and smell of this ritual.

Top Fuel Dragster

A Top Fuel Dragster is the fastest-accelerating vehicle on the planet. Period.

When the engine is tuned just right, the clutch adjusted just right and the track conditions just right, a Top Fueler will travel the quarter-mile from a standing start in about 4.5 seconds. With optimum conditions, this car will go from zero to 100 mph in under one second, to 275 mph in three seconds, and clock over 330 mph by the time the parachutes are deployed at the end of the quarter-mile.

Progression and Development

A Top Fuel car, or dragster, has always been a long-wheelbased vehicle with minimum body work over a specially-constructed chassis. With the most powerful engine and the lightest weight, dragsters have traditionally been, and continue to be, the quickest cars in drag racing.

Since its inception, the foundation of this car has always been the same. However, there have been many changes, both for speed and safety over the decades, but the biggest change in dragster development was the introduction and adoption of the front-driver, rear-engined configuration, which took hold in the early 1970s.

After some serious crashes with the older front-engined designs (including a nasty accident involving Don Garlits in 1970 (see pages 32–33), a workable rear-engined car became commonplace. This design, spearheaded by Garlits, offered a vast increase in driver safety simply by putting the driver out of harm's way if the engine or drivetrain exploded. The new design also offered unlimited visibility.

In the late 1970s, at the behest of west coast Top Fuel driver Jerry Ruth, dragster chassis builder Al Swindahl built Ruth the prototype chassis on which today's cars are based. Ruth was tired of banging his head on the roll cage, and so Swindahl incorporated a larger cage into the integrity of the chassis. Swindahl also lengthened the chassis, and put more space between the cockpit and the engine. The car that Ruth debuted was not as aerodynamic as other dragsters of the day, but it was lighter and so well-balanced that other teams realized this was the design to have. Today's cars, whether built by Hadman or McKinney or Attac, closely follow Swindahl's design.

Another major development in dragster design has been an increase in the length of the car. Although present sanctions allow a wheelbase of between 180 and 300 inches, most cars are closer to the longer limit as the cars are easier to handle, and rarely get out of shape. Today's Top Fuel drivers guide their car down the track with finesse and a light touch on the steering wheel, an altogether different approach from driving a shorter-wheelbase, front-engined car.

While aerodynamics does not play as big a role in Top Fuel as it does in Formula One cars, there are wings, spoilers and other body modifications that work mainly to apply downforce on the rear wheels to enhance traction.

Brandon Bernstein tucked inside the cockpit of his Top Fueler. It may be tight in there, but that is the point. Notice the substantial roll cage, almost toy-like steering wheel, multi-point harness and computer and electronic equipment.

While it may appear that little has occurred in dragster development over the years, the basic package of today's car remains a solid platform for designers and engineers to further enhance in the quest to get to the finish line first.

Chassis and Safety

The dragster is built of exotic, lightweight materials on a 300-inch (25-foot) wheelbase. The weight of the car when race-ready must be a minimum of 2,225 pounds.

The car is constructed not only for speed, but to offer maximum protection for the driver. A very solid roll cage, which is built as an integral part of the car's chassis, provides a Top Fueler racer with a secure cocoon in case of an accident. If a high-speed

Fast Facts

The extraordinary world of fuel racing is filled with extraordinary facts and figures. Comparing other types of automotive facts with Top Fuel or Funny Car racing is almost futile, but here are some interesting items that provide some perspective on this type of vehicle.

- The rear slicks on a fuel car are usually discarded after two runs.
- A fuel car produces about the same horsepower as the first five rows of a NASCAR Cup race.
- The 100 gallons-per-minute fuel pump on a fuel car is capable of filling an 18,000 gallon swimming pool in three hours.
- The rear wing on a Top Fueler reportedly produces up to five tons, or 10,000 pounds of downforce at 300 mph. That's like having three good-sized cars sitting on the back of the race car.
- Under full throttle, a fuel engine consumes the same amount of fuel as a fully loaded Boeing 747.
- Fuel engines eat spark plugs at an alarming rate. By half-track, the electrodes in the plugs are gone, and the only way to stop the engine is to shut off its fuel supply. There is no ignition to turn on and off as in a regular street vehicle.
- During the launch of a fuel car, the driver sustains close to five Gs of gravitational pull, more than a space-shuttle astronaut.
- The power-to-weight ratio of a Top Fueler is 3.37 horsepower per pound, close to 20 times better than a new Corvette.

Sell The House

Obviously, running a vehicle of this nature is not cheap. At $22 per gallon, a fuel car will use 15–20 gallons per run, costing $330–$440. That means if a fuel car runs eight passes at a major event, it could burn 160 gallons of nitro, costing over $3,500. The 12-inch rear-end assembly is worth about $20,000. The data retrieval system will set you back up to $25,000. A pair of slicks is about $1,100. Each of the clutch discs is worth about $125, and you're fortunate to get more than three runs on a disc. Superchargers cost $15,000. A fuel engine ready to be installed will set you back at least $80,000, but you must have a hauler full of spares as the engine is torn down after every run. To purchase a race-ready Top Fueler or Funny Car will cost between $200,000 and $250,000.

At the end of the day, fuel teams competing at national meets need budgets of close to $2 million to compete regularly. When the cost of transportation, crew, accommodation, spares, and other logistics are factored in, each time a fuel car goes down the track, the cost is a minimum of $4,000.

And that's if nothing breaks.

mishap occurs, the driver, who is tightly strapped into this cockpit with a seven-point harness, usually suffers only minor injuries, if any.

Onboard fire extinguishing systems are mandatory, as well as engine and drivetrain containment devices (straps, blankets) for breakage and explosion protection.

Three hundred feet of strong, lightweight, chrome moly tubing comprise a dragster chassis, which, on average, weighs about 600 pounds. The cockpit is situated a little more than halfway back in this chassis and the engine placed at least a foot behind the cockpit. The rear wheels are placed right at the rear of the chassis, several feet behind the engine.

The large rear wing sits high and to the rear of the back wheels, mounted on long struts, and is an essential part of the chassis. It is built of carbon fiber, is 1,500 square inches in size, and can provide up to 10,000 pounds of downforce for the car. The maximum height of the wing assembly is 90 inches from the ground, and although adjustable, it cannot be altered during the actual racing.

What body there is on a Fueler is comprised of lightweight but very strong materials such as magnesium and carbon fiber. The body panels are constructed in such a way as to allow for easy removal and replacement. The car body is also designed to prevent the driver's body from coming in contact with the car's wheels,

Fuel Engines

The heart of a Top Fuel Dragster or Funny Car is the 500-cubic-inch engine. There are engines in drag racing with larger displacements, but two major factors with these aluminum-based powerplants provide the tremendous horsepower ratings: what's inside and on top of the engine, and the fuel used to power the engine.

A fuel engine is filled with the lightest, strongest components in the industry. Based on the V8 Chrysler Hemi-head engine used in the large Chrysler and Imperial models, today's engine block is of machine-billet aluminum, as well as the cylinder heads, which hold two valves per cylinder, with the intake valves made of solid titanium.

Valve sizes are 2.45 inches for intake and 1.925 inches for exhaust. Copper gaskets and stainless steel o-rings seal the heads to the block. The crankshaft and camshaft are made of billet steel; pistons are

tires, exhaust system or track surface. Windscreens are required, while fairings (coverings) around the front wheels are prohibited.

Top Fuelers have no suspension, with the axles being directly mounted onto the chassis. The steering shaft to the front wheels is constructed to collapse and break away to the side of the car to prevent driver injury in case of frontal impact, and a quick-release steering wheel is mandatory.

Small, narrow tires are mounted on the front wheels. The rear slicks are 17.5 inches wide, (36 inches in diameter, with a circumference of 115 inches) and can balloon up to 10 feet in circumference during a burnout. In most situations, the slicks contain 4 psi of air.

Brakes are employed on the rear wheels only, and the 11.5-inch diameter rotors are made of carbon fiber. The brakes are activated by the driver with a hand lever at the end of the run, and along with the two parachutes, will slow down the car with a negative five-G impact.

Another area of development in Top Fuel has been the implementation of computerized data retrieval systems, but computers that would enhance a car's performance are strictly forbidden. Devices on the cars are used to record the functions of the car while racing and in no way affect the car's operation. This recorded data is then used by the team for tuning, adjustments and replacements on the race car.

of forged aluminum, as are the connecting rods. All parts are bolted together using aircraft-specification hardware.

The supercharger is of a General Motors design, originally made for its line of industrial two-stroke diesel engines used in trucks, buses, locomotives and construction equipment. This Roots-type blower is of a 14-71 configuration, and this refers to the GM nomenclature of 14 as the largest blower built (case length) for the 71 series of engines (71 cubic inches per cylinder).

This supercharger is geared to run in an overdrive mode in relation to the engine revolutions, and this percentage is adjusted according to track and race conditions. When the engine is running wide open at about 8,500 rpm, the supercharger is spinning at over 12,000 rpm, and this can consume up to 900 of the engine's 7,500 horsepower.

Fuel enters the engine at a terrific rate, up to 100 gallons per minute, using constant fuel injection with over 40 injectors.

The fuel is ignited with the help of two spark plugs per cylinder, fired by two 44-ampere magnetos, enough current to weld together steel plate.

A wet sump oiling system is used, and contains 16 quarts of SAE 70 grade mineral or synthetic racing oil. A titanium oil pan is bolted to the bottom of the engine.

Harnessing all this power and getting it to the rear wheels continues to be one of the class's most developed areas, as builders and teams work on applying this power with a minimum of traction loss.

Today's cars employ a timer-controlled clutch system with several clutch discs and steel floater plates. The centrifugal pressure is applied gradually in a series of infinitesimal stages controlled through a hydraulic throwout bearing.

This pressure is applied until a one-to-one ratio between the engine and drivetrain is achieved, which is usually around three seconds. There is no transmission in a fuel car, and the rear-gear ratio final drive is 3.20:1.

The Ultimate Fuel

Nitromethane is an industrially-produced chemical of propane, treated with nitric acid. It is a monopropellant, a term meaning that it carries its own oxygen. Once this fuel is ignited, it becomes a volatile force inside an engine like no other. The crackling sound and acrid, eye-searing fumes nitro produces is the epitome of drag racing.

Used in dry cleaning, medicines and model airplane engines, nitromethane has a higher oxygen content than regular gasoline. During one stroke of an engine, 8.7 times more nitro can be burned than gasoline. For one pound of gasoline burned, 15 pounds of air is needed: for one pound of nitro, 1.7 pounds of air is needed. Nitro also absorbs engine heat, which helps in engine cooling.

Nitro was developed for rocket engines around 1930, and was applied to high-performance automobiles such as Germany's Auto Union Grand Prix cars of the 1930s and the land speed record run car of John Cobb at Bonneville in the late 1940s. Drag racers were quick to pick up on the use of nitro, but taming its capabilities proved costly, as the wrong percentage of nitro in an engine could literally explode the engine with such force that pieces were never found.

Early fuel cars ran on a diet of close to 100 percent nitro, mixing in a little methanol, usually under 10 percent. But reliability became an issue, so this percentage was limited to 85 percent nitro by the sanctioning bodies, including the NHRA.

There has been a strong movement to change this figure to 90 percent. Fuel teams stress that with nitro's quicker flame front at 90 percent (flame broadcast in the combustion chamber), parts breakage would lessen. A higher nitro percentage would also provide a longer burn rate from the fuel along with a longer power stroke in the cylinder, providing more power and torque.

The boss still gets his hands dirty. Racing great Kenny Bernstein makes some adjustments with his Funny Car during some down time between rounds at Las Vegas. Notice the large containment blanket on the supercharger.

Funny Car

While a Top Fuel Dragster may be the fastest-accelerating car in the world, a Nitro Funny Car is not far behind, and it provides the loudest, most explosive and most colorful racing in all of motorsports.

Witnessing two Funny Cars at full throttle is a sensational experience: the grandstands rumble and shake, and your hearing tries to cope with the assault of two 7,500-horsepower engines maxed out to within a hairsbreadth of exploding.

• nitromethane

• none

• 500 ci – 7,500+ hp

• high 4 secs
• 320 mph

• 17.5"

• 2,250 lbs

Using the same powerful engines as a Top Fueler, but with the engine sitting in front of the driver on a chassis less than half as long as a Fueler, the car is a beast to handle down the track. The driver fights constantly with the steering to keep the car straight as the back tires take on a life of their own, struggling to maintain traction.

A product of the all-out unlimited exhibition-type cars that emerged in the late 1960s, this class has evolved into the most difficult car to get down the quarter-mile.

A Funny Car is a little over 200 pounds heavier than a Fueler, but sub-five-second times and 300-mph-plus runs are common.

Funny Car Anatomy

From their altered-wheelbase, stock-appearance roots, today's Funny Cars are comprised of a chassis, a one-piece, flip-up car body and a 500-cubic-inch engine. The car's wheelbase ranges from a mandated 100 to 125 inches in a frame built of about 180 feet of chrome moly tubing welded together. The bare chassis weighs about 125 pounds.

Then, such items as front spindles, steering box, fuel tank, floorpan, engine and rear-end mounting plates are added, along with control levers, clutch pedal assembly and roll bar pads.

A Funny Car body costs around $10,000. They are carbon fiber, and must resemble a late-model, two-door automobile. (In theory, anyway. Like today's NASCAR Cup cars, it's hard to tell the make of the car body unless you see the manufacturer's nameplate and badges painted on the car).

The body is 60 inches wide, weighs about 90 pounds and has a very narrow cabin, with the driver's cockpit situated in the center of the body. The roof may be chopped (lowered) two inches, but it must be at least 32 inches in width.

Both the NHRA and IHRA allow some streamlining, but wheel wells must maintain the radius and contour on which the car body is based, and the use of wheel fairings (covers) is prohibited. There is a pair of large panels above each rear fender on the deck of the car, but the large strut and wing assembly used on a Top Fueler is not allowed.

There is a front-hinged escape hatch in the car's roof to permit easy driver exit in case of an emergency, and the taillight area of the car may be hinged with rectangular flaps for air venting.

Windows are made of Lexan, a tough clear material developed by General Electric and now produced by plastics manufacturer SABIC. The side window has a round, six-inch hole in it to stuff through a fire hose in case of emergency. There are also small windows on each side of the firewall, allowing the driver to view the engine's valve-cover area in case of fire there. The rear bumper on the body has slots in it for the parachute release to open the pair of parachutes, which sit on the back of the car.

Unlike in a rear-engined dragster, the driver of a Funny Car sits behind the engine, and as such there is a great deal more safety equipment built into the car to protect the driver. The car's firewall and dashboard are made of high-grade steel or aluminum. The driveshaft, which passes underneath the driver from the engine to the rear-end assembly, must be covered completely with steel of 1/16-inch thickness or 1/8-inch thick aluminum. This cover must also surround the driveshaft couplers, and be fastened to the chassis.

Driver safety is paramount in a Funny Car, and the fire extinguishing system mandates at least a 20-pound system, five pounds of fire suppressant into the driver's compartment, and 15 pounds into the engine compartment, distributed through outlets in front of each of the engine's eight exhaust headers. The entire body inside is also sprayed with a fire-retardant coating. Funny Car drivers must wear clothing produced with the highest fire rating, including gloves, boots and a head sock.

While mechanical cables and hydraulic or pneumatic lines may be installed within the car's frame rails, any electrical wiring must be externally mounted on the frame rails of a Funny Car.

Unlike a Top Fuel car, a Funny Car employs a four-wheel brake system with carbon fiber rotors of up to 11.5 inches in diameter on the rear wheels and front rotors up to 10.5 inches in diameter. The brakes are activated with a hand lever by the driver, but the car's primary braking is through the use of two parachutes, which can produce up to a negative five-G condition when deployed.

Close-up of the rear wing and parachute system on Robert Hight's Funny Car. The rear wing wasn't always as prominent on Funny Cars, but in today's racing, the down force the wing provides is absolutely crucial in getting these 300-mph beasts down the track.

Mark Niver's Top Alcohol Dragster is pulled through the lanes to compete in the Lucas Oil–NHRA Division 7 meet at Las Vegas in November of 2008.

Alcohol Cars

Next to nitro-powered dragsters and Funny Cars, the alcohol-powered versions of these two classes are the quickest in drag racing. Although considered Sportsman (as opposed to Pro) classes in the NHRA, these cars are akin to their nitro cousins in appearance and size. Neither the Alcohol Funny Car class nor the Alcohol Dragster class compete in the IHRA.

Developed from gasoline-powered cars in the 1970s as a lower-cost alternative to fuel cars, dragsters competed with Funny Cars in a class known as Pro Comp, but today participate separately.

Top Alcohol Dragsters travel down the quarter-mile with speeds in the 260- to 275-mph range, with Alcohol Funny Cars hitting between 250 and 260 mph at the top end. The cars may not be quite as fast as fuel cars, but they can be just as exciting.

While these automobiles are named "Alcohol," the Top Alcohol Dragster and Alcohol Funny Car use a mixture of alcohol and methanol. Ethanol is another fuel used occasionally in the engines of these cars.

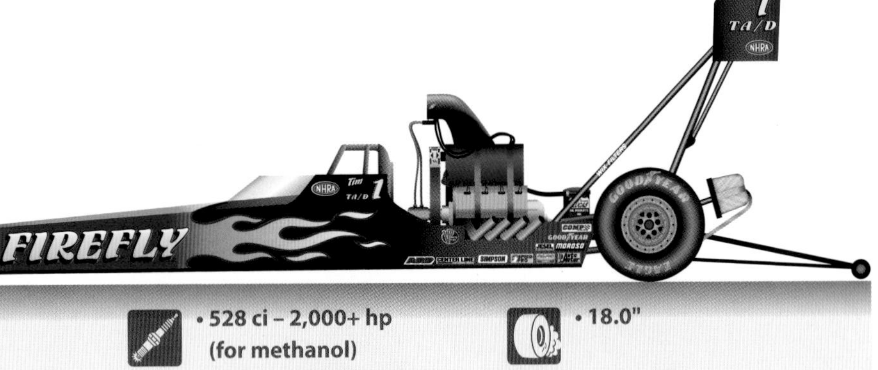

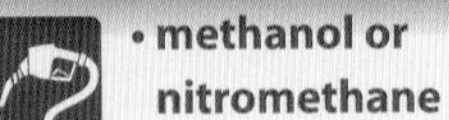

- methanol or nitromethane

- three-speed (for methanol)
- none (for nitro)

- 528 ci – 2,000+ hp (for methanol)
- 456 ci – 2,000+ hp (for nitro)

- low 5 secs
- up to 270 mph

- 18.0"

- 2,000 lbs

Alcohol Dragster

Sitting on a wheelbase of 150 to 300 inches, a Top Alcohol Dragster (TAD) may be powered with a methanol-burning supercharged or a non-supercharged injected engine fed with nitromethane, the same fuel as Top Dragsters and Funny Cars.

There are three engine/weight options for the dragsters. A non-supercharged, nitromethane-burning car has an engine displacement of 410 to 456 cubic inches, and the car must weigh a minimum of 2,125 pounds. The nitro percentage allowed in the NHRA is 96 percent, except at Denver's Bandimere Speedway, where 100 percent nitro is allowed because of the altitude at the event's location.

A car equipped with a supercharged engine employing a Roots-style supercharger can have a maximum engine size of 528 cubic inches with a minimum weight of 1,975 pounds.

The final variation is a supercharged engine with a screw-type supercharger. Here the maximum engine size is 466 cubic inches, and the car's minimum weight is 2,050 pounds. Larger engines may be used with this combination, with an additional five pounds in weight for each additional cubic inch.

Magnetos of 44-ampere capacity fire the spark plugs, and on the supercharge cars restraint straps of fireproof material are mandatory. Programmable ignition systems are allowed.

Depending on whether the engine is fuel injected or supercharged, different transmission and rear-end drive ratios are employed. Cars with a screw-type supercharger are allowed a maximum 4.58 gear ratio, cars with a Roots supercharger are allowed a maximum 4.72 gear ratio and nitromethane injected cars are allowed a maximum 2.90 gear ratio. Any TADs using a "small-block" (under 400 cubic inches) with either-style of supercharged engine are allowed a maximum 4.90 ratio gear ratio.

While a transmission is not allowed in a nitro-burning injected car, the supercharged cars may employ an aftermarket planetary transmission of three speeds, which must be manually shifted by the driver.

Front suspension on a TAD is optional, and brakes are employed on the rear wheels only. Wheelie bars are allowed.

Rear tires are a maximum of 18 inches wide and are allowed a 118-inch maximum circumference. Front wheels and tires must be at least 13 inches in diameter.

A rear roll cage shroud is mandatory to protect the driver in a rear-engined car, along with a deflector plate of aluminum, steel, or titanium between the driver and the engine. The car chassis may be painted, but cannot be plated with chrome or another surface covering such as cadium (for metal hardness or decoration), and all wiring is to be external of the car's frame rails, while hydraulic or pneumatic cables may be installed within the frame rails.

The Top Alcohol Dragster of Jim Whiteley at Las Vegas late in 2008. Compare the width and height of the rear slicks during a burnout to the still slicks on page 96. With close to 2,000 horsepower spinning the tires, the once partially deflated slicks are now full of heat and energy causing them to expand.

The car's body is fabricated of steel, carbon fiber, or fiberglass. While a small (17 inch by 17-inch) air deflector plate is allowed behind the cockpit, ground effect panels on the car's body of any kind are prohibited. The area of the rear wing must equal 1,500 square inches, and the maximum height of the wing cannot exceed 90 inches from the racing surface.

In terms of cost, racing a TAD is expensive, but less so than a Top Fueler. A competitive car will cost $150,000 to $200,000, and the performance of the car is in the low five-second range, with speeds of 270 mph.

Safety requirements for the TAD cars are very similar to the nitro-burning Top Fuel dragsters, including on-board fire extinguishing equipment, dual parachutes, and driver safety apparel. Drivers of front-engined supercharged cars of this class must wear protective clothing with burn rates equivalent to what is used in the Funny Car classes, which is higher because of the engine placement that adds a greater degree of risk. A head and neck restraint (HANS) device is mandatory for all competitors in the class.

Alcohol Funny Car

An Alcohol Funny Car (AFC) may be a little slower than a nitro Flopper, but it can be more difficult to drive. A large part of the car's charisma comes from the fact that the driver must shift through the gears manually while trying to keep the front-engined, short-wheelbase car traveling straight down the strip.

Using the same carbon fiber body as a nitro Funny Car, the body sits on a chrome moly chassis with a wheelbase of 100 to 125 inches—less than half the length of the wheelbase of a dragster. The busy driver tries to get the car's power to the back wheels without spinning the slicks while watching the engine revs in anticipation of punching the next shifter button.

AFC engines are supercharged, using either the screw-type or Roots-type blower. In NHRA competition, the maximum engine size for a car with a screw-type supercharger is 528 cubic inches, and the car must weigh a minimum of 2,300 pounds. Using a Roots supercharger, the engine size is limited to 565 cubic inches, and the car must weigh at least 2,200 pounds. Engines run on alcohol or methanol, and are permitted two magnetos of up to 44 amperes each, along with two sparkplugs for igniting the mixture,

- methanol

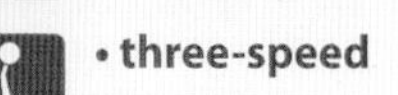
- three-speed

- 528/565 ci – 2,500+ hp

- mid 5 secs
- up to 260 mph

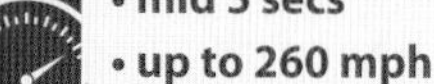

- 18.0"
- 2,200–2,300 lbs

Clowns of the Quarter Mile

Similar to the clowns who provide entertainment between events at a rodeo, or the halftime show at football games, exhibition cars at drag racing events are a popular diversion from regular competitive racing.

The two most prominent types of exhibition cars are jet-powered vehicles and wheelstanders. Both these cars have been around for decades, and both still get the fans excited when they take to the track.

Neither type of vehicle participates in regular sanctioned competition, although there are regulations and safety procedures

which is fed through a supercharger with a maximum overdrive of 1.92 for a screw blower and 1.70 for a Roots blower. Nitrous oxide is prohibited.

The car's clutch must be manually operated, and a full-floating or live-axle rear end is mandatory, with gear ratios between 4.30 and 4.58. The planetary three-speed transmission may be pneumatically shifted, but each gear change must be activated by its own shifter button.

Car bodies are made of composite materials and must be of a coupe or sedan type originally mass-produced by an auto manufacturer, domestic or foreign. Bodies must be a minimum of 60 inches in width. There are some aerodynamic panels such as rear deck spoilers and rocker panel extensions allowed on a Funny Car body, but fairings and airfoils are prohibited, along with covering the car's wheels. Beltline moldings along with headlight and taillight housings or indentations must be incorporated in the body to provide car recognition. The taillight area at the rear of the car may be hinged for air venting purposes.

As with nitro floppers, the alcohol version has an escape hatch in the roof to permit driver exit if needed. And as with the nitro cars, the driver of an AFC sits in the center of the car.

New for the 2009 season is a mechanism that allows a car's body to be removed from the rear of the car. This manual release, in the interests of driver safety, must be highly visible and easy to employ if the car's body must be removed in a dangerous situation.

The strictest of safety and fire prevention requirements are mandated for the cars and the drivers in this class. A driver must wear clothing of the highest-rated fire retardant material, which allows a margin of 40 seconds before second-degree burns. The gloves and boots are rated for 30 seconds. Arm restraints, and energy absorbing foam seat are mandatory, as is a HANS (head and neck restraint system) device. The seat upholstery, driver harness and underside of the car body must be coated with flame retardant.

Along with a large blanket under the engine to contain parts and fluids in case of engine failure, parts such as the supercharger must employ containment straps in case of an explosion. Belt guard shielding for fuel and oil lines is mandatory.

The fire extinguishing system must

that have been put in place by both the IHRA and NHRA.

Capable of speeds of over 300 mph, a jet car offers the ultimate in noise, smoke and speed. Originally a jet engine was installed in a specially constructed dragster or Funny Car, but today just about any type of body is used, including semi trucks, ambulances and limousines.

No matter what body is on a jet-powered vehicle, the ritual is the same. The vehicle is fired up behind the starting line, and in a flurry of smoke and increasing noise, the vehicle is brought up to the staging area. When staged, the vehicle leaves the line, slowly at first as the engine's thrust builds up, and by half-track, the vehicle is a blur with a huge flame shooting out the back. A jet run at night with the fire and smoke is very popular with the crowd.

There are about 50 jet vehicles in North America today, and these are in high demand for bookings at tracks. Quite often a pair of jet vehicles will be booked in and will match race each other. At one time a regular fast car such as a Top Fueler would match race a jet, but that rarely occurs today as the costs associated with booking a high-profile Top Fueler is an expensive proposition for most local race tracks. Also, due to the tight scheduling and the large number of national IHRA and NHRA meets, there is little time for teams to concentrate on anything but the national tours.

People who go to a drag race for the first time will remember the antics of a wheelstander more than any other event of that day. A mainstay of exhibition racing, one of these vehicles will attempt to run the entire quarter-mile on its rear wheels only. With a flair for driving outrageous-looking vehicles and pure showmanship, wheelstanders provide the crowd with a humorous diversion from rounds of regular racing. The vehicle will have the engine in the rear to help with the transferring of weight to the back wheels, and the driver will get the vehicle up on its back wheels at the starting line and power down the track in this manner. The driver will sit at the extreme front of the vehicle in order to see, or sometimes there will be a window in the bottom of the body shell to aid the driver.

Originally car bodies were used, as well as the early cab-over-engine pickups, but eventually just about every type of vehicle was built as a wheelstander, including police cars, tow trucks, school buses and even tanks.

contain a minimum of 20 pounds of fire suppressant. Of this total, 15 pounds are directed into the engine compartment with a nozzle in front of each bank of exhaust headers. The remaining five pounds are dispersed into the driver's compartment with a nozzle at the driver's feet.

And, similar to a nitro-burning Funny Car, an AFC has fire windows on either side of the car's firewall near the engine valve covers to warn the driver of a fire.

As with the Top Alcohol Dragster, an Alcohol Funny Car is less expensive to build and maintain, but is by no means a cheap venture. Car bodies alone can cost $8,000, and engines at least $75,000. A competitive car will cost upwards of $200,000, and for that money you'll get a ride down the quarter-mile in less than six seconds at speeds up to 260 mph.

A peak under the body of an Alcohol Funny Car shows the electronics and engine-management equipment in a modern race car. There is also some fire extinguishing equipment between the two front wheels.

Pro Modified

In a world of wild-looking and exciting cars, some of the most exhilarating are in the Pro Modified class. Pro Mods are certainly the most visually interesting, offering a wide range of body styles, from early 1930s' Willys coupes to modern Corvettes and muscle cars.

With up to 2,700 horsepower, these front-engined cars with their short 115-inch wheelbase have grown in popularity and are favorites whenever they show up at a drag strip. Although close in speed and times to Alcohol Funny Cars, Pro Mods retain a sense of kinship with regular street cars with their fully functional body doors, and are known as the "world's fastest door slammers."

The class is an extension of the IHRA's Top Sportsman class, and was started around 1989. The first Pro Mods, such as Charles Carpenter's 1955 Chevy, were powered by big-block, nitrous-injected engines of 1,200–1,500 horsepower. Other early proponents of the class included Johnny Rocca with his 1949 Mercury, and the 1937 Chevy of Jim Oddy (who built his engines with superchargers, taking the class to a new level).

By 1990, when Tim McAmis won the first IHRA Pro Mod title, cars were running low to mid-seven elapsed times with speeds of around 200 mph.

Today's Pro Mods are capable of sub-six-second runs at over 240 mph.

One reason for the success of the class is the wide variety of allowable modifications to the basic car, giving builders and racers a chance to try new ideas and setups not found in other classes. It is truly a class where ingenuity and hot rodding of the highest level come into play.

Engines and Drivetrain

There are three types of engines allowed in the Pro Modified class, and the three are subject to displacement size and car weight. Turbocharged engines have a 650-cubic-inch maximum, and the car must weigh a minimum of 2,700 pounds. Cars with nitrous-oxide-fed engines have a minimum weight of 2,425 pounds, but engine size is unlimited. A supercharged car is subject to a 527-cubic-inch limit and a 2,650-pound weight. These variations are maintained by the sanctions to help keep a level playing field. While there are turbocharged cars in the class, they, for the most part, have still not reached their potential; nitrous cars are players in the class, but the blower (supercharged) cars have remained dominant and have overcome the weight handicaps to produce the best quarter-mile times. And the most victories.

No matter what engine used, it is placed in a chassis in front of the driver with a setback of no more than 10 percent of the car's wheelbase. Both wedge-head and Hemi-head cylinder-head designs are allowed, and gasoline or methanol are the only fuels allowed.

Non-supercharged cars may use any number of carburetors, and injectors are allowed on any type engine. Nitrous cars are limited to a maximum of two 15-pound bottles of nitrous oxide, and are used only after a car has performed its burnout. Supercharged cars are limited to a 20 percent blower overdrive setup, and the maximum length of the drive pulley to the leading edge of the rotor is 15 inches.

The clutch must be manually operated by the driver's foot, and no electronic, pneumatic or hydraulic assist in operating the clutch is allowed. Two or three disc clutches are allowed.

A three-speed transmission is employed, and is manually shifted by the driver with a separate button shifter for each gear change. These buttons, usually air-operated, are situated next to the driver's right hand, and are punched in sequence as the car reaches its engine redline in each gear. All cars have a reverse gear.

The driveshaft between the transmission and the rear-end housing is fully enclosed and covers the driveshaft couplings as well. An automotive-type rear end is used, and a full-floating or live axle assembly is mandatory. Gear ratios vary depending on the sanction and track (quarter-mile versus eighth-mile), but the final drive ratio for supercharged cars ranges between 4.30:1 and 4.56:1.

Chassis and Suspension

Pro Mods are built in a manner similar to the other professional classes, with tubing welded together, including a strong and extensive roll cage as an integral part of the chassis. Early cars were built with rigidity in their frames, but this thinking has been altered somewhat to allow for some chassis flexing to allow a car to track better down the strip and maintain a higher degree of traction.

The four-link rear suspension setup is now bolted to plates on the frame rather than welded, which allows the car to flex with varying track conditions, and allows for adjustments. The firewall has also received attention, and is built stronger to help distribute engine torque through the car more efficiently.

Four-wheel brakes are mandatory, and suspension systems allow one shock absorber per wheel with a minimum of one-inch wheel travel. Wheelie bars are limited to 104 inches in length. Rear wheels are limited to 16 inches maximum, and all tires must be situated underneath the car's bodywork.

Body and Interior

One of the most admired aspects of the Pro Mod class is the variety of car body styles in use. Nostalgia-type cars such as the 1957 Chevy, 1953 Corvette, 1941 Willys and 1953 Studebaker will face off against such cars as early

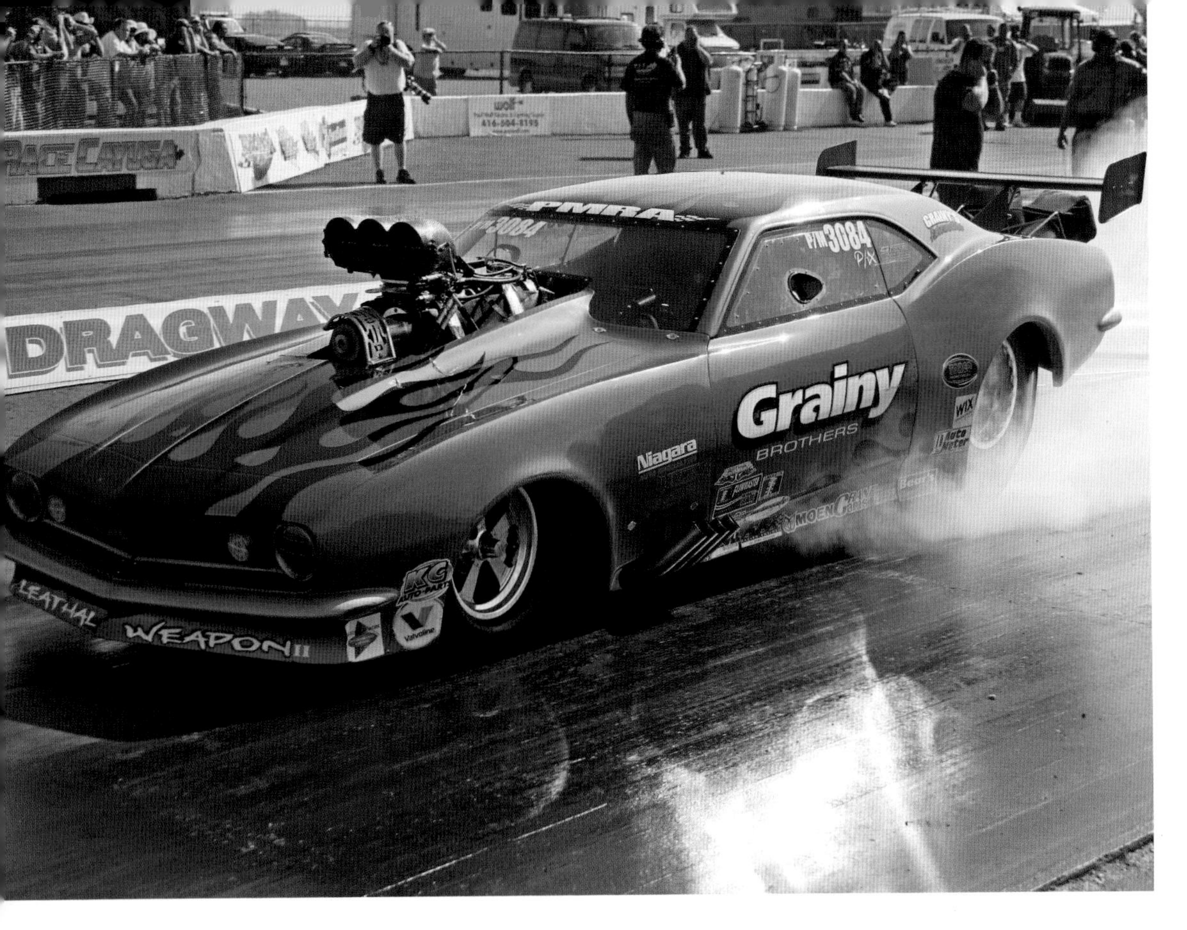

Pro Modifieds come in a variety of body styles, but the 1967–68 Chevy Camaro body is the most common. The small wing on the back of this car is about the only aerodynamic influence allowed in the class. This Pro Mod is raced by the Grainy Brothers, long-time doorslammer competitors.

1970s' Dodge Challengers, 1992 Chevy Luminas and split-window 1963 Corvettes. Pickup truck bodies are also allowed in the class.

The most prominent body style of late has been the 1967–68 Camaro/Firebird, which is more aerodynamically suited to the 240-mph speed the cars are capable of, and are more stable than other body styles at this speed.

No matter what style is used, the body is made of fiberglass or carbon fiber. There is a big weight difference here in the materials, as a carbon fiber body is 30–50 percent lighter, weighing 50–60 pounds compared to the 115–135 pounds of fiberglass for the same body shell. One-piece bodies are not allowed, and the body must have two fully functional doors that can be operated internally and externally.

Pro Mods are mostly devoid of any aerodynamic body panels except for a rear wing or spoiler which may not be higher than the car's roof. Two small hinged openings are allowed at the rear of the body. Side windows and windshield are of shatterproof material, and door windows must have a minimum four-inch opening adjacent to the driver for a fire hose in case of emergency.

The hood scoop on non-supercharged cars may not extend more than 14 inches above the car's hood. A functional taillight is mandatory.

Interior and Safety

Pro Mod drivers must wear protective fireproof clothing, including suit, gloves and boots. The HANS (head and neck restraint) device is also mandatory. The fire system in a Pro Mod contains at least 20 pounds of fire suppressant, with one nozzle directed at the driver and at least two nozzles on the engine and fuel cell. A fresh-air breathing system for the driver is also mandatory.

Strides have been made to incorporate comfort in the cabin by Pro Mod builders. A Pro Mod driver is a busy person while racing, making shifts with one hand while trying to steer straight down the track with the other, and then deploying the parachutes. Items such as the length of the throttle control and location of other controls in the cockpit have been addressed for easier manipulation. With the driver's view hindered by either the supercharger or hood scoop, better sight lines out the windshield are also being developed.

Builders and Costs

There are several outfits that build Pro Mod cars, from a basic chassis, to a turnkey car. The most prominent builders are G-Force Race Cars, Vanishing Point Race Cars, and Tim McAmis Race Cars. A complete Pro Mod chassis runs between $85,000 and $90,000, and engine prices are between $75,000 and $85,000. So, along with other items for the car, an investment of over $200,000 is quite normal for Pro Mod teams in high-level sanctioned competition.

Pro Stock

In the world of drag racing, cars in the Pro Stock class most resemble the automobiles we drive on the street. But the visual appearance is the only thing these 200-mph-plus full-bodied cars have in common with their street brethren. Cars and competitors race in a class where technology and attention to detail is paramount and which is virtually unequaled in all other forms of motorsport.

With such stringent rules and regulations, Pro Stockers are so evenly matched that a qualified field of 16 cars at an event will have elapsed quarter-mile times within hundredths of a second between the number one qualifier and the 16th-place car.

Pro Stock cars retain a full body complete with windows, headlights and taillights in their original factory positions. The cars must be shifted manually and, running on high-octane gasoline, can obtain speeds of close to 220 mph in the 6.30-second range, even with very little in the way of aerodynamics.

Engine and Drivetrain

The heart of a Pro Stock car is its engine, which is limited to 500 cubic inches in NHRA competition and up to 840 cubic inches for IHRA racing.

The powerplant is also the area of a Pro Stock car that receives the most attention. Big-block V8 engines with wedge heads of General Motors and Ford design can be utilized, as well as a Chrysler Hemi-head design. All blocks must be made of steel for NHRA racing, although cylinder heads and intake manifolds are of aluminum. Aftermarket engine blocks, such as GM's DRCE corporate big-block, are allowed.

All Pro Stock engines must retain their original two-valves-per-cylinder arrangement, with a single spark plug for each cylinder. The use of lightweight engine components and exotic materials such as titanium are not allowed.

Much of Pro Stock engine development and emphasis revolves around the cylinder heads. Engine builders spend literally hundreds of hours preparing the heads with sophisticated porting techniques to acquire the most efficient fuel/air mixture possible. Two large, highly-modified four-barrel carburetors sit on top of the engine, usually on a custom-built intake manifold, designed and built to match the flow requirements of the cylinder head design. All of these components work together as an integral group.

Sitting on the carburetors is a large, tall hood scoop, a trademark aspect of the class.

A competitive NHRA Pro Stock engine produces close to 2.5 horsepower per cubic inch, or over 1,300 horsepower in total. Compression ratios are in the neighborhood of 17 to 1, and the 118-rated octane gasoline goes through the engine at a rate of 7.5 gallons per minute.

A race-ready engine costs between $175,000 and $200,000.

The multiple disc clutch setup in a Pro Stock is an area where races can be won or lost. The clutch must be set up properly for track and race conditions, and its tight tolerances must be maintained between each run.

The four-speed gearbox from the early 1970s of Pro Stock racing has given way to a five-speed box. The IHRA allows air-shifted transmissions of a planetary design; the NHRA mandates a five-speed clutchless manual gearbox. The clutch is used here for launching the car, and not the actual shifting.

An automotive-type rear-end assembly found in regular production cars is required. Aftermarket axles are also required, while a full-floating or live axle assembly is optional.

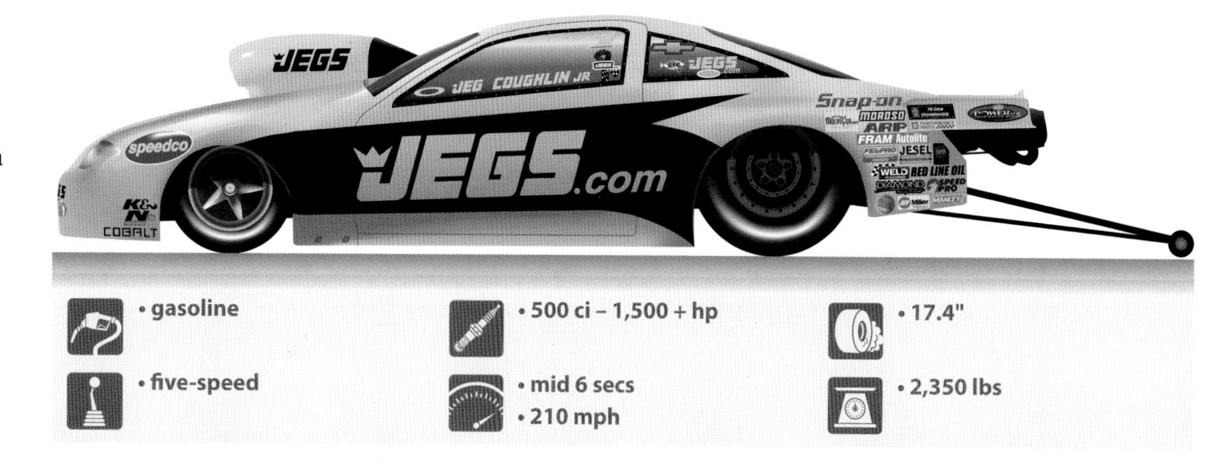

It takes a little imagination, but other than the overhang extending from the trunk lid, this Pro Stock would closely resemble its street-model roots. Like the street version, this car also runs on gasoline, but uses carburetion and not fuel injection.

Chassis and Body

As with Top Fuelers and Funny Cars, a Pro Stock chassis is comprised of chrome moly steel tubing. While a dragster chassis is built with about 300 feet of tubing, a Pro Stock requires about 100 more feet due to the car's suspension and roll-cage design.

The car's wheelbase is between 104 inches and 105 inches in length depending on the car model. Minimum weight required in NHRA racing is 2,350 pounds, and 2,400 pounds for IHRA racing.

Automotive-type suspension is used, and the front suspension utilizes the McPherson-type struts with control arms. The early ladder-bar and three-link rear suspension has been replaced with the present four-link setup, which allows unlimited adjustments for track and race conditions. Adjustable coil-over shock absorbers are used.

Pro Stock cars stop with the help of four-wheel disc brakes of carbon fiber material, single calipers on the front and dual calipers on the rear. Stock-type steering in its conventional location is required.

The 17-inch-wide rear slicks must fit entirely within the car's body, and are usually filled to about 5 psi for racing. The narrow front tires carry up to 32 psi for better rolling resistance.

Car bodies are a mixture of materials resembling late model domestic or foreign cars with two or four doors. Popular body styles include the Chevy Cobalt, Ford Escort and Dodge Stratus. Other than the huge hood scoop and a spoiler extension on the rear deck, a Pro Stock is quite identifiable with its manufacturer's origins.

The roof and rear quarter panels of a Pro Stock body are made of steel or carbon fiber. The rear spoiler is of aluminum. The body must retain its stock appearance with no alterations to the original factory contours. Doors must be functional from both inside and outside the car. Car bodies must conform to the sanctioning body templates.

Stock floors may be replaced with material such as aluminum, but must remain stock in appearance and location. A welded floor pan of steel from the firewall to behind the driver's seat must be installed. Full windows are required, matching the car's original shape and contour, but may be made of approved lightweight material.

At the back of the car, wheelie bars of 80 inches in length are used, along with two parachutes.

A rolling chassis, which would include everything except the body, engine and drivetrain, weighs about 1,000 pounds, and will cost up to $125,000.

Driver Safety

Pro Stock cars are built with a complex and strong roll cage integral to the car's chassis. Recently, the even-stronger Funny Car roll cage has been instituted to provide further protection.

A driver competes in a Pro Stock car completely clad in fireproof clothing, including gloves and shoes, and gets strapped in using a five-point restraining system with three-inch wide belts. The HANS (head and neck restraint system) device is mandatory.

The roll-cage bars are padded, and a window net on the driver's door is also mandatory. The car's fire extinguishing system must be a minimum of five pounds of fire suppression chemical, with one nozzle in front of the driver's feet and another nozzle in front of the engine.

Sportsman Classes

Home to the hardcore, Sportsman racing is an essential component to drag racing. With thousands of racers and dozens of classes of cars, from regular cars with license plates driven to the track to high-horsepower dragsters, the spirit of drag racing is found within these dedicated weekend racers.

Sportsman cars compete regularly at their "home" track, plus travel throughout their region as set up by the sanctioning body. They also compete at national events, but it is the regional or divisional racing that makes up the majority of competition.

The two major sanctioning bodies, the NHRA, and the IHRA, offer similar classes and car makeup, and drivers will race their cars, with minor alterations, in both sanctions. To do this, a driver must have a competition license in both the NHRA and IHRA, and the car must be inspected and certified for both sanctions.

The NHRA's Comp classes are comprised of Dragsters, Altereds, and some Modified classes, such as Super Modified and Pro Modified. The IHRA has countered with its Top Sportsman class and Top Dragster class. The Super Gas and Super Comp classes in the NHRA are comparable to the IHRA's Quick Rod, Super Rod and Hot Rod classes.

Both Super Stock and Stock are very similar in makeup in both sanctions.

Stock Classes

The Stock classes in drag racing have been around since the 1960s, and encompass a huge variety of vehicles, from the 130-mph muscle cars of the mid and late 1960s through to today's front-drive, family-type sedans, which are fortunate to make 75 mph in the quarter-mile. The class is comprised of a series of subclasses, using an alphabet nomenclature. The quickest and most powerful cars are the A/S (A-Stock) class, and this system continues down through the alphabet, to W/S. This system is based on a car's power-to-weight ratio. An "A" behind the category designates an automatic transmission-equipped vehicle, such as C/SA for a C-Stock Automatic.

The handicapped starting system devised allows a slower car, such as an E/S car, to get the green light just before a faster A/S car at the line. The slower car could be some distance down the track before the faster car starts and tries to catch his opponent before the end of the quarter-mile.

The classes of Stockers allow level-entry racing and racing on a modest budget. The cars are virtually showroom stock, using factory parts for the particular make and model raced. Cars must be 1960 or newer, be factory-assembled and must have been originally available in an auto dealership.

Cars with a "V" designation are for four- or six-cylinder autos only. Class "W" is restricted to four-cylinder cars.

Mechanical parts may be upgraded with some aftermarket items, but the majority of a Stocker must keep OEM (Original Equipment Manufacture) parts in order to retain the car's corporate identity.

A car's original heating/air conditioning system may be removed, as well as any emission devices. All window glass must be retained and be functional. Windshield wiper blades may be removed.

A car in a Stock class must utilize all functional aspects of a street car with no chassis or body alterations. Slicks, up to nine inches in width, are permitted, as are some traction-handling devices and changes to the rear suspension. Quicker cars (A through

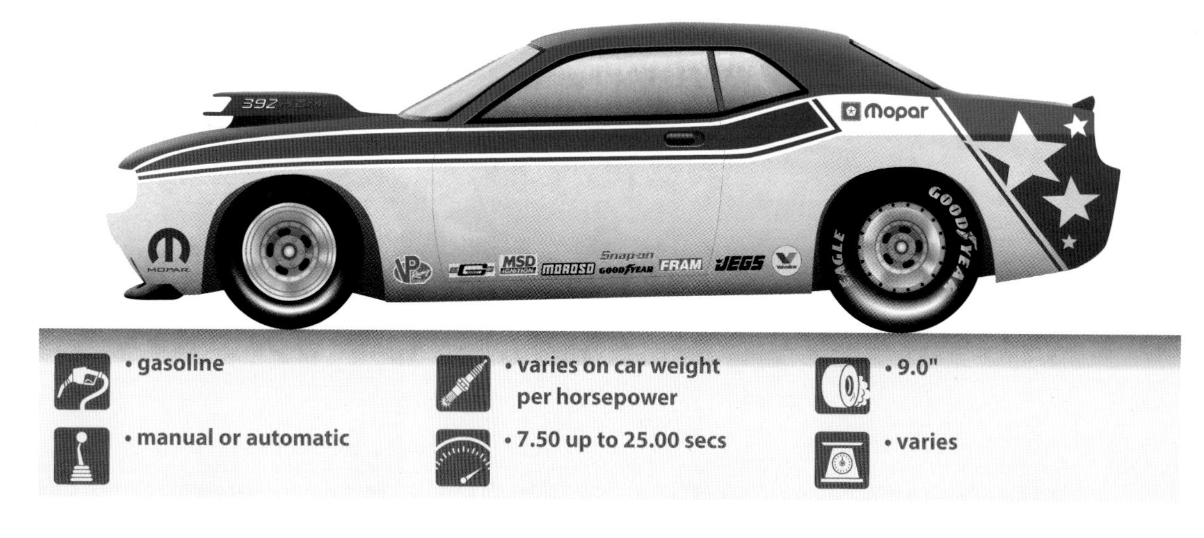

M) must have a roll bar, and classes A through J must have sanctioning body-mandated driver restraint systems.

Speeds and times for today's Stockers range from under 10-second runs at over 130 mph for an A/S car to 16-second runs at just over 80 mph for a W/S car.

Super Stock Classes

The Super Stock classes are somewhat modified versions of the Stock classes with engine modifications and suspension upgrades.

This has been a very popular class for many years, and continues to feature some of the most powerful production vehicles ever built.

Car types may be both domestic and foreign, but are restricted to factory-assembled models readily available to the public.

Based on class designations utilizing a horsepower-to-weight ratio, Super Stock cars are externally similar to a regular street car, but contain numerous engine, powertrain and suspension modifications. Cars are restricted to gasoline only, and nitrous oxide is not allowed.

Most of the revisions allowed to a Super Stock car are for enhanced power, but provide more strength and durability in the makeup of the after-market equipment, along with lighter weight. While modifications may be made, the basic engine, transmission and other driveline components must retain stock placement, and in many cases, stock dimensions. Absolutely no body modifications are allowed, and the car must preserve its original appearance, stance and dimensions.

The cars compete on a handicap system with an indexed scale like the Stock classes. The index for an SS/A car is 9.95 seconds, while at the other end of the scale is the SS/P designation with a 12.80-second index.

Along with a large number of "pure" Super Stock categories, there are subcategories for GT classes, trucks and Modified versions. Both the NHRA and IHRA have Super Stock classes for front-drive conversion cars.

Regulations for cars of the GT and Modified classes are similar to Super Stock, but may use any size or model engine as long as it is the same make as the car. This allows a racer to fit a large V8 engine into a subcompact car. Multiple carburetor setups are allowed in some cases, as well as after-market racing transmissions. Weight-saving body panels may be substituted in place of original sheet metal in several instances, but the vehicle must retain a stock appearance.

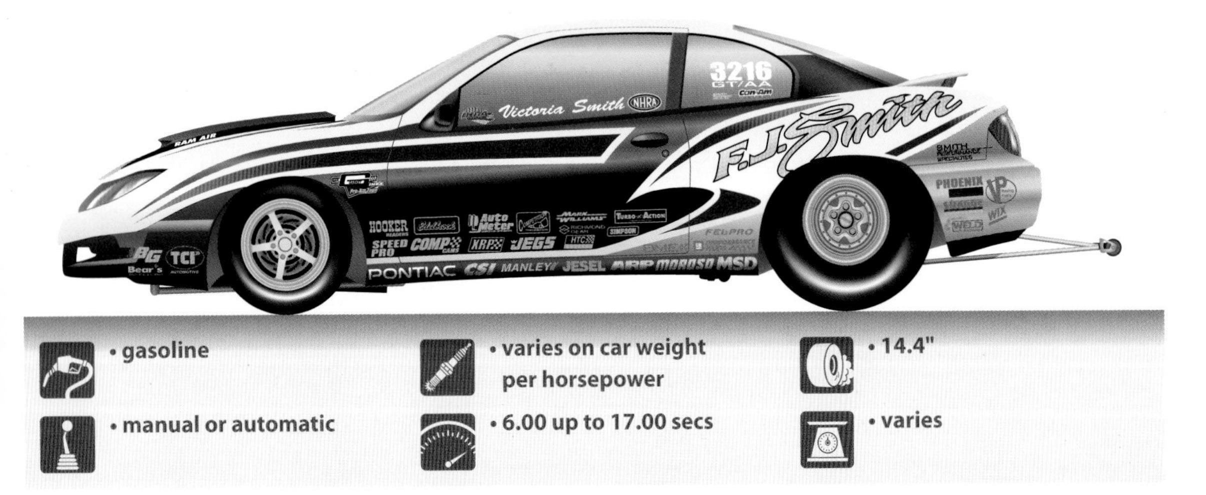

Sportsman (IHRA Specific)

Top Sportsman is the fastest class of full-bodied Sportsman cars, which has no limitations on engines or body customizing. This class delivers some of the most innovative and radical-looking race cars. Speeds of over 200 mph are well within the range of the class.

The class runs on a dial-in system, but the maximum time is 7.8 seconds for national events and 8.0 seconds for regional races. The engines may be supercharged, use nitrous, or be turbocharged. Car weights vary from 2,000 pounds for small-block, non-nitrous cars to 2,600 pounds for supercharged, big-block cars. State-of-the-art electronic devices are permitted.

Many Top Sportsman cars do double duty, and get tweaked to run Pro Modified, as the differences between the two categories are that miniscule.

Top Dragsters are the fastest class of cars in Sportsman racing, comprised mostly of rear-engined dragsters with a minimum 200-inch wheelbase. Front-engined dragsters and roadster-style cars are also allowed. As with the Top Sportsman class, nitrous, turbocharged or supercharged big- and small-block engines are allowed. Car weight starts at 1,400 pounds for a four- or six-cylinder carbureted car to 2,000 pounds for a supercharged, big-block entry. Clutchless transmissions are allowed.

The maximum dial-in for the class is 7.70 seconds for national events and 8.0 seconds for regional events. These cars are well capable of six-second, 225-mph runs.

The next three classes in the IHRA's hierarchy are the Quick Rod, Super Rod and Hot Rod. The cars run through a 8.90-second, 9.90-second and 10.90-second class index, respectively.

Dragster, Funny Car, Altered and full-bodied car bodies are allowed in Quick Rod. Cars must have a 90-inch minimum wheelbase. Superchargers and multiple carburetors are allowed, as is mechanical fuel injection. Fuel may be gasoline, alcohol, methanol or propane. Nitrous oxide is not permitted. Cars may use any type of transmission. The top cars in the class are capable of speeds in the mid 180-mph range, and up to 48 cars will be on hand at a national event.

The Super Rod class is comprised of full-bodied cars with functional doors, or street roadster bodies. No dragster, Funny Car or Altered-type cars are allowed. As with the faster Quick Rod cars, this class is allowed supercharging, fuel injection and multiple carbs, along with any transmission. Maximum wheelbase for the class is 125 inches. Running as close to their 9.90 index as possible without breaking out, Quick Rod cars will hit in the 160-mph range.

The Hot Rod class is an interesting mix of full-bodied entries with functional doors and other items that relate to the car's stock status, such as bumpers and grilles. No open-wheeled vehicles such as dragsters are allowed. Fenderless street rods are also not allowed. The class is open to convertibles, however. As with the other faster Rod classes, engines may be supercharged, fuel injected or have multiple carbs, but once again, nitrous is not allowed. Cars in this class, which could tally as high as 40 per national event, and running as close as possible to their 10.90-second index, will attain speeds up to 145 mph.

It may not be as elaborate as a professional team pit area, but the pit for a Sportsman car team is just as functional, and it's the team's home and workshop for several days. Here a crew works on a supercharged roadster.

Sportsman (NHRA Specific)

The NHRA's Competition Eliminator (Comp) class comprises a wide variety (96 indexes) of race cars, which compete in a handicap starting system to equalize the competition. Cars run on indexes of just over seven seconds to just under 10 seconds. For example, a car designated A/D (A/Dragster), which would be a high-horsepower dragster, has a 7.04-second index, while a 9.67-second index is used for an I/SM (I/Super Modified) car, a slower car with less horsepower than an A/Dragster.

The quicker cars of the class are Dragsters, Altereds and Funny Cars with large V8 engines. Superchargers and turbochargers are allowed in some of these classes. Methanol fuel is mandatory in the quicker cars, but racing gasoline is used in the majority of the classes.

Along with the quicker Gas Dragster class, which only runs gasoline, there are Econo and Nostalgia dragsters in Competition Eliminator racing. These cars are usually front-engined cars, similar in appearance to the early nitro-burning fuel dragsters of the 1960s and early 1970s. They may look similar to the older cars, but are right up to date in terms of technical and safety requirements.

Super Modified cars have naturally aspirated engines using carburetors only, and are two-door passenger car styles built in 1967 or later, including front-wheel drive conversion cars. When car manufacturers started building front-drive midsize cars in the early 1980s, drag racers omitted this front-wheel drive setup in favor of the traditional front-engine, rear-wheel drive setup for better traction.

The Altered Truck classes in Comp are restricted to 1997 or later mid-size, extended cab pickups which may not be altered in any manner.

The NHRA's Super Comp, Super Gas and Super Street are very similar to the IHRA's "Rod" classes using the same time indexes.

The Super Comp class cars run on an 8.90-second index with a Pro tree, weighing a minimum of 1,350 pounds for V8-powered cars. Most cars in this class are dragsters, but full-fendered cars such as Funny Cars and Pro-Stock appearing cars are allowed. Front-engined Altereds, usually with a fiberglass nostalgia-type body such as a "Bucket T" or "Bantam Roadster" are also allowed. Engine modifications are virtually unlimited, but the car must race to the 8.90-second index.

Running with a 9.90-second index, Super Gas cars are full-bodied with functional doors and a minimum weight of 2,100 pounds for V8 cars. The class rules stipulate the car must have left-hand steering, so no open-wheeled vehicles such as dragsters are allowed in Super Gas. Cars in this class appear close to their stock roots, with doors, engine hoods, grilles, windshields and bumpers.

As with Super Comp, a heads-up

Bracket Racing

Bracket, or ET (elapsed time) racing, is the backbone of drag racing. Every weekend, thousands of amateur and hobby racers drive their cars to the strip, put on a helmet and drag race. It is from this entry-level class that a racer's career also starts, and if he or she has the passion and the wherewithal to build and drive a faster car, Bracket racing is the starting point.

Devised with indexing and a handicap starting system, a good Bracket racer learns quickly that speed is not the most important aspect of winning races. To be successful at Bracket racing, consistency is most important. A good racer gets "dialed-in" (establishes the elapsed time the car

start is used in Super Gas, with a .4-second Pro tree.

Super Street vehicles appear very similar to street-driven stock vehicles. They are full-bodied with functional doors, hood, grille and windshield. No fenderless cars such as dragsters or Altereds are allowed. The vehicles compete with a 10.90-second index.

Street rods, panel trucks and sports cars are allowed in the class. Minimum weight for four-cylinder cars is 1,200 pounds, for six-cylinder cars is 2,000 pounds and for V8-powered cars is 2,800 pounds. And as with the other "Super" classes, a heads-up start is used, but this time with a .5-second Pro tree.

Justion Beaver cleans the tires on his Chevy Nova Super Stocker during the NHRA Division 7 meet at Las Vegas in 2008.

will travel in the quarter-mile) and stays close to that dial-in without going faster, or "breaking out."

There are several classes in Bracket racing depending on the performance capabilities of the vehicles. At NHRA-sanctioned tracks, the Super Pro class is for cars that can run the quarter-mile in 11.99 seconds or less. The Pro Class is 13.99 seconds or less, and the Sportsman class is for cars running 12.00 to 19.99 seconds. The IHRA's program is similar, with cars in Pro/Comp running at 8.90 seconds, Top ET for cars under 11.90 seconds and Mod ET for cars under 13.00 seconds. Street ET is for cars over 12 seconds.

In Bracket racing, several variables keep drivers from obtaining an artificial edge when racing. The following rules and systems keep the racing clean, competitive and skill oriented.

Handicap System

Operating on a handicap system, slower vehicles have the ability to compete on an even playing field with quicker and faster counterparts. The slower vehicle will receive an advantage at the start, equal to the difference between the two vehicles' performance predictions, or dial-in times, which are established before racing begins. After the cars are staged, the countdown yellow lights on the Christmas Tree will start first for the slower vehicle (the car with the highest pre-determined elapsed time) while the faster car (lower elapsed time) must wait until his or her sequence starts.

Breaking Out

In most cases, the vehicle that gets to the finish line first wins. However, if a vehicle goes quicker than its performance prediction, it is determined to have broken out of its dial-in time. A breakout racer is disqualified. If both vehicles run under their projected elapsed time, a "double breakout" occurs, and the driver running closest to his or her dial-in is the winner.

Cutting a Light

A driver can win a race despite having posted slower elapsed times and speed totals. In some instances, a winning driver can use a quicker reaction time to the green starting light to overcome an opponent's greater performance advantage on the track. If a slower car (one with a higher dialed-in time) has a better reaction time starting the race, that driver has the race lead over his opponent right from the start. The opponent must try to make up for this time loss. This is true for all classes in both Sportsman and Pro, but comes into play more in the Sportsman classes as the car that leaves the line last must not only try to beat his opponent, but not go faster that his dialed-in time at the end of the track.

Fouls

In other instances, such as a foul start (red light), crossing the center line or making contact with an outside track boundary, drivers are automatically disqualified.

Top Drivers

Not only did Tony Schumacher win the inaugural NHRA Carolina Nationals in 2008, but the victory gave him the most Top Fuel victories in NHRA history, eclipsing the mark set by Joe Amato in 2000.

53
ONY SCHUMACHER
ST NHRA TOP FUEL VICTORIES
NHRA
POWERADE
DRAG RACING SERIES
U.S. ARMY
HARDY
U.S. ARMY
ARMY STRONG.

Greg Anderson

In the world of NHRA Pro Stock, three drivers have dominated the class since its inception.

In the early 1970s, after the class was established and sorting itself out, Bob Glidden was the man to beat. In the 1990s, Warren Johnson was virtually unstoppable in Pro Stock, eventually winning 96 national events, surpassing Glidden's 85 victories.

Anderson in April of 2008; It was ten years earlier that Anderson began driving Pro Stock after working many years in the class for Pro Stock guru Warren Johnson.

And the Pro Stock driver of the new century is Greg Anderson, who has won three championships since 2003, and has never finished the season lower than third since 2002. He won 12 of the 23 nationals in 2003, with an outstanding 67–11 win-loss record, for his first NHRA world championship.

But in 2004, this Minnesota native, born in 1961, took 15 wins, an NHRA record. With a win-loss record of 76–8, he won his second Pro Stock title. He also qualified number one 16 times in 2004, another NHRA record.

Anderson only won eight events in 2005, but it was enough for his third championship. He finished 2006 and 2007 in second place by the narrowest of point margins.

In the early 1980s, Anderson helped out his father, who was running a Modified Eliminator car in Minnesota. A fellow racer of his father's, John Hagen, gave the young Anderson a job working on his Pro Stock car.

When Hagen, Anderson's mentor, was killed in a racing accident at Brainerd, Warren Johnson, one of Hagen's NHRA Division 5 competitors, invited Anderson to work for his Pro Stock team in Georgia. Anderson learned from Johnson, who was becoming one of the best in the class.

While on Johnson's team, Anderson received his Pro Stock license in 1995, but did not use it for several years. He continued to work for Johnson, always hoping he would get a ride with the team.

But the ride never came, and with a meager budget, Anderson set out on his own to race in 1998. He believed his mechanical and set-up knowledge was strong, and that he would become a good driver, but lack of funds kept him struggling for several years.

Anderson's fortunes turned around in 2002 when businessman Ken Black provided the funds for a properly financed assault, and the winning has not stopped since.

In his first full year of competition, Anderson won two events (Englishtown and Columbus), and with four runner-up finishes, he placed third in the 2002 season, a long way from the 15th spot the previous year.

In 2003, he hit his stride, winning a dozen events, earning 14 number-one qualifying awards and setting records in the class at 19 racetracks.

If 2003 was a good year for Anderson, then 2004 was exemplary as he won a record 15 events (matched only by Tony Schumacher in 2008) and won the championship by 742 points, the largest margin in NHRA Pro Stock history. That season Anderson also took home the prestigious Driver of the Year Award, presented to the top driver in American auto racing. He was only the second NHRA racer ever to do so since the inception of the award in 1967; John Force, in 1996, was the first NHRA driver to win.

While Anderson didn't win double-digit races in 2005, his eight victories were enough to take his third championship. 2006 was all of a blip on the radar for Anderson as he only won three events. Even still, he finished second in the points race.

With eight wins in 2007, Anderson was number one for most of the year. From September at Indy until three races later at Richmond he was second, but a

win at Las Vegas gave him a slim 34-point advantage going for top place into the final event at Pomona.

Anderson lost in the first round, and watched Jeg Coughlin go through the ladder to win the race and the title for 2007.

Anderson was confident of his chances in 2008, especially after grabbing victories at Pomona, Houston, Englishtown and Norwalk to start the season.

"If we can maintain this pace and come out of the western events [Denver, Seattle and Sonoma] in first place, we'll be in good shape," he said after his Norwalk win. "But we'll take these races one at a time and try to do our best at each one. I just know that we're heading in the right direction now and that's a good thing."

Anderson won in Denver, giving him at least five victories in five of the last six seasons, but had some problems in the remaining events. He finished 2008 on a high note, getting the right combination and winning the Pomona race, but it wasn't enough to put him on top, and he finished second in NHRA Pro Stock points.

After the Pomona race, Anderson felt he had pressured himself too much in his quest for the title.

"I probably tried a little too hard and thought too much about it and put too much pressure on myself and just kind of stopped having fun racing," he is quoted as saying. "Today, the pressure was off, and I just came out and had fun, and, poof, the car performed great, and the driver performed fine, and we won a race again."

As the most dominant Pro Stock driver of the new century, Anderson has set a pace few of his competitors have been able to keep up with, let alone surpass. And that's a good thing for Anderson.

Shown here at Las Vegas early in 2008, the three-time NHRA Pro Stock champ placed second behind Jeg Coughlin for the season.

Brandon Bernstein

In a sport of families and dynasties, the name Bernstein is perhaps the most renowned.

Drag racing icon Kenny Bernstein announced his retirement at the end of the 2002 NHRA season, but there was a hitch. The six-time champ had qualified his Top Fueler number one for the prestigious Bud Shootout, which was to take place at the season-closing Pomona national event.

Continuing the family tradition, Brandon Bernstein, son of Kenny, now drives the Budweiser-sponsored Top Fueler. He is always a threat, and has played spoiler several times, although he has yet to win a championship.

Rain postponed the entire event until February 2003, and Bernstein had officially retired.

So, instead of Kenny coming out of his very short retirement, his 30-year-old son Brandon got into the cockpit of the Budweiser/Lucas Oil dragster for the delayed Shootout, and in his first competitive outing in a Fueler, finished runner-up.

And it's been a winning ride every since. This second-generation driver has never finished below seventh in the season standings except for 2003, when he only ran eight races.

And although he only competed in eight events in 2003, he won three of them, at Pomona, Gainesville and Bristol. He won another three in 2004, a pair in 2005 and four in 2006.

With a solid win-loss record of 39 and 19 in 2006, Brandon Bernstein was victorious in four events, taking out Melanie Troxel at Houston, Cory McClenathan at Columbus, Tony Schumacher at Brainerd and Rod Fuller at Dallas. He had three runner-up spots for the year, losing in the final to Doug Kalitta at Topeka, and Tony Schumacher at St. Louis and at the U.S. Nationals at Indianapolis.

Obviously, the team had its game plan together for the 2006 season, and finished third in the standings, up considerably from a seventh-place finish the year before. Bernstein had dyed his hair at the beginning of the 2006 season, and although it probably didn't make him go any faster, he thought the new look would be good for a change.

"We're going to shake everything up this year," Brandon is quoted as saying just before the 2006 NHRA opener at Pomona, where he introduced his new platinum hair color. "I don't think the hair will make the car run any faster, but it has given the team new energy to come up with a lot of one-liners for me."

"Shaking things up" was a family trait. Brandon Bernstein's father, Kenny, started his racing career in the mid-1960s, always in a fuel car, whether dragster or Funny Car. Born in Texas in 1944, Kenny Bernstein's interest in racing had been a sideline to his business interests and entrepreneurial endeavors. In his early years, he represented several women's clothing lines, and built up an auto wrecker business with 18 tow

truck and vehicle recovery units. He then sold the tow trucks to start a restaurant, eventually building a string of establishments in the early 1970s, with the racing sidelined. When he returned to racing in the late 1970s, he was a regular on the NHRA and IHRA Funny Car circuit. He won the IHRA Funny Car title in 1979, and was in that sanction's top 10 almost every year for the next 10 years. He also won his first NHRA race in 1979, defeating John Force at the Cajun Nationals at Baton Rouge.

From that time on, he was the man in Funny Car competition, winning the NHRA crown four times, from 1985 through 1988. When he switched to Top Fuel, he was never out of the hunt, and took that title in the NHRA in 1996 and 2001.

Aside from these stellar accomplishments, the elder Bernstein will be remembered for two major items in drag racing: he brought a major brewery to the sport as a team sponsor, and he was the first driver to break the 300-mph barrier when he ran a 301.70-mph pass at Gainesville in March 1992.

He continued to race successfully well into the new century, and came out of a short retirement to drive a full Funny Car schedule in 2007, finishing 14th.

The team's emphasis, however, is now focused more on the driving career of Brandon, who first started driving the Budweiser/Lucas Oil dragster in 2003. Born in 1972, Bernstein worked on his dad's team during summers while attending university. When he graduated in 1996, he joined the team full time, and started driving an Alcohol Dragster a few years later.

In 2001, he won the NHRA's Division 7 honors in the dragster, and then went back to crewing on the team car in 2002. When he started driving a year later, the Bernstein tradition of winning continued to the next generation.

The younger Bernstein has not filled his father's shoes by winning a championship. Yet. He came close in 2007 with five wins, two runner-ups, and a 37–15 win-loss record—good enough to end the season in third place.

Bernstein had trouble duplicating his 2007 season in 2008. He continued to qualify and snagged a trio of runner-up placings at Gainesville, Englishtown and Norwalk, but ultimately couldn't muster the times needed to be the best on the track.

He qualified second at Seattle, and went to the final, but lost to Tony Schumacher, and then didn't get beyond the second round in the next five races. Later in the year at Dallas and Memphis Bernstein made it to the semi-finals and was sitting sixth in points after the Memphis race.

But a pair of first-round losses and a quarter-final round loss at the season-closing Pomona event dropped Bernstein to seventh place for the season.

When Bernstein returned for the 2009 NHRA opener at Pomona, he no longer had the luxury of working with team crew chief Tim Richards or tuner Kim Richards (formerly Kim LaHaie), the husband and wife duo who helped the team to 33 wins in the past seven seasons, wrenching in his garage.

Kenny Bernstein has treated his racing team as a business first and foremost, and as such has provided his son with everything needed to win. Will the younger Bernstein be as prominent a driver as his father? Only time and a lot of winning rounds will tell.

Bernstein and the familiar Budweiser racing suit. 2009 will mark 30 years of Budweiser/Bernstein sponsorship—the longest in the history of motorsport.

Laurie Cannister

Laurie Cannister has approached her drag racing career with enthusiasm, professionalism and the belief that all racers are the same, whether they are men or women.

"We all put our fire suits on one leg at a time. I want to be treated as a straight-up competitor."

And Cannister has proven herself a strong competitor. After a five-year absence from racing, the 2000 Pro Outlaw Champion raced three races in the 11-race IHRA Alcohol Funny Car circuit in 2007 taking one victory and finishing ninth overall in the season standings.

Cannister began her professional driving career in the now-defunct IHRA Super Eliminator class, also known as Pro Outlaw. She was known as a strong competitor behind the wheel of her small-block-powered dragster and she cemented her reputation by capturing the Pro Outlaw World Championship in 2000. Cannister became the second woman in the IHRA—and the fourth woman in all of drag racing—to win a professional class world title.

After her championship, Laurie and her husband Dale decided to move up to alcohol racing and toured an Alcohol Funny Car for the next two seasons. Her success was limited, but considering

she had to learn and master a race car with an entirely different execution from her dragster, the experiment was a relative success.

"They are two completely different driving styles," Cannister notes about racing a rear-engined dragster and the short-wheelbase front-engined Funny Car. "With dragsters it's all finesse and guiding the car. You point and shoot. Driving a Funny Car is like wrestling with an alligator," she says. "You're constantly fighting with the steering. It's just an animal. That's how you have to drive them."

The team ran out of its own pocket, however, and due to lack of funding had to call it quits after the 2002 season. Laurie and Dale kept involved in racing by crewing for another team, the hope of getting back into their own ride never far from sight.

When Trevor Lebsack could not pilot his car at an IHRA national event in Texas in 2007, Cannister was asked to take over the seat. She didn't win the race, but she did qualify, and felt she was ready to return if a steady ride could be obtained.

The phone call came later that year when the owners of her previous Funny Car, Kevin and Wendy Sims, wanted to get into the sport full-time. The Sims asked the Cannisters if they would be interested in Laurie driving and Dale wrenching.

The Cannisters accepted the Sims's offer and joined the Kalbones Racing Team for the final two IHRA meets of 2007. The team was hoping to test its competitiveness at these two events with the possibility of a full season effort in 2008 if all went well.

Right off the trailer at Budds Creek, Maryland, the team knew it had the right combination as Cannister won the event, taking the victory over perennial class winner Mark Thomas. She then qualified number one at the IHRA season finale at Rockingham, North Carolina.

To prove she was going to be a player on the 2008 IHRA Alcohol Funny Car circuit, Cannister won both opening rounds, taking the wins at San Antonio and Rockingham. As the season rolled on Cannister was almost unstoppable, taking six of the 10 IHRA races for 2008, and finishing runner-up twice.

She knew she had the AFC title sewn up going into the second-last event of 2008 at Epping, New Hampshire. Cannister didn't win that race, but she did win the season-ending race at Rockingham.

"It's a really awesome feeling," she said a few weeks after the series final. "We've been living on this high since we knew we had the points race wrapped up at Epping."

Cannister's successful return to racing has been the result of a solid team effort, including a strong rapport with husband Dale. They have been married for 19 years, and think as one when it comes to racing.

"When we get up to the staging area and get ready, I get strapped in and the last thing before the car is fired up and the body comes down is that Dale reaches in and holds my hand.

Facing page: Cannister in 2008 IHRA competition. With the cancellation of the IHRA Alcohol Funny Car class for 2009, Cannister will race in the NHRA.

Above: Cannister doesn't sit around between races. Her duties include engine work, and she is shown here with husband and team crew chief, Dale Cannister.

"After I make my pass I'll tell him about the run and we discuss any problems. Then we go over the computer readouts. We'll go over them, plus discuss what I thought about the run. We get along well with this exchange of information."

It helps that Cannister is mechanically inclined. Between rounds her duties in the pits include maintenance on the right side of the car's engine.

She also spends time between rounds with the fans and signing autographs and acting as a role model of sorts by offering encouragement to younger racers such as Junior Dragster drivers.

"I just love it," Cannister says of her job. "It's pretty cool."

Jeg Coughlin

It had to be in the genes. Jeg Coughlin, the youngest of four brothers, grew up in a world of performance and fast cars. Coughlin's father, Jeg Sr., was an early Ohio Gasser racer who also competed in the Pro Comp, Funny Car and Top Fuel ranks. The senior Coughlin also started a speed shop in his native Ohio, which has become one of the automotive aftermarket's biggest enterprises.

Young Edward James Coughlin (Jeg) and his three older brothers all took to the drag strip. John, Troy and Mike Coughlin have all competed in a variety of classes, from Super Stock to Pro Modified to Super Comp.

By 1990, young Jeg was an experienced racer, and at 20 years old he won his first major event: the 1990 Super Gas division at Columbus. While racing Super Gas and Super Stock, Jeg Jr. helped on his father's Top Fuel team and worked on his Bachelor of Arts in business. By 1997 he was a busy racer, and became the first driver in NHRA history to win national events in four different categories—Pro Stock, Super Stock, Comp and Super Gas.

Growing up in a racing and auto-related family, Jeg Coughlin's star has shone brightly, including capturing the 2008 NHRA Pro Stock championship.

Coughlin got serious in 1998, running all NHRA nationals with his Pro Stock car, and finished second at the end of the season. He had four wins that year against tough competition, including Jim Yates and both Warren and Kurt Johnson.

He won five national events in 1999, two against brother Troy in final rounds, and two against the "Professor," Warren Johnson. He once again finished second in points.

The year 2000 was a watershed year for the Ohio native. He won the first six of seven national events on his way to capturing 10 of the 23 races on the tour. He established a resounding 62–13 win-loss record on his way to winning his first NHRA championship.

For the next five years Coughlin was a player in Pro Stock, winning another championship in 2002 with eight national event wins. In 2004 and 2005, he placed sixth in the standings, and then backed away from his pro career for 2006, competing in only three races.

That isn't to say Coughlin didn't race. An avid Sportsman class racer, he competed in several meets, including some Super Pro and Top Dragster events.

He then returned in 2007 to active NHRA Pro Stock racing with Victor Cagnazzi, owner of the JEGS.com Chevy Cobalt. And it was quite the year, as the two-time champ played catch-up, trying to get ahead of Greg Anderson who was number one in points almost all season.

Going into the final 2007 event at Pomona, Coughlin was second in the points race with 3,102 points and Anderson was leading with 3,136 points. Coughlin knew he had to be perfect to get enough points to win another championship.

Anderson's fate at Pomona would be left up to others to decide, as he was eliminated by Justin Humphreys in the first round. Coughlin meanwhile roared his way through the ladder in eliminations, beating Larry Morgan, Richie Stevens and Mike Edwards, only to face Humphreys in the final.

By winning the first two elimination rounds, Coughlin added 40 points to his overall total—six more points overall than the eliminated Anderson's 3,136—which meant that before Coughlin raced the final against Humphreys, he had already won his third Pro Stock championship.

And knowing this, Coughlin went out and beat

Humphreys in the final round, giving him four victories on the year.

"What a feeling," Coughlin is quoted as saying after winning his first two rounds and earning enough points to win the title. "It was a tough battle against the best racers in the world, but we got it done as a team and I couldn't be prouder of the entire Victor Cagnazzi Racing organization.

"It's incredible how it all fell into place," Coughlin went on. "The pressure was enormous for all of us, and I think my previous experience might have really helped me there. Last year I only ran three Pro Stock events at the end of the season. The rest of the time I was running a bunch of those high-dollar Bracket races and those things are so intense. That's kind of what it felt like these past two races."

Coughlin's 2008 started off with a bang as he won the Gatornationals early in the season, but he struggled through the mid portion of the tour and was sitting fourth in points going into the Reading event, the 17th race of the season, which he won. Three races later at Dallas he finished runner-up to Greg Stanfield, and was leading the points. A win at the second Las Vegas event gave him his third victory of the year and enough momentum to stay atop the Pro Stock ladder, with the closest competitor, Greg Anderson, 123 points back. All Coughlin had to do in order to take the Pro Stock crown was qualify at the season-ending Pomona event. He did that and not much more, as he was eliminated by Allen Johnson in the first round.

But Coughlin was getting ready for the next season.

"We have a new Cobalt coming and we'll get out sometime this winter and get her broken in," Coughlin was quoted as saying after Pomona. "For now, we're going to come together as a team and enjoy this championship. It takes an incredible amount of work to get to this point and everyone at Victor Cagnazzi Racing should be extremely proud of this trophy."

With 41 NHRA Pro Stock and 13 Sportsman class event wins to his credit, the youngest member of this racing family now has 54 Wally trophies (the brass-finished award named after NHRA founder Wally Parks) for his fireplace mantle—something he can really brag about at the next Coughlin family picnic.

Coughlin took part in the preseason Pontiac Pro Stock Showdown at Las Vegas in 2008 before he began his quest for the 2008 NHRA championship.

Larry Dixon

One of the longest unions in drag racing came to an end late in 2008, a union that had lasted over 20 years.

The 42-year-old Dixon joined his second career organization late in 2008 when he left Snake Racing to join top crew chief Alan Johnson and the Al-Anabi team.

Legend racer turned owner Don Prudhomme, and Top Fuel star Larry Dixon, who drove the Snake Racing dragster, parted ways, apparently not with smiles and handshakes. Dixon bought out the remainder of his contract with Snake Racing, while Prudhomme stated the 2008 season ended on a "bittersweet note."

Dixon placed second in the 2008 NHRA Top Fuel standings, but before he won in the season-ending Pomona event, there were rumors that he would be leaving the team that he had become an integral part of.

When the new Alan Johnson–Al-Anabi Racing team was organized, Dixon's name was in the hat, and after some weeks of speculation, he joined the new Top Fuel team for the 2009 season. Prudhomme named 2008 IHRA Top Fuel champion Spencer Massey to drive Dixon's old ride.

Dixon, born in 1966 and a two-time Top Fuel champion, had been with the legendary Prudhomme since 1988, first working on the engine for Prudhomme's Funny Car team. When he went to work on Prudhomme's Skoal-sponsored Flopper, he was 22 years old, ready to get his hands dirty and continue to learn the world of nitro competition.

As the son of former Top Fuel ace Larry Dixon Senior, the younger Dixon, who was born in California and now resides in Indiana, grew up with drag racing as a big part of his life. He had spent several years helping in his father's racing efforts, and although he figured he would drive some day, he performed his duties and bided his time.

"I loved the whole nuts and bolts of working on a car," he has been quoted as saying. "Everybody working together as one to try and make our package better than whomever we're competing against. I didn't have any money to bring to the table. I just had a lot of drive and hopefully a little talent."

Back in the late 1980s, Prudhomme was still winning races, but the emerging John Force overshadowed his former dominance. When Prudhomme's team switched over to a Top Fuel car in 1991, it won three national NHRA events. After the 1994 season, the veteran put Dixon in the car after he earned his Top Fuel ticket in Gainesville that year.

"I obviously didn't think working on the Funny Car would snowball into a driving job," explained Dixon. "I figured Snake would be driving as long as Chris Karamesines has." (Now in his 70s, Karamesines has raced in Top Fuel since the 1950s and continues to compete.)

But Prudhomme's choice of a driving replacement was a good one. In 19 races for 1995, Dixon won four events: Phoenix, Gainesville, Englishtown and the prestigious U.S. Nationals at Indy. He placed third in points and was named NHRA Rookie of the Year.

Victories were scattered about over the next five years, but the team was consistent, finishing eighth in the points in 1999, third for 2000 and second in 2001.

Dixon won the opening round of the 2002 NHRA season at Pomona, and the victory started a run of nine wins to handily capture his first championship. Not only did he win nine of the 23 events, Dixon was runner-up in five of those races, and produced a 57–13 win-loss record.

The team continued in the same manner for 2003, starting off with another Pomona win. There were four more wins by mid-season and then three in a row in the latter half at Denver, Seattle and Sonoma. Once again he was runner-up five times. He also qualified number one at four of these races, down from his career high of seven the year before.

The next three seasons were not as fruitful as the earlier ones for Dixon. He finished the 2004 season

Dixon in his new ride at Firebird International Raceway in Phoenix in 2009. Dixon opened his first term with Al-Anabi Racing by being the top qualifier in the second and third events of the season, going all the way to win the class title at the third.

in sixth with two wins (Englishtown, Memphis), and rallied in 2005 with a second place in the championship points standings with three wins: (Las Vegas, Englishtown, Indy).

The next year, 2006, was not a good season for the team. There were no wins, only one runner-up (Englishtown again, his third trip to the final there in three years), and he failed to make the field in Dallas. But he did get some rounds in during the season, and finished seventh in points.

After 12 years of Miller Lite sponsorship, the brewery pulled its association with the team, to focus on NASCAR Cup racing. There was SkyTel sponsorship for the Prudhomme team in 2007, and then for 2008 the team was sponsored by U.S. Smokeless Tobacco.

No matter the financial backing, the team continued to be a major player in the competition. For 2007, Dixon slowly but surely made winning rounds, including the important final round at Chicago and Englishtown, and was second in points. For the remainder of the season he qualified well, and when he won at Dallas, he was at the top of the division. In the final three events of 2007, Dixon made the show but never got past the second round at each race, and finished the year fourth in the standings.

Dixon's 2008 was a successful year with four runner-ups and two victories, at Phoenix and the season-ending event at Pomona. He was number one qualifier four times in 24 events: Topeka, and then three in a row at Indy, Charlotte, and Dallas. Although he was fifth in points going into Pomona, his final round victory over Rod Fuller pushed him back up to second in the Chase behind Tony Schumacher.

Dixon did not qualify for the 2009 NHRA season opener at Pomona, while Prudhomme and Massey made the show, losing in the first round. But Dixon is ready to make his mark with his new team.

"I had a great time at Don Prudhomme Racing for the number of years that I was there, but it was time for a change," Dixon said before the season opener in February 2009. "Between crewing and driving, I was there for 20 years, so that's half my life. I have a great opportunity driving for Alan Johnson and his Al-Anabi Racing team, and I'm really looking forward to the challenge."

Ashley Force

John Force always said he hoped his son would take over the family business. Force didn't have any sons, but one of his four daughters has admirably carried on the family heritage. Born late in November 1982, Ashley Force grew up in the world of drag racing, and is perhaps the daughter destined to follow in her father's footsteps.

Ashley Force, seen here in 2006 with a Wally trophy for the NHRA Southern Nationals Top Alcohol Dragster class, has won events in two disciplines, as she became the first woman to win a major NHRA Funny Car race in 2008.

When she won the Funny Car final in Atlanta in 2008, and became the first woman to win a major race in the NHRA's Funny Car division, Ashley Force was definitely walking proud. This shy young woman has emerged as a fresh new face in the high-performance world of drag racing.

Force has now gone from the pressure of succeeding in racing to the pressure of celebrity status. Even with guest appearances on television shows such as Jay Leno's *Tonight Show* and ABC's *Good Morning America*, Force has tried to downplay her success. She has consented to photo shoots for several publications, but posed for *Penthouse* in her full fire suit. She had problems when asked to sing during a promotion for Old Spice, one of her team's major sponsors. "I'd rather drive my Funny Car at 300 mph, without a parachute, than sing karaoke," was her comment.

Force's short career behind the wheel of her Castrol GTX Ford Mustang has now passed through the initial stage of her driving skills and experience. The pressure of the indoctrination into a Funny Car has been in a fishbowl environment, but she now feels comfortable.

"It's been perfect how it's worked out. When I first tested in Dad's Funny Car, I had the best people in the sport working on the car in Austin Coil and Bernie Fedderly. They've seen my Dad through all his championships, and Austin has been with him for all his wins, but I was always intimidated by them.

"Even as big a goofball as Dad is, he's still a great driver," the younger Force has said about her early time on the team. "He knows how to do it. How hard it must have been for them because I knew almost nothing and I always felt scared that I was going to mess up and make them mad at me."

But that didn't happen. "They never did get mad," she continued, "but as a new driver you always thought of that."

Through her relationship with current crew chief Dean "Guido" Antonelli, Force's transition has worked well. Antonelli was also a new player in the long-established team.

"With Guido I feel more relaxed and a lot less nervous because we're both in the same situation. When you have two people that are both kind of new to it, I think it makes it flow a little better. When problems do occur, they aren't such a big deal."

Although Ashley has been racing since the end of her high school days, her mother Laurie (and wife of the 14-time champion John) insisted she proceed with her post-secondary education. Ashley raced on weekends and acquired a Bachelor of Arts degree in communications.

She also continued with her education in racing. Before the Funny Car, Force was a dominant Top Alcohol Dragster racer, winning several events, including the 2004 U.S. Nationals. She finished fourth in points the same year and was named Rookie of the Year in the Lucas Oil Drag Racing Series. During her three years with the dragster (2004–2006), Force had 38 starts, went to nine final rounds, took five of those finals and had a 67–33 win-loss record.

In her first year of Funny Car competition in 2007, she finished 10th in the points race, a solid record considering it was her rookie year in the class, and she did not compete in two rounds of the 23-event schedule. After a couple of first-round oustings, Force took a pair of semifinal rounds, and by mid-season was seventh in points, After three events in which she did not qualify, she was 14th, but another pair of semifinal rounds late in the year boosted her back to 10th. A final-round appearance at Las Vegas, losing to Tony Pedregon, also helped her in the standings.

Force performed better in 2008, and was third in the standings halfway through the season. The highlight of the year was her win at Atlanta, as she took out Dad in the final. She also recorded three runner-up finishes, at Houston, Las Vegas and Memphis. After a third-round loss at Chicago, she suffered four first-round losses in a row dropping her considerably in the standings. With a couple of better showings at Sonoma, Reading and Charlotte, she regrouped for a respectable sixth place showing in the NHRA Funny Car standings for the season.

After the season-ending Pomona race where Force qualified third and then went two rounds before being eliminated, she was reasonably pleased with her efforts and the efforts of her team.

"It is what it is," Force said at the time. "We really had a good day today, even the run we lost on I don't know that we would have done anything differently. At least that is how we ended our year, not on something stupid that happened or broke or I did something wrong. We had a good finish and a good car. We'll just start again in a few months."

Ashley Force at the SummitRacing.com Nationals in Las Vegas. With the familiar Force-family sponsor, GTX, Ashley placed sixth in the NHRA standings for 2008.

John Force

By any standards John Force is an incredible person. He has been and continues to be an incredible drag racer. He has sustained the demanding lifestyle of a professional drag racer for decades. He has withstood the physical and mental stresses of driving a race car that accelerates and goes faster than most people can imagine. He has withstood the emotional distress of a fellow team member and protégé killed in the sport, and has continued on. He has also introduced his children into the sport knowing the dangerous possibilities they face.

John Force looks on during the SummitRacing.com Nationals at Las Vegas Motor Speedway. With more victories than any other driver, John Force continues to drive, and win.

John Force has also marked his spot in racing history with the most incredible record in drag racing: a record that far exceeds any other in the sport and one that may never be equaled, as in May of 2008, he recorded his 1,000th competitive-round win at the NHRA Midwest Nationals in Madison, Illinois.

Force was already the iconic figure of drag racing when he suffered his worst crash in September 2007. While he was convalescing from the 300-mph calamity at the Texas Motorplex, many thought he would stop driving. Many thought he would just operate his team of Funny Cars, which included his daughter Ashley and son-in-law Robert Hight.

But after 31 years of racing, Force waited for his broken hands and feet to heal so he could get back into his nitro-burning Ford Mustang.

"What else would I do?" said the 59-year old ex-truck driver during his three-month mending period. "Drag racing is all I know. It's what I love."

This 14-time NHRA Funny Car champion was born in California in 1949. Since he started racing in 1974, he has been behind the wheel of a Funny Car. His first car was purchased in Australia through some family connections, and even though he didn't have a license to drive that Vega Funny Car in Australia, he was the first to break the 200-mph barrier there. He then quietly returned to California before track officials chased him out.

Force was hooked. He lived the life of a professional racer but had no budget, lots of enthusiasm, and the will to do just about anything to race.

"Anything for gas money to the next race," he has said. This included promotional gigs such as dressing up as a clown for appearances at Wendy's (an early sponsor), and getting in front of a television camera for local commercials.

His first final-round appearance in NHRA competition was in 1978, losing to Kenny Bernstein at Baton Rouge. It was also his only appearance that year. With six starts in 1979, he made two final rounds. By 1985, he was coming off a 1984 AHRA Funny Car championship and was in a dozen NHRA races. He didn't win any national events, but placed fifth in the NHRA standings that year.

Force's career caught a break in the mid-to-late 1980s thanks to two major events. He obtained sponsorship from Castrol Oil in 1986, which continues to this day. And the two dominant Funny Car drivers of the day, Don Prudhomme and Kenny Bernstein, left the Funny Car ranks late in the decade to go Top Fuel racing.

Force made good use of the two opportunities,

and from 1985 until 1989, he was never lower than sixth in the standings. He won his first NHRA national event in 1987 in the Grand Nationals at Sanair, Quebec, beating Ed McCulloch in the final. The next year he recorded three wins (Pomona, Brainerd, Columbus), finishing the season in third place. He had only one win in 1989, at Reading, and finished sixth in the standings.

But for the next 13 years, he was unstoppable, capturing 12 championships.

The early 1990s were a defining era for Force. A large part of his success in winning the 1990 and 1991 championships was due to the efforts of Austin Coil as crew chief.

Coil, who won back-to-back Funny Car titles in 1982 and 1983 with the Chi-Town Hustler and Frank Hawley driving from his Chicago base, went to California in 1985 to join Force, and has been with him since.

He later acquired the mechanical talents of Bernie Fedderly, who is also still with the team. Fedderly's background as crew chief for Top Fuel aces Terry Capp and Gary Beck gave this former Albertan the credentials for working with nitro cars, and he left

Force finishing a burnout early in 2008. Teamed with Bernie Fedderly and Austin Coil, Force was unstoppable in the 1980s and 1990s with 14 Funny Car championships.

The master sits and waits his turn. Born in 1949, Force has talked about retiring in 2010.

the Larry Minor–Cruz Pedregon team in 1992 to work with Force.

The Force team's 1992 season was its only losing season between 1990 and 2002, as driver Tony Pedregon rallied with five victories in the final six races to clinch the championship.

Force bounced back, however, and in 1993 won 13 of 18 nationals and his first of 10 consecutive NHRA Funny Car titles. He won six of that year's first seven races, along with his first U.S. Nationals at Indianapolis. The next year (1994), he became the winningest driver in Funny Car history with 10 season victories for a career total of 42, seven more than previous title holder Don Prudhomme.

Force wasn't done setting records there. In 1996, as he won 16 of 19 national events, he was the first to break the 4.90-second time barrier with a 4.889-second run at Topeka, Kansas. He won 65 elimination rounds that year and was the number-one qualifier in 13 events. His career year was made all the sweeter as he was named U.S. auto racing's Driver of the Year, the first drag racer to ever receive the honor.

Force went on to win two more championships, the last coming in 2006.

Throughout all his successes, Force has never strayed far from his humble roots. He is known for having one of the grimiest driving suits in the sport, and is never afraid to get his hands dirty and help out his crew. He is well-liked by the fans, the media and his competitors. He has signed more autographs than anyone in the sport, and has a strong rapport with his fans, never shying away from impromptu photo sessions between rounds.

Force has also never shied away from speaking his mind in front of the media. His interviews are spontaneous, truthful, and delivered about as quickly as one of his five-second trips down the quarter-mile. Not only the most charismatic driver in the sport, he is probably the most quotable, as he always has something to say.

As one of the major teams in drag racing, John Force Racing has fielded multiple-car teams for several seasons. Along with Force himself, he has

included in his team such stars as Tony Pedregon, Gary Densham, Eric Medlen, Robert Hight and daughter Ashley Force. The team suffered greatly in March of 2007 with the death of Medlen at a Gainesville testing session.

Force missed six events in 2007 due to his crash in Texas that year, but was back in his car for the 2008 season. He did not have a great year in 2008, posting only one victory (in Topeka), and one runner-up (in Atlanta). After Charlotte, the fourth race he failed to qualify at in 2008, Force was 10th in points. He bounced back late in the season with a couple of semi-round wins, and finished the year seventh in the NHRA Funny Car ranks.

While Force will continue racing, the death of Medlen and his own serious accident have changed the veteran's priorities and redirected his seemingly endless energy.

Working with the NHRA, the SFI (SEMA Foundation Inc, the organization that issues and administers standards for auto racing), the Ford Motor Company, chassis builder Murf McKinney, and John Medlen (Eric's father and team crew chief), Force is committed to building a safer Funny Car.

Known as the Eric Medlen Project, testing is conducted at the team's Indiana shop facility. With the redesign of the car's chassis, the first major update in Funny Car design in over two decades, the group is working with a newly-developed nitro-powered Ford engine to make the heavier but safer car competitive.

Force also realizes he cannot race forever, and is taking steps to ensure the racing dynasty he has will not disappear when he retires from racing in 2010.

"It's all about the kids now," said Force, about not only the younger drivers on his team but the mechanical crew as well. "I'm still going to race as hard as ever to win the championship. That won't change. But my main job now is to continue to train these young drivers so that they won't have to go through what I went through.

"It's the changing of the guard," he continued. "I know I can't go on forever and I want this team to continue to compete at the same high level in the future."

Force doing a burnout in the well-known Castrol Funny Car. This scene has been playing since 1986 when Castrol first sponsored the up-and-coming Force. The sponsorship has now grown into a Force-family right.

Robert Hight

As part of the John Force Racing dynasty, Funny Car driver Robert Hight is a member of the most successful team in drag racing. And although he is married to the boss's oldest daughter, Adria, this son-in-law of racing icon John Force has certainly earned his place in the family business.

Hight, seen here in May 2008, has built quite a name for himself while driving for John Force Racing, the team owned by his father-in-law.

This former Force crew member, who had no experience behind the wheel of one of the sport's most powerful cars, proved to be a natural when he started racing in 2005. He finished fifth in the class standings for that year. He also earned the NHRA Rookie of the Year honors in 2005 with the help of national event wins at Houston and Denver, plus a pair of runner-up finishes.

In 2006, Hight had three victories, first at Pomona, and then back-to-back wins at the U.S. Nationals and at Dallas, to take second place in that year's standings.

The driver of the Auto Club/Castrol Ford Mustang won three more events in 2007 and placed second again, a mere 19 points behind champ Tony Pedregon.

By the midway point of 2008, Hight had opened up the year with another Pomona victory, this time over Cruz Pedregon, qualified number one at Las Vegas and Norwalk and was fourth in the points race.

Hight believes his experience as a trapshooting marksman has helped his racing career. He was a state champion at 15 in the sport, and at one time was considered for a spot on the U.S. Olympic team, but relinquished that dream to pursue racing. He has said the pressure in shooting, along with learning to retain his focus, have been beneficial to his driving.

"I definitely think that dealing with the pressure of shooting helped my driving. The pressure in racing is a lot more intense. In shooting if you screw up, basically the only person you hurt is yourself. But when you screw up in the race car, you're not just letting yourself down, you're letting down everyone else on the team. That's real pressure."

Born in northern California in 1969, Hight earned degrees in business and accounting, but upon graduation wanted to get into drag racing rather than work in the trade he was schooled for. So he went to work for the Force team in 1995 as a clutch technician, and for the next five years settled in as a full-time member of this winning team.

He also started to get serious with Adria Force, and they were married in 1999. In 2004 the couple presented the boss with a grandchild, Autumn Danielle Hight.

Hight's opportunity came after some personnel changes in 2003 and 2004. Tony Pedregon left Force after the 2003 season and Eric Medlen was given the ride. A former crew member, Medlen did well in the car. Hight was offered a ride in the team's third Funny Car in 2005. In 2007, Ashley Force joined the team as a driver.

Tragedy struck the team early in 2007, when Medlen was killed in a testing exercise at Gainesville. When John Force was injured in a crash in September 2007 and could not race for the remainder of the season, Hight and Ashley Force carried the team banner in competition.

Hight gave his 2007 season a good shot, posting two of the fastest times (4.646 seconds and 4.636 seconds) in the class's history. He also won more rounds than any Funny Car driver in 2007, with a total of 34. Champion Tony Pedregon was next with 30 winning rounds.

Hight lays down a crowd-pleasing burnout while qualifying for the SummitRacing.com Nationals at Las Vegas Motor Speedway.

But at the start of 2008, Hight was determined to do better.

"What we learned last year [2007] was that every point is important," he said. "We had our chances, but we didn't do what we needed [to win the championship] and that's the thing that has given us motivation for this new season."

Hight's 2008 progress continued into the latter half of the season, as the team won at both Sonoma and the U.S. Nationals at Indianapolis. But the Pedregons would get the better of Hight, as Cruz beat him in the final at Las Vegas in the autumn of 2008, and Tony bested him in the first round at the season-closing Pomona race, relegating Hight to a fourth-overall finish in the Funny Car standings.

Hight, a true John Force racing disciple, will rededicate himself to improving for the 2009 season. He knows that becoming a champion is a 24/7 commitment.

"To be competitive you have to live it like John Force has," Height is quoted as saying. "It is so all consuming. You have to wake up every day thinking about how you can win, what you can do to make your car better, and what you can do to make yourself better. You get down to the last race and your hopes are so high. I can't wait to start again to get back out here and try to get on top again. That is our goal to win a championship and get John Force Racing back on top. We know we can do it. We just have to work harder."

Mike Janis

Mike Janis races at only 10 events a year, but those 10 events consume a great deal of his time.

"Racing is everything with me," said the Pro Modified standout and veteran, waiting for the first round of qualifying for the 2008 Mopar Canadian Nationals at the southwestern Ontario IHRA facility of Grand Bend. "There really isn't anything else. There's no fishing, no nothing. Sounds like I'm pretty boring."

Pro Mod veteran Mike Janis celebrating in 2008. Janis has won a pair of IHRA championships in the Pro Mod division.

Based in the Buffalo suburb of Elma, New York, this long-time Pro Mod driver is anything but boring when he gets into his car.

With two IHRA World Championships in Pro Mod (2001 and 2004), Janis has focused his driving in the highly competitive class for the past 10 seasons, initially competing against the early giants of the class, including Scotty Cannon, Al Billes, and the formidable team of Jim Oddy and Fred Hahn.

Born in 1956, Janis has been involved with racing cars and machines ever since he can remember. His father, Jim Janis, started a speed shop in the Buffalo area with partner Tony Centra not long after Mike was born, and the duo also established Jan-Cen Motorsports. Eventually, Mike and his brothers took over the business. Concentrating on snowmobile and ATV sales and service, Jan-Cen continues its reputation as one of the foremost race-engine builders for Pro Mods and other doorslammers.

Janis's first Pro Mod cars were nitrous-powered, as were most of the cars in the class in its early years. He was successful at match racing and some local series at the time, but was struggling in IHRA competition until he stepped up with a supercharger for his car.

Another Western New Yorker, Jim Oddy, was already established as a top Gasser builder and racer when he got into the Pro Mod class, and took the class to the next level.

"Oddy was running an Outlaw Pro Mod with a blower," said Janis. "This really got them going in the class." And Oddy, with driver Fred Hahn, were a tough team to beat.

Around the turn of the century, Janis started with an Alan Johnson engine, got some help with the fuel management system for the blower-powered car, adjusted his driving style to the different engine, and started winning races.

After some starts in the new car, Janis said driving a blower car was easier and smoother, with the supercharger offering consistent power from the start of the race until shutting off the engine. He also said the early cars were much stiffer than today's Pro Mods.

"You don't want a rigid car," he explained. "We made our Corvette [one of his earlier Pro Mods before some modern Chevy Cobalt bodies] a soft, flexible car. That car is still running, now in the ADRL, and must have 1,000 runs on it."

Janis won four IHRA nationals in 2007, placing second in the points championship. Since 2001, he has not been lower than fifth in the standings at year's end. For 2008, Janis qualified at all his events in the tough Pro Mod ranks, but did not win any races. He made it past the first round on all but three races, was a second-round loser in another four, and got to the semis three times. He finished fifth in points for the year.

The difficulty of maintaining a competitive edge has increased dramatically over the past several years, according to Janis, as other teams enter the popular, crowd-pleasing division.

"Today, the class is much more competitive," Janis said. "Everyone has caught up. It has also turned into a money class."

Next to fuel cars, the Pro Modified class is very popular with the fans as the short, front-engined cars offer some of the wildest rides down the quarter-mile. Although the Pro Mods are a mainstay of the IHRA program, the NHRA has approached these cars with caution, and they are not regular players in the world's largest drag racing sanction. Nevertheless, there have been special Pro Mod events held in conjunction with some NHRA national events, where the sponsoring entity invites top cars into the show.

And for 2008, racing parts supplier JEGS sponsored the Pro Mod invitational series run at selected NHRA events, but Janis decided not to take part in the series, concentrating on the IHRA events.

"I couldn't do both [JEGS and the IHRA series] in 2008," Janis explained. "I have a pretty hectic season. These 10 or 11 races per year are plenty."

Janis rides with major funding from automotive OEM (Original Equipment Manufacturer) supplier Eaton Corporation, and Aeroquip Performance Products. His 1967 Firebird-bodied Pro Mod was built by Dan Page Race Cars and is powered by a 526-cubic-inch Jan-Cen Hemi powerplant, which produces about 2,700 horsepower.

And with all that power, Janis is content to stay in the Pro Mod ranks and has no aspirations to climb into a fuel car.

"As you get older, you're more relaxed," he said. "The little things don't bother you. I'm content to be where I am. I never had the urge [to get into a fuel car]. I've always wanted a doorslammer."

Janis racing in 2008 with the wheels up on his Eaton sponsored 1968 Firebird.

The Johnsons

There are several family teams in professional drag racing, but none have had the success or staying power of Warren and Kurt Johnson. This father and son duo has been the heart and soul of the NHRA's Pro Stock division.

Warren Johnson

Born in 1943 and hailing from Minnesota, the elder Johnson ran the strips of that state, winning his first race in 1963 at Minnesota Dragway with a 1957 Chevy, and started building engines for other racers. He took a Camaro to the U.S. Nationals at Indy in 1971, qualified 28th in the 32-car Pro Stock field and was taken out in the first round.

Warren Johnson watches the competition at the NHRA Winternationals. Nicknamed "The Professor" for his work with cylinder heads, Johnson was invincible in Pro Stock for many years.

He participated fulltime at NHRA Pro-Stock racing in 1976 and finished second overall in points. He stayed in the top 10 for the next two years, and then went over to the IHRA, winning back-to-back Pro Stock titles in 1979 and 1980.

Back on the NHRA tour for 1982, he won his first race in that sanction at Englishtown. He also won at Fremont and Irvine in 1982.

Johnson and his family moved to Georgia at this time to race more often in the warmer climate. From 1982 through 1990, he won at least once during each NHRA season, and always finished in the top five in points.

In the early 1980s, Oldsmobile started a serious racing program in Pro Stock. Impressed with his reputation for building winning Pro Stock engines, the automaker had Johnson head up the effort. With the new 500-cubic-inch engine size limit in the NHRA, Johnson and Oldsmobile became invincible, winning the championship in 1992, 1993, 1995, 1998 and 1999. His association with General Motors was cemented, and continues to this day.

With GM's involvement, Warren Johnson has been able to maintain an edge in innovation and technology for the class. He continues to prepare the cylinder heads and intake manifolds for the team's cars. He has been given the name "Professor" and with just cause: In 1997 he became Pro Stock's first driver to exceed 200 mph with a 200.13-mph pass at Richmond. He was also the first to exceed 180 mph (in 1982) and 190 mph (in 1986). Johnson's career mark of 96 NHRA event wins is the most ever in Pro Stock racing, and 11 more than Pro Stock luminary Bob Glidden.

Johnson won his sixth title in 2001 with six event wins, but has not dominated the class since that time. Driving his GM Performance Parts Pontiac GXP in 2008, Johnson failed to qualify at two events, and his best showings were a pair of semifinal rounds at Chicago and Memphis. He placed 11th in the 2008 NHRA Pro Stock points, his second finish outside of the top 10 since 2001.

But his legacy today is just as strong as it was 15 years ago. Johnson's mechanical prowess and innovation have made the Pro Stock class what it is today, and his contribution to the sport has no peers.

Kurt Johnson

Although Kurt has not won six NHRA championships, he has been a dominant force in the class. Born in 1963, Kurt Johnson started his racing career by sweeping his father's shop floor and loading cars into the hauler. He learned the world of Pro Stock drag racing with the best of teachers and classrooms, and by 1990 was helping to build engines—and in 1992 he crew-chiefed for his father and enjoyed the success of a class title.

After attending Roy Hill's racing school, Kurt got into his own Pro Stock car, debuting at Pomona in 1993. He had learned well, taking three national NHRA wins that season (Seattle, Reading, Dallas) along with four runner-ups to finish his rookie season second to father Warren. All four of his runner-up races that year were against his father.

And while his father has set speed records in Pro Stock, Kurt too set a milestone for the class, becoming the first to run a sub-seven-second run with a 6.988-second clocking in May 1994 at Englishtown.

The younger Johnson finished second overall three more times since his debut season, and finished a disappointing sixth in 2007.

For 2008, Johnson won three NHRA events, St. Louis, Chicago, and Brainerd. He was also runner-up three times, including the season-ending Pomona race, where he fouled out in the final to winner Greg Anderson. Johnson placed third in the Pro Stock points for the season.

"I felt we had a car capable of winning the championship," Johnson said in a post-race interview at Pomona, "but as close as the competition is in this category, you have to run well at every race, with everything falling into the right place, as well as keeping the bad luck at bay.

I think we have a really good team right now, and we're looking forward to coming back next year to attack the competition."

A perennial contender, Kurt has built a reputation of his own in Pro Stock as a knowledgeable, tough racer. Nothing could bolster his status more than a class championship to go along with his handful of runner-up finishes.

Dad might even let him win this time.

Continuing with the Johnson winning ways, son Kurt, seen here at the Pontiac Pro Stock Showdown in 2008, has always been a threat in the NHRA Pro Stock wars.

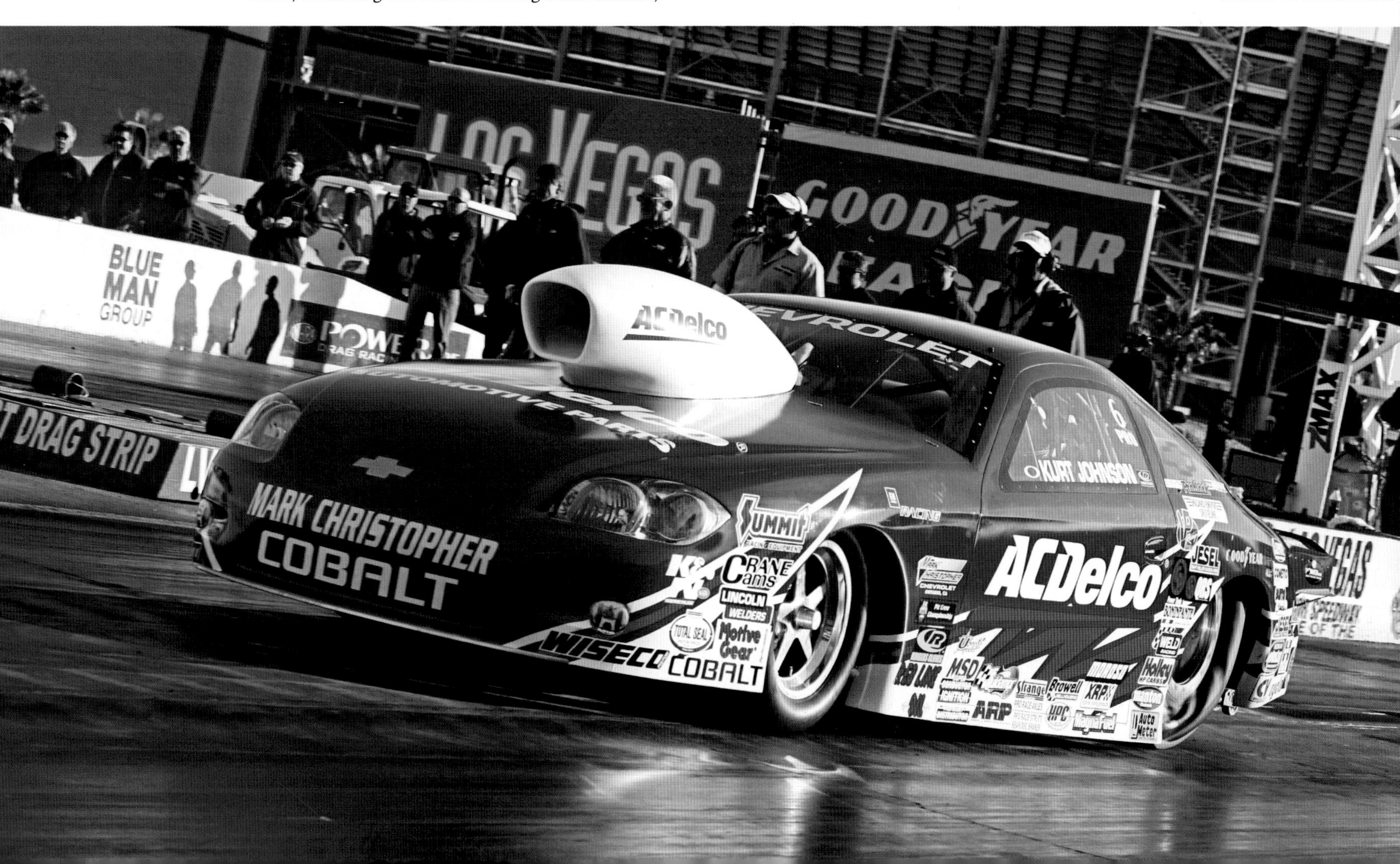

Doug Kalitta

Doug Kalitta is one of very few contestants in professional drag racing who has raced in another type of motor sport.

Doug Kalitta strapped in and ready to go at the NHRA Torco Racing Fuels Nationals in 2007. Notice the black duct tape blinders on the visor of his racing helmet.

Before he climbed into a dragster in the late 1990s, the Mount Clemens, Michigan, man spent his weekends racing in USAC (United States Auto Club) Midget and Sprint Car racing. He was good at it. So good, that he won the USAC National Sprint Car title in 1994.

But as a nephew of legendary drag racer Connie Kalitta, drag racing seemed a natural, and since 1998 he has been a major player in Top Fuel racing.

"I'm often asked if I miss Sprint Car racing," Kalitta said in an interview. "As long as I'm racing toward the front with the opportunity to win an event, and maybe the series championship, I don't care what kind of race car I'm driving. Sprint Car racing is really fun, and sometimes I do miss it, but nothing compares to the acceleration of a Top Fuel dragster."

Kalitta has come close to winning the coveted Top Fuel title in the NHRA. Since his debut, he has never placed below 10th in the standings. He finished second in 2003, 2004 and 2006, the last two years behind Tony Schumacher. He captured five national rounds in both 2005 and 2006. He lost the 2006 title by a mere 14 points to Schumacher.

Born in 1964, Kalitta spent most of the 1980s working with Uncle Connie's Top Fuel team. He went dirt racing in 1990, and continued with it until 1997, when he was asked to take over the driving duties of the Kalitta dragster when Connie wanted to leave driving.

He got his first taste of success in 1998, with a victory at Sonoma. He also won the same race in 1999, and in 2000 won at Gainesville, Englishtown and, in what was becoming a habit, Sonoma, again. He took another three wins in 2001 and 2002. In 2003 and 2004, Kalitta won four events in total, finishing both years in second place with the same 42–19 win-loss record. In 2003, he qualified a class leading nine times as number one.

In 2007, Kalitta and his Mac Tools dragster were part of a four-car assault on the fuel ranks from Kalitta Motorsports. His teammates Hillary Will and Dave Grubnic also drove dragsters, while cousin Scott Kalitta raced a Funny Car after a successful career in Top Fuel.

Kalitta lost crew chief Rahn Tobler at the start of the 2007 season, and the team had its problems adjusting to this loss. Although making power was not an issue, getting the 7,500-plus horsepower through the clutch and to the racing surface kept the team guessing with set-ups. Grubnic's crew chief Jon Oberhofer helped in the effort, as did former Top Fuel champ Dick LaHaie, brought out of retirement to get the car back on track.

Kalitta's 2007 was a year of frustration. His highest qualifying position was second (at the second Las Vegas event) but that was a rarity. He qualified only eight times in the top 10, and didn't make the field in two events. All was not black though. He won the final round against Melanie Troxel in Richmond, and was runner-up to Rod Fuller at the next race in Las Vegas. With his first-round loss in the season-ending

Kalitta getting off to a hot start during qualifying at the SummitRacing.com Nationals at Las Vegas Motor Speedway in 2008; he would be eliminated in the semifinals.

Pomona event, he finished 10th for the season.

But Kalitta was confident 2008 would be a better year.

"We're ready to go racing," he said just before the opening round of 2008 at Pomona. "Our Mac Tools team has worked so hard during the off-season to get our 'Big Red' car ready to go in 2008. I can't say enough about how hard all the guys have worked to get our car not only ready, but to win."

Unfortunately for the Mac Tools team, Kalitta's 2008 season was closer to 2007 than it was to his five-win 2006 season. He was hampered by a DNQ and a string of first-round losses. He did race a few semifinals over the course of the year, but his only major highlight was finishing second to Tony Schumacher at Indianapolis.

"It's tough to get to the finals in Indy and not be able to bring home the trophy, but it was still a great weekend for the Mac Tools team," said the Ann Arbor, Michigan, racer. "Indy is the biggest race in the world and we made the finals, so it's still a good day."

The remainder of Kalitta's 2008 season was disappointing after Indy. While he did qualify for the remaining six races, he was a first-round loser in five of those events.

The entire Kalitta team went through a lot in 2008 with the racing death of Scott Kalitta at Englishtown. For Doug Kalitta, as long as there is racing, there is fun to be had. Hopefully for Doug, and the entire Kalitta family, the fun will return to racing in 2009.

The Pedregons

Tony Pedregon

Tony Pedregon won the 2007 NHRA Funny Car championship. The honor was his second Funny Car title, but his first as a car owner.

Tony Pedregon with a Wally Trophy in 2006, the year before he won his second NHRA Funny Car championship in 2007.

"It's very gratifying to win this with my own team. I did it as a driver in 2003, but this win, in front of my family, friends and sponsors is great," Pedregon said in an interview after the final event in his native state of California.

Although Pedregon was number one in points in the previous three national events, Robert Hight had a chance of catching him going into Pomona. Hight, driving one of the John Force Racing Team cars, was less than 100 points behind Pedregon going into the event. Hight went all the way through his side of the ladder, eliminating Phil Burkart in the final to win the event. Pedregon was eliminated in the first round. Fortunately for Pedregon, Hight failed to set the national ET (elapsed time) record at the event, missing an extra 20 bonus points that would have allowed him to become the 2007 champ.

After winning the title, Pedregon was quick to thank his team. "We had our ups and downs, but we kept pressing and we were very consistent. Dickie Venables, my crew chief, and my entire team worked so hard to get us this championship."

Born in 1965, the younger Pedregon grew up and followed in his father Frank's footsteps, the senior Pedregon being a dominant fuel racer in his day. Tony started his NHRA career in a Top Fueler in 1992. After a dismal 1994, during which he did not qualify for any of the four events he entered, he ran 12 events behind the wheel of a Larry Minor-owned Funny Car, and has been racing in that class since. In 1996, driving for John Force Racing, he made seven final-round appearances, five of them against Force. He also took his first NHRA event win that year, beating Force at Atlanta.

For the next several years, Pedregon played bridesmaid to Force in the season championships. Force was the champ each year from 1993 to 2002. During that time, Pedregon was never out of the top 10 in points, and posted second-place finishes in 1996, 1997, 1999 and 2002.

But in 2003, Pedregon won eight nationals and amassed a 47–15 win-loss rating to win his first national championship, the first non-Force title since 1992.

In 2004, Pedregon left the Force team to start his own Funny Car effort. The team didn't win any races that year, placing eighth in the standings. The next two years the team slowly gained momentum taking five wins over the two seasons. The team was up and down in 2007, but always in contention. Tony took hold of the points lead with three races left in the season and stayed there to win his second championship.

He started his title defense strong with four wins in 2008 at Gainesville, Chicago, Norwalk and Brainerd, but wound up fifth in the Funny Car points as he struggled down the stretch. While Tony didn't win the 2008 title, the championship stayed in the family with his brother Cruz taking the class victory. "I didn't win [the championship], but I feel like I did," he said after the Pomona race. We're a close family. I'm happy for him."

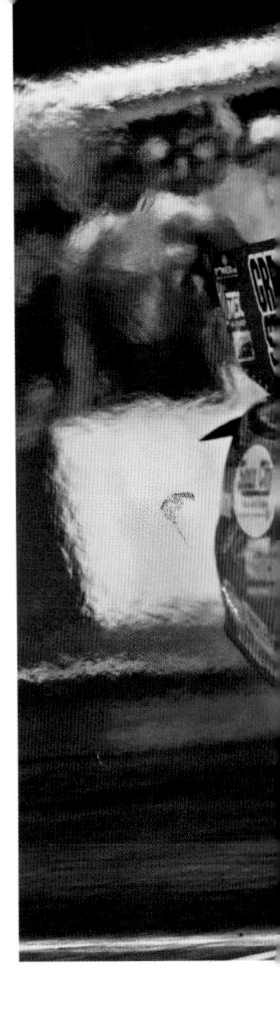

Brother Cruz Pedregon picked up where younger Tony left off in 2007, winning the Funny Car title for 2008. He credits consistency to his winning efforts.

Cruz Pedregon

During John Force's reign as Funny Car champ in the 1990s, Cruz Pedregon was the only other driver to win this title in the decade, taking the championship in 1992.

It would take another 16 years for him to get back into the winner's circle.

The 1992 title was the first NHRA championship for the elder Pedregon brother, a former kart racer and ESPN broadcaster. In the late 1980s Cruz, who was born in 1963, started in NHRA competition with an Alcohol dragster, and then went to an Alcohol Funny Car in 1990. After a single year (1991) driving a Top Fuel car, he got into a fuel Funny Car, won six events—and the championship.

He competed in the class throughout the 1990s, staying in the top 10, and won 16 national events from 1993 to 2000. He only raced eight times in 2000, and did not compete at all in 2001. The next year he was back racing, but with limited success. Over the next five years, he posted only one victory: Las Vegas in 2006.

There were few highlights for the 2007 season, as Cruz did not qualify for seven of the 23 national events, finishing the season in 12th place.

2008 saw a more consistent Cruz, qualifying more often, and more consistently going into later rounds. When he placed runner-up at Charlotte, Cruz found himself in first place. Two races later he was dropped to sixth place, as Robert Hight and Tim Wilkerson duked it out for the top spot. But with three races left in the season and no run-away winner, Cruz stormed ahead, taking all three events and beating Wilkerson by less than 100 points for the title.

"I'm worn out," he said after his Pomona win. "There was so much leading up to this race and so much happened today, I feel like I don't have any emotion left in me. I can tell you this, I have the best crew chief in the business with Rahn Tobler and he's only been tuning Funny Cars for a little over a year. I have the best teammate in the world with my brother Tony, and I have a hard-working crew that always gives me a great race car.

"What a way to end the year," he continued. This is the best day of my professional career, without a doubt."

Tony Schumacher

Winning races in the highly competitive Top Fuel division is difficult. Winning a national championship is a great accomplishment. To win six championship titles is taking success to a new level. In a field that has tremendous depth in its contestants, Tony Schumacher has assembled the new standard.

At the end of the 2008 season, not only had he claimed his sixth championship, and fifth in a row, but he had, since 1996, competed in 268 races, winning 56 events—a Top Fuel victory record. He was runner-up in 32 of those contests, qualified number one 56 times, and since 1999, has failed only once to make the starting line up. His win-loss ratio is 455–204.

The Sarge with one of his many trophies. This one is from his Indy win in 2006, his fifth Nationals victory at the time.

Obviously, Schumacher is a very talented driver.

Born in Illinois on Christmas Day in 1969, the son of former Funny Car driver Don Schumacher, Tony's racing pedigree is as strong as anyone's in the sport. A part of his success has been obtained through the total professionalism of the Don Schumacher Racing Team, which has set the benchmark for producing the near-perfect environment in drag racing. It is through solid business acumen, a strong desire to win and the best in equipment and personnel that has produced this winning effort.

Don Schumacher was one of the toughest Funny Car drivers in the early 1970s. Not only did he travel heavily on the match race circuit, competing with his familiar "Stardust" named Barracuda Funny Car, he was a strong competitor in regular competition, winning the 1973 AHRA Funny Car championship as well as numerous NHRA and IHRA titles in the class.

After witnessing the solid racing career of son Tony, which began in the NHRA's Sportsman classes in the early 1990s and moved through the classes from the exhibition circuit to Alcohol racing to Top Fuel, the elder Schumacher once again wanted to go racing. In 1998 with his son driving, Don Schumacher Racing was formed.

The partnership has been one of the strongest and most successful in drag racing. It certainly has prospered through the understanding that a successful venture in auto racing must have a successful business plan.

And the Schumacher team has benefited from this philosophy right from the start. When the team acquired the financial backing of Exide Batteries halfway through the 1998 season, the team put the money to good use, winning the 1999 NHRA Top Fuel championship.

In 2000, the team got together with the United States Army, which has been an outstanding public relations partnership for both parties ever since.

Schumacher's dragster is emblazoned with his title sponsor, and Tony himself has been nicknamed "The Sarge," complete with that rank's chevrons on his racing helmet.

Tony Schumacher won four NHRA nationals in that first year of Army involvement, including the U.S. Nationals. He was also in the final round and runner-up in six of the 21 events of 2000, finishing second in points. For 2001, he placed eighth in the standings with no wins and only one runner-up round. He placed third in the standings in 2002 and 2003 with six event wins in total for the two years.

In 2004, the team was a juggernaut, winning its second championship. Schumacher set the then single-season record for Top Fuel victories with 10. His round win-loss record for that year was 60–13.

Not only did Schumacher win nine events in 2005, once again taking the points championship, but

The U.S. Army Top Fuel team did everything right in 2008, winning 15 of 24 NHRA events and another championship.

Top: Another round won by the U.S. Army team, this time at the CarQuest Auto Parts Winternationals at Pomona in 2008.

Facing page: The Sarge: the stripes for the rank of Sergeant adorn Schumacher's helmet, driving gloves, fire suit and car.

he set the single-season record for five consecutive victories (Reading, Chicago, Dallas, Las Vegas, Pomona). He also set single-season records for round wins (20), and number-one qualifying positions (11).

In 2006, Schumacher once again rewrote the record books on his way to yet another championship by picking up 13 number-one qualifying positions. He won five races, including the all-important final event at Pomona, where entering the race he was second to Doug Kalitta in points. Schumacher needed to make every round count, and he beat Melanie Troxel in the final round at Pomona to overtake Kalitta and win the championship by 14 points. Pomona put Schumacher in the company of greatness, as the victory placed him beside Top Fuel legend Joe Amato as the only two Top Fuel drivers to win three straight NHRA titles. He also equaled drag racing icon Don Garlits's career NHRA Top Fuel win count of 35, good for fifth on the all-time list.

For 2007, Schumacher played catch-up. It was an exasperating year for the team. Schumacher was either eliminated in the first round, or won the event. In the final 12 races of 2007, he was taken out in the first round in six events.

Schumacher and the team, who sat in fourth place overall, knew they had to be perfect and also have a little luck when they raced at the final event at Pomona. When points leader Rod Fuller was eliminated in the first round by Bob Vandergriff, some of the pressure was off, but Schumacher, who

had eliminated Alan Bradshaw, Morgan Lucas and Brandon Bernstein to get to the final, was matched up against Vandergriff.

Vandergriff ran a respectable 4.681-second pass in the last race of the day, but Schumacher gave himself and his team another championship, running a 4.486-second time to take out Vandergriff.

Schumacher and the U.S. Army car got right down to business in 2008, capturing the opening round at Pomona, backing that up with wins at Gainesville, Bristol, Chicago and Englishtown. He earned his 52nd career NHRA Top Fuel win when he defeated Doug Kalitta in the final round at the U.S. Nationals at Indianapolis in September 2008. He won 11 of the first 18 events of the year, including six in a row, breaking his own record for consecutive victories (five) that he set in the 2005 season.

In his post-race comments in Denver, Schumacher was elated with the performance of his team in 2008. "I guess we've managed to put together the best start ever for this team," he said. "It's pretty amazing, to be honest. We just want to ride this wave as long as we can.

"Winning races never gets old, I can guarantee you that."

After Indy Schumacher won another five events to capture 15 of the season's 24 races, good enough to tie him with Pro-Stock star Greg Anderson for the most events won in a single season. His incredible year also made him the third drag racer to ever be honored with the Driver of the Year Award, presented to the top driver in American auto racing.

But the glory for Schumacher may be harder to obtain come the start of the 2009 season. Ace crew chief and tuner Alan Johnson has left the Schumacher camp to start his own team with a Top Fueler and a Funny Car. But Schumacher realizes the implications of this, and said at the end of the season the team will be prepared.

"We'll have an adjustment period," he said. "But, we'll be working real hard to maintain the standard of excellence that our soldiers have to come to expect from us. The goals will be clear—to win races and to contend for another title. There's no other way to approach it."

Melanie Troxel

Melanie Troxel made a big career move at the start of the 2008 NHRA season. After driving dragsters for 10 years, she made the move to a fuel Funny Car. Although she had raced Top Fuelers for several years, she knew she had work ahead of her in piloting an 7,500-horsepower front-engined beast.

"It's been a big learning curve," she said about the driving differences in the cars. "It's a totally different style. I've had to break all my habits from driving in Top Fuel."

But at the Thunder Valley Nationals in Bristol in May 2008, Troxel was inducted into a very elite club. She won the Funny Car class at that event, becoming only the second woman (behind Ashley Force) to win in the fuel Funny Car ranks.

Troxel also started a club of her own with her Bristol victory—as the first woman in NHRA history to win a major race in both Top Fuel and Funny Car. The Indiana resident won her first two Top Fuel races in 2006 and added two more in 2007.

Troxel has said she always wanted to race a Flopper, and when the chance came during the 2007–08 off-season, she became part of Mike Ashley's Gotham City Racing Team.

Now, with some time in the car, Troxel says she is more comfortable, but still has a ways to go.

"It takes quite a few passes to get used to the differences in the cars," she said. "I struggled a lot at first. My biggest problem was to overcome the steering. There is more finesse with the Top Fuel car. With the Funny Car you must react quicker. It is a car that requires more. For a couple of races I was not having any fun."

Troxel's father Mike was one of the best Top Alcohol Dragster drivers, and her mother Barbara was an aircraft mechanic. As a young child, Melanie spent a lot of time at the track. Born in 1972, she first raced at 16, and began her professional career driving a Top Alcohol Dragster like her father, in 1997, winning a pair of NHRA nationals two years later.

Troxel made the switch from Fuelers to Floppers in 2008, and joined the elite club with a win at Bristol.

Troxel got into a Top Fueler in 2000 as part of Don Schumacher's team, and raced a limited schedule for the next several years. During her time in a Top Fueler, Troxel put down some impressive numbers. In 2005, she became the fastest woman in NHRA history, with a 4.458-second pass at Dallas, and in Atlanta a year later recorded a 331.04-mph speed. She was beginning to get noticed, and began to receive accolades for her performances.

Her first 2006 win was at the season opener in Pomona, and she recorded three runner-ups before her next win of that year at Las Vegas. For the first half of the 23-race season, Troxel remained in top spot, and even with a pair of runner-ups late in the season, she had to settle for fourth in the standings.

After Troxel took her second NHRA win in 2006 and became the first Top Fuel driver to record five consecutive final-round appearances, she was nominated for two ESPN awards: one in the Female Athlete of the Year category, and the other for Driver of the Year. Also in 2006, she was named Sportswoman of the Year by the Women's Sports Foundation.

Even with four Top Fuel wins to her credit, Troxel did not win a round with her Flopper until her Bristol victory. After competing at Englishtown late in June 2008, Troxel was candid about her progress.

"The good news is that we've got a good consistent car, and we are really miles ahead of where we were just five races ago," she is quoted as saying. "We're basically where we need to be and the team is peaking at a great time."

Troxel's semifinal round loss at Indianapolis was the highlight of the latter half of 2008. She suffered three first-round losses in a row after Indy, and was a second-round loser in the final three races, placing 11th in the Funny Car points for the season.

"We lost a good, close race in the second round," she said after Pomona. "We're not disappointed with that by any means. We would have liked to have won the race, but it is still a pretty strong finish."

Her husband, Tommy Johnson Jr., has been one of the top Funny Car drivers in recent history, and it is certain the pair spend a lot of time discussing their racing careers. He, too, is a former Top Fuel driver, but has been racing a Funny Car for close to 10 years. They have not competed against each other, but when and if this occurs, it will be a milestone in drag racing, as no husband and wife have yet raced each other in Funny Car competition.

Competing in a 24-race series across the country from February to November leaves little time for visiting family and other social duties, but Troxel says she wouldn't have it any other way.

"I want this lifestyle," she admits. "I love every aspect of it. I love traveling and not having a nine-to-five job."

Race fans are eagerly awaiting Troxel's Funny Car return, as sponsorship problems stalled her ride in early 2009. With a résumé like Troxel's it shouldn't be long before she is back behind the wheel.

Troxel, shown here at Las Vegas early in 2008, was the first woman in NHRA history to win in both Top Fuel and Funny Car.

Tim Wilkerson

At the halfway point of the 2008 NHRA season, Tim Wilkerson found himself leading the Funny Car points race. Since he started racing in 1996, the Illinois native had never found himself in this position.

Obviously, Wilkerson is a talented driver. Born in 1960, the father of three started his career in 1979 racing a 1963 Plymouth. Ten years later he was driving an Alcohol Funny Car, and by 1995 had a pair of NHRA Division 3 titles to his credit. He entered the world of nitro in 1996 with a fuel Funny Car.

That first year in the nitro car he ran a sub five-second pass (4.945-seconds) and topped 300 mph, the first Funny Car rookie to do so.

He went to the final round at the 1997 U.S. Nationals, losing to Whit Bazemore. In 1998 he finished the season in seventh spot, and ended 2003 and 2004 the same. He also won the 2003 U.S. Nationals at Indy.

What is incredible about the Wilkerson effort is that it has none of the multimillion-dollar sponsorship backing of his competitors.

"Our Levi, Ray & Shoup Impala is running well," explained Wilkerson in an understatement just before the running of the 2008 Norwalk event. "We're not hurting parts. I seem to be making pretty good tuning decisions, my driving has helped us a few times and the crew is doing a super job right now.

"So, I'd say everything is working in our favor right now."

Although he qualified number one in the first two races of 2008, he was taken out in first-round action. He went to the semis at Gainesville, made a couple of rounds in Houston, and then beat Ashley Force in the final at Las Vegas for his first Funny Car win since 2004.

The team was determined to regroup for 2008 after finishing 2007 in 15th spot with several semifinal-round races. The team also did not qualify for seven of the season's 23 races, including three in a row: Denver, Seattle and Sonoma during mid-season.

Wilkerson, who has had financial help from the information technological firm of Levi, Ray & Shoup, Inc. since 2000, says there is no special magic to win at this level.

"We're going to focus on doing what we did there towards the end of last year [2007], which was going down the track more than anything," Wilkerson said at the start of the 2008 season. "Hopefully it will work out for us. That's my prognosis for the year."

Wilkerson also said he knew there was strong opposition ahead.

"The problem we face is that there used to be 14 good cars in the country and we were sixth or seventh. And now we have 20 good cars and we're 12th or 13th. That's not acceptable, and we're going to try and fix that. We know it's not going to be a picnic but we're going to go out there and sure try and shake it up."

With four wins in the first 18 races in 2008, Wilkerson certainly shook things up in the Funny Car ranks.

Wilkerson, tucked in and ready to race, finished the 2008 season in second place, 93 points shy of winning his first ever NHRA Funny Car championship.

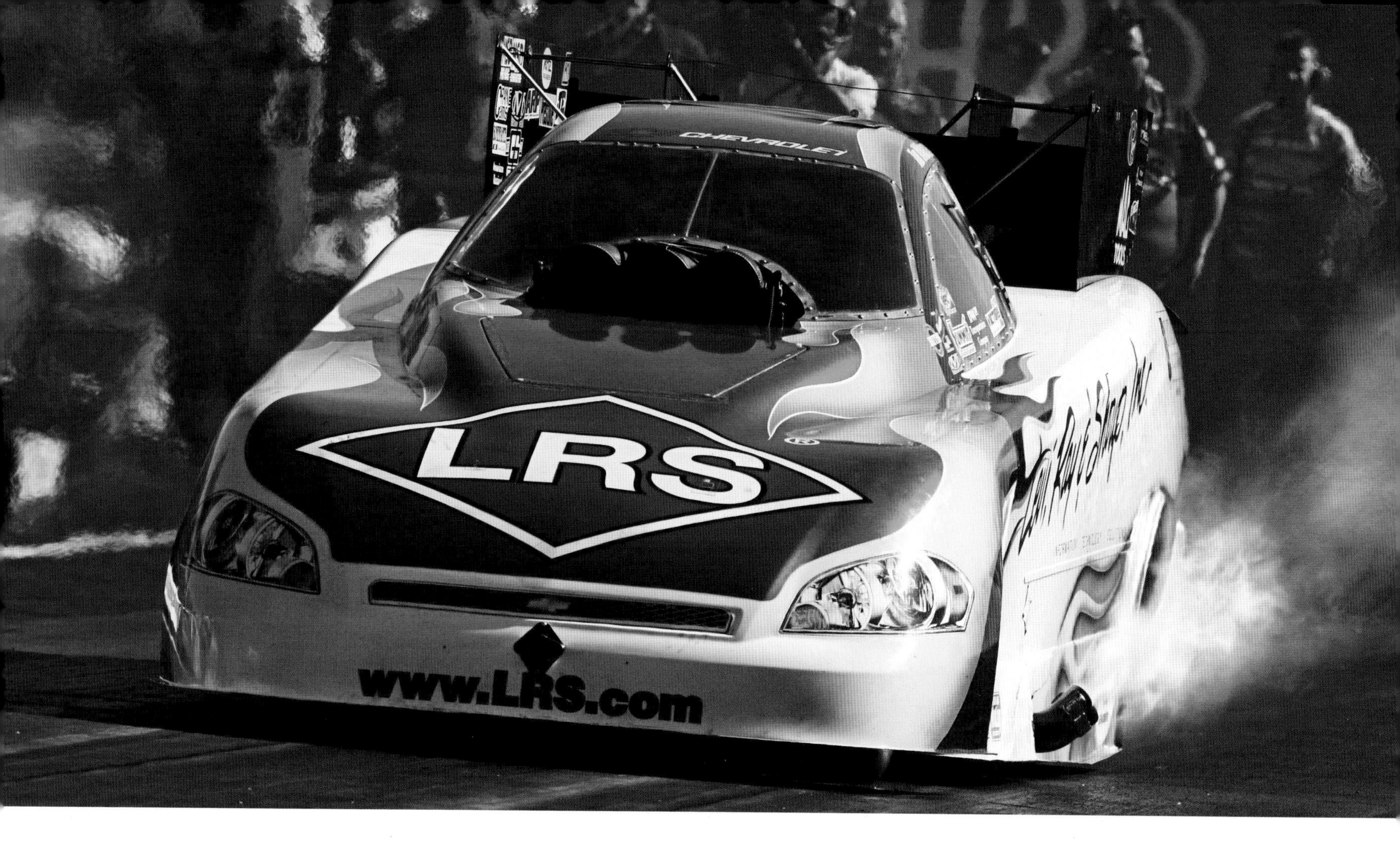

Wilkerson at the SummitRacing.com Nationals at Las Vegas Motor Speedway in 2008. Wilkerson won the event over Ashley Force by 0.029 seconds.

After a first-round loss at Charlotte, Wilkerson found himself once again in the driver's seat, winning the Dallas and Memphis rounds. Unfortunately, in the final two races of the season, when the team needed the points most, Wilkerson had two opening round exits at Las Vegas and Pomona. He ended up placing second in the standings, less than 100 points behind Cruz Pedregon. But although he did not capture the title, he was pleased with his season.

"It's been a terrific year for our team and my group of young guys," Wilkerson is quoted as saying after Pomona. "They just do a superb job. You can see it in how my car is prepared and I can't be more proud of them."

Tim Wilkerson has proved a private entry can be competitive, in part, thanks to his three-step goal:

"First, we need to qualify for the race," he explained. "We don't have to top qualify, even though that's been great in helping our points. The second step in achieving our goal is to go rounds. We have to go past the first round in order to keep going. And if we do that, maybe we can fulfill our third step, which is to win the race. We need to keep on track and keep up our momentum, and hopefully we can be a thorn in everybody's side again."

Wilkerson has said he and his team have been treated differently as a top-running effort.

"It's interesting being first," he stated. "They take you a little differently than when you were just a guy that went down the race track from time to time."

"But we need to keep our eye focused on the ball and hopefully we can keep our momentum up and keep those others behind us."

Hillary Will

Born in California in 1980, Hilary Will is now living her dream. And when she won the NHRA Summernationals at Topeka in June 2008, thoughts of her former career as a financial analyst were probably the furthest from her mind.

Hillary will race, that's for sure, as she posted the world's fastest time recorded by a woman at 334.65 mph at the CarQuest Auto Parts Winternationals in 2008.

At the time, Will also acknowledged her induction into an elite group: "This is definitely the year of the woman racer," she proclaimed. "It's an honor for me to be mentioned with all of the great women who have won and raced."

With the Topeka victory, Will became only the eighth woman to win an event in Top Fuel, and one of only three women (along with Funny Car drivers Ashley Force and Melanie Troxel) to win a major event halfway through the 2008 season.

"Words cannot describe how I feel right now," Will said after her win. "I have dreamed of this day for so long and it's finally here. We knew we had everything to win, and today everything went our way."

Will's Topeka victory was her first final round since Memphis in 2006, and the 55th NHRA event of her career.

Driving the Ken Black–Connie Kalitta KB Dragster, she has come a long way from Bracket racing in her native state in the late 1990s. Although she jumped into the faster cars of the Super Gas and Super Comp classes at the turn of the century, she also earned her Bachelor's degree in economics.

In 2004 Will, after forming a race team with her father Steve, drove a Top Alcohol Dragster and did well in the class, winning several NHRA divisional events.

Her efforts did not go unnoticed. She was given the opportunity to drive a Top Fueler by the newly formed drag racing team of Ken Black, a Las Vegas businessman, and Connie Kalitta, a veteran racer who owns and operates the Michigan-based Kalitta Motorsports, which is where the Black-Kalitta team made its home. After attending an earlier IHRA race to support team member Doug Kalitta in 2006, Will made her debut in a Top Fueler at the IHRA's Skull Shine Nationals in Norwalk.

She won the event, becoming the third woman, behind Shirley Muldowney and Rhonda Hartman-Smith, to win an IHRA Top Fuel title.

That same year, Will and her KB dragster went to all 23 NHRA national events, and qualified at each. She experienced many first-round losses in 2006, but went to the final at Memphis, losing to teammate Doug Kalitta. She finished 10th in points.

After a 14–23 win-loss record in her rookie year of 2006, Will had problems in 2007. She qualified for all but one of the 23 nationals, but rarely in the top 10. She was eliminated 14 times in the first round, seven times in the second round, and lost to Larry Dixon at Englishtown, her only semifinal-round appearance of the year.

The season-ending round of racing at Pomona had been typical of the team's efforts in 2007. Will ran a 4.524-second pass, losing to Dixon, who posted a 4.522-second clocking.

She placed 13th in the 2007 points standings.

"This was another heart-breaking loss for our team, and I hate to end the season this way," Will was quoted after the Pomona race. "But we did run a few good runs and we're looking forward to next season.

"I think what we did this weekend will actually give us confidence going into 2008," she continued.

"I wish that things started next week, because I'm ready to go."

After some personnel changes and regrouping back in Michigan, Will and her team qualified fifth at the 2008 opener at Pomona, got into the second round, and was fifth in points. At Gainesville, she went three rounds before losing to Brandon Bernstein. There was a first-round loss to Kalitta at Houston, a pair of semifinals at Las Vegas and Atlanta, and two semifinals at St. Louis and Bristol, losing both to the dominant Tony Schumacher. After Norwalk, she was seventh in points.

But the Topeka race was all hers, as she eliminated Doug Herbert, Morgan Lucas, Cory McClenathan and Larry Dixon to take the victory.

"It's a huge relief for me and my KB Racing LLC team to finally get a win. We've been through a lot together, and we've been through some really tough times, but going through the down times makes us all appreciate this accomplishment even more."

Will qualified and performed well for the rest of the 2008 season. She managed a runner-up against Tony Schumacher at Richmond, which put her second in points, but a second-round loss at Las Vegas and a first-round loss at Pomona drove her back to fourth in the standings as she finished the year behind Tony Schumacher, Dixon, and McClenathan. She said after Pomona she was somewhat disappointed but still positive with her showing for the season.

"We really wanted to be No. 2 but we're still ecstatic about our year," Will said. "We finished 13th last year so fourth is fantastic."

Will's 2008 success has turned bittersweet, as she was left off the KB Racing roster for 2009 due to team budgetary constraints. With Will's talent, it is not a question if she will race Top Fuel again, but when.

Will, racing in 2008, placed fourth in the NHRA standings that year, her best finish to date.

Del Worsham

In 1991, Del Worsham became the youngest driver to win an NHRA Funny Car title. He was 21 years old, and in April of that year bested racing icon Kenny Bernstein to win the class at the Southern Nationals in Atlanta. Three months later he was pitted against veteran Tom McEwen in the final at Englishtown, and once again the win light came on in his lane. He placed sixth in points that year.

Worsham had never raced any car before 1990, let alone a nitro-burning Funny Car. But Worsham has never held back, as demonstrated not only by his debut in the sport, but in getting established the previous year.

"There I was, just a 20-year old kid at the Dallas Motorplex, and I needed two pro drivers to watch me run and sign off on my license," Worsham is quoted as saying. "Why mess around?" he continued. "I marched right over and asked Kenny Bernstein and Don Prudhomme. It was actually a huge thrill for me to have those two legends at my licensing test."

Although he had never driven before 1990, Worsham was far from a novice in the sport. His

father, Chuck Worsham, bought an Alcohol Funny Car in 1978, and the young Worsham helped on the team and learned the world of drag racing.

The team toured on the NHRA circuit with the elder Worsham wrenching and Art Hendey driving. It was during this time that young Del, who was born in 1970, became more than just a gopher assistant with the team. By the time he was 13 he could work on a car with authority.

By 1989, Del felt he could have a career in drag racing, and when Hendey moved on, Chuck thought his son would be a promising replacement to drive the Funny Car. The power for the car was also changed, as the team decided to try its hand with nitro.

Worsham received his competition license for a Funny Car after some unusual in-seat training, as he explained:

"Most people start out drag racing slower cars, and work their way up to faster and faster speeds. You can't do that with a Nitro Funny Car, they kind of have only two speeds: flat out or stopped. So instead of working my way up speedwise, we worked my way up distancewise. I learned how to do a burnout, how to stage, then went 60 feet, then 100 feet, then 300 feet, and so on. By my first full pass, I was getting pretty comfortable."

There was some actual racing with the car late in 1990 to gain more knowledge and experience, and then Worsham went at it right away for 1991—getting named the NHRA Rookie of the Year.

As funding allowed, the Worshams competed as much as possible. The team ran as an independent venture for the first few years, a difficult undertaking in the most expensive class in the sport. In 1995, the team ran the full season, qualifying at 10 events and finishing 16th in the points. In 1996 Worsham was in five semifinal rounds, finished seventh in points, and drove the only private (non-sponsored) car in the top 10.

In 1997, the team acquired the primary backing of Checker Schuck's Kragen Auto Parts.

"We all had a goal to win a championship and knew we'd need a company that could believe in a group like ours," Worsham has stated. "With Checker Schuck's Kragen, we found that company. Nothing has really been quite the same since."

With financial help, Worsham has captured 22 NHRA event wins since 1997. His best season to date was in 2004, when he won at Phoenix, Gainesville, Columbus, Dallas and Chicago. Previous to that he won four events in both 2001 and 2002.

In 2006, he didn't win any races, placing 11th in the standings. In the previous eight years, he had always been in the top 10—for half of those years he finished in the top five.

Worsham didn't win any races in 2007 either, but he was a consistent runner qualifying for all 23 races, including a number-one qualifying spot at Reading.

For 2008, Worsham had mixed success. He failed to make the field in the opening two rounds, but rebounded with a win in the final at Houston for his first win in three seasons. Worsham placed 13th in Funny Car points for 2008, out of contention for the Countdown but still able to play spoiler.

Unfortunately, Worsham did not qualify for three of the final four events, including the season-closing Pomona event. It was a bittersweet time for Worsham, who knew his 12-year sponsorship with CSK Auto was coming to an end.

Worsham signed on for 2009 as the Funny Car driver for the newly formed Alan Johnson Al-Anabi Racing Team, which is comprised of one Funny Car and one Top Fueler.

"I've been running our family team for so many years, and have been a big part of team operations in addition to driving the car," Worsham is quoted as saying after he found out he would be a part of the new team in September 2008. "I am definitely looking forward to letting Alan handle running the team so I can just be the driver and hopefully have some great success focusing on that one aspect. I'm looking forward to it."

Above: A familiar sight, Worsham in his CSK Auto-sponsored garb. Worsham was chosen to drive for the new Alan Johnson–Al-Anabi racing effort in 2009.

Facing page: The veteran Worsham in his new ride, the Al-Anabi Racing Toyota Funny Car.

Women in Drag Racing

Racing is a sport that offers an even playing field for both men and women. It is the only sport, with the exception of horse racing, where women can compete in the same arena with the same equipment and the same rules.

Most forms of auto racing have been very slow to accept women competitors, if at all. There never has been a serious attempt by a woman in NASCAR or Formula One racing, and only recently has a woman succeeded in Indy Car racing.

Drag racing, however, has had females in competition since the 1960s, and several have done very well since Barbara Hamilton became the first woman to receive an NHRA license in 1964, and Shirley Shahan became the first woman to win a major NHRA title, capturing the Stock Eliminator class at the 1966 Winternationals in California.

While there were other women in the early years, Shirley Muldowney fought and won on and off the track to establish herself as a major player in the sport. She overcame bias and sanctioning obstacles to reach the top of her profession, winning the coveted NHRA Top Fuel championship three times. Muldowney is profiled in the "Legends" section of this book.

In 1979, Amy Faulk won the NHRA Super Stock class. NHRA Pro Stock Motorcycle racer Angelle Sampey has also won three championships

Ashley Force, seen here at the 2008 Las Vegas Nationals, posted the fastest Funny Car time for 2008 on the new 1,000-foot track length with a 310.05 mph run.

ASHLEY FORCE 10
MAC TOOLS
BRAND SOURCE
Old Spice
Castrol
GTX
JOHN FORCE
Ford
RACING
Whirlpool
MITSUBISHI ELECTRIC
MSD
WELD
GOODYEAR
NAPA
AUTO PARTS
belts hose
ROCKST
ENERGY DRIN
STANDARD ABRASIVES
LVMS.COM

Melanie Troxel in April of 2006 with her Top Fueler and her second Wally Trophy, taking the class at the SummitRacing.com Nationals in Las Vegas. In 2008 Troxel captured her latest Wally, this time in a Funny Car. She is the only woman to win both an NHRA Funny Car title and Top Fuel title.

(2000–2002). Others include: Erica Enders, Super Gas champion at Houston in 2004, Shelly Anderson, who won four Top Fuel NHRA races between 1993 and 1996 and continues to race in Pro Modified, and Judy Lilly, who captured four Pro Stock titles including the 1972 Winternationals and the 1973 Gatornationals. In all, there have been over 40 NHRA national events won by women, from Top Fuel on down through Stock. The only class in NHRA racing where a woman has not won is Pro Stock.

Early in 2008, Ashley Force became the first woman to win an NHRA Nitro Funny Car national event, and in May 2008, Melanie Troxel, a former Top Fuel Dragster driver, won the Funny Car title at Bristol. Troxel is the first woman to win major NHRA events in the sport's top two classes.

So when it's pointed out that Indy Racing League open-wheel racing star Danica Patrick became the first woman to win a "major" racing event by capturing the Indy Japan 300 in 2008, the drag racing world can smugly sit back with the knowledge that their sport has had women as winners for decades.

The women who have raced in the past and those who compete in drag racing today have a love for the sport and the same competitive drive as the men. The fire in their hearts and the focus in their eyes are just as strong. They want to be remembered as racers, and racers only.

One of the sport's greatest ambassadors, Bunny Burkett has been a crowd favorite for decades in her series of pink Alcohol Floppers.

Bunny Burkett

Bunny Burkett celebrated a large part of her 31st year of racing in a hospital bed. Driving her pink Alcohol Funny Car in a match race at Beaver Springs Dragway in September 1995, Burkett's car was hit by her competitor as he got loose and came over into her lane.

After getting clipped, her car went sailing at top speed off the track and into the Pennsylvania woods. She was in a coma for three weeks with most of her body smashed.

For the next year, Bunny began her slow but steady recovery. She gathered up her inner strength and, as her body healed, her determination to get back into a race car grew. In 1997 she made a return to the drag strip.

A native of West Virginia, the former Carol Hartman married Mo Burkett who took her to drag races in Virginia. By the time she was 19, she was driving a Mustang at the track. A job at the Baltimore Playboy Club supplied enough money to get a new race car to feed her habit. The Playboy hostess position also supplied the name "Bunny" as she has been known ever since.

The Super Stock Mustang gave way to a Pro Stock Pinto in 1973, and this car was later traded for her first Funny Car, and the team went professional. Since 1975 she has competed in the Funny Car ranks.

Traveling up and down the eastern U.S. seaboard, she drove in regular IHRA and NHRA competitions, while at the same time becoming one of the most popular match racers ever to sit behind the wheel of a race car.

It was in 1986 that Burkett had perhaps her best year racing. She earned the IHRA Alcohol Funny Car title that year, and NHRA Division 2 honors.

When she returned to racing in 1997 after her accident, Burkett and her "Hemi Honey" only ran in a few events, but whenever Bunny entered a match race or competed in selected IHRA events, the applause was almost as loud as her car when she lit up the slicks in one of her famous burnouts.

In 2006 Burkett suffered another personal tragedy—breast cancer and a double mastectomy. Then early in 2008, she took a fall and underwent a hip replacement. But she has always bounced back and returned to what she loved most, racing.

"I was back racing my car one month and four days after," she said about her return to the track in 2007 after the cancer surgery. "I don't plan on retiring. I love what I'm doing and enjoy it thoroughly." She has also stated that if given the opportunity to drive a Top Fueler or Fuel Funny Car she would do so in a heartbeat.

Burkett has a legion of fans, and has understood right from the start of her career that interaction with the fans is important. While the crew of her "Bunny and the Boys" Funny Car thrashed in the

A quiet personality who has let her racing do the talking, Amy Faulk has persevered for many years in Super Stock, most notably winning the 1979 NHRA Super Stock title. Here she poses with the trophy for "Best Appearing Car" at Gateway International Raceway in Madison, Illinois, in June 2003.

pits, Bunny was always center stage talking with the fans, signing autographs and posing for photos. She has been one of the sport's greatest ambassadors.

With such determination, the question is not if Burkett will get back behind the wheel of her beloved Funny Car, but when.

Amy Faulk

Amy Faulk had to bite her tongue many times and prove herself on the track. Faulk, who lives in Tennessee, got started in the early 1970s, and had to have a special woman's permit to race. This entailed the signatures of two track owners and three licensed drivers.

She started driving a Super Stocker, and with the help of husband Kenny, gradually perfected her skills, and won the NHRA's Super Stock title in 1979. In 1983, the team moved into a Comp Eliminator car, and she won a national event in Atlanta. Then they campaigned an alcohol dragster for the next year, but another car collided with Faulk during a race and with limited funding, the dragster was abandoned. She went back to driving door cars, and continues today to race in Stock Eliminator.

Faulk has said that she approached the male bias of those early years differently than the outspoken Muldowney, preferring to prove her point quietly. There was a time when she thought of going racing professionally, but she and her husband declined, deciding to race on their own terms, which included racing for the sheer joy of it.

Aside from winning the 1979 NHRA Super Stock crown, Faulk was the first woman to win NHRA titles in multiple classes (Super Stock, Comp and Top Alcohol Dragster).

Kathy Fisher

Not only does this Ohio native race in an IHRA Sportsman class as much as possible, she is a host in several television productions featuring all kinds of motorsport, including drag racing. And as an alumnus of the noted Frank Hawley Drag Racing School, where she acquired her SC/QR (Super Comp/Quick Rod) license, Fisher now works in the sales and promotion side of the Florida-based school.

"Drag racing is definitely my life," she notes. "Just about everything I do is involved with the sport."

Fisher comes from a family of drag racers. Father Denny Hague, an early 1970s IHRA record holder with his 1966 Chevelle, got her hooked, and she drove a bit when she was 15. "I've been around racing since I was born. I think it was injected into me in my mother's womb. I started racing again in 1999 with my new Camaro and have continued since."

Now, with the help of husband Kevin, whom she married at Marion County International Raceway in 2000, the television personality competes in a dragster in the IHRA's Quick Rod class, running down the track at about 170 mph in just under nine seconds. While her main focus has been competing in the IHRA's Division 3, where she has been a consistent

Not only does Kathy Fisher race a dragster, this Ohio native hosts several television programs featuring drag racing, and performs public relations duties for several teams.

top-10 finisher, she estimates she will compete in about 20 events per year, traveling within a day's drive of home.

Fisher will go to some NHRA divisional events, but sticks mostly to the IHRA tracks, such as the Milan and Martin tracks in Michigan, Epping in New Hampshire, and the Ontario tracks of Grand Bend and Toronto Motorsports Park in Cayuga.

Fisher has no desire in going to a faster class of car, claiming the rear-engined dragster suits her just fine. "I'm not interested in going faster. I like to breathe the fresh air sitting out in front in my dragster."

Kathy Fisher has done well in her class, and is proud of her achievements in the big-block Chevy-powered car. She was the IHRA Quick Rod champion in the IHRA Canadian Nationals at Toronto Motorsports Park in 2007, and has been in the sanction's Summit All-Stars program as part of the top eight in her division.

As one of the few women racing at this level, Fisher noted there is little, if any, animosity from her male competitors. "There's a handful of old-school guys with an attitude," she said, "but that's few and far between. I noticed that things really changed in the mid to late 1980s."

She has also noted that as the cars and racing get more expensive, there is less prejudice. "Back in 1999 there were a few jerks, but that was local, not at the national or divisional levels. I realize that women in racing are still a minority, and I'm part of it, but that's okay. I'm too busy at the track to take much notice."

Not only does Fisher race at the track, she makes sure everything is in order before she and her husband, who also races, head off to the strip. She estimates her car is worth about $45,000, and to campaign the car takes another $35,000 to $45,000 per season, and all this falls on her shoulders. Once at the track, she is not only busy prepping the car for racing, she is walking around the pits wearing her interviewer hat.

"This is a business for us, and I run it as a business," she says. "I have to account for all the spending," and adds that 16-hour days are not uncommon as she performs her various duties.

Drag racing may not consume 100 percent of Kathy Fisher's life, but it comes close.

Aggi Hendriks

Racing a jet-powered dragster was a big lifestyle change for Aggi Hendriks, who ran a plant store in New Westminster, British Columbia, before strapping herself into one of these exhibition cars and touring from drag strip to drag strip.

The first woman to acquire a jet car license, Hendriks began a drag racing career of over 20 years traveling across North America in 1981.

Teamed with Wayne Knuth, Hendriks piloted a 1,275-pound dragster that developed 4,500 horsepower from its General Electric J85 jet engine. The 27-foot-long car, known as the "Odyssey," propelled her down the track at speeds approaching 300 mph in just over five seconds.

With no formal sanctioning in drag racing, jet cars were, and still are, used for exhibition runs, something different for the fans from the regular racing. The cars were usually teamed in pairs for match racing, either with another jet car, sometimes a Top Fueler or Funny Car, in a best two-out-of-three series of runs.

Driving the Odyssey, Hendriks earned a reputation as a solid performer, winning notice from both the NHRA and IHRA, whose approval she needed to be able to run on sanctioned tracks. The majority of her time was spent match racing against some of the best in regular drag racing, including Don Garlits and Shirley Muldowney.

"Shirley and I raced a lot," said Hendriks. "We developed a big fan base, and a lot of my time at the track was spent signing autographs." Hendriks said she treated her racing career differently than a regular competitor. She realized she was in the entertainment side of drag racing, and made the most of it. "It was all about creating a business. Exhibition racing is a business. You do the best you can to entertain the fans."

Some of the highlights in her career include racing Muldowney in special "Mother's Day" events, which would receive a great deal of promotion. "The Mother's Day events were popular. I remember Shirley and I would match race in places like Louisiana, and then after, we'd all go out and have dinner together. It was a time when racers were all like a big family."

The first woman to get her jet car license, Aggi Hendricks had her own odyssey traveling across North America match racing her jet car.

Hendriks continued to race on a part-time basis, driving the "Queen of Diamonds" jet car for Al Hanna until 2002. But after 21 years she decided to park the car for good, stepping away from any involvement in the sport. She now lives in Oregon.

"Racing was a large detour in my life. My life was on hold for many years. It was a lot of hard work but it was a life I enjoyed."

Paula Murphy

Paula Murphy raced just about everything with four wheels. She drove Art Arfon's jet car at Bonneville, as well as a Studebaker Avanti, and set over 300 speed records on the salt flats. She drove one of the Granatelli-built Novi Indy Champ cars, and took a ride in Richard Petty's Grand National Plymouth stock car.

A native of Cleveland, Ohio, with a degree in Physical Education from the University of Cincinnati, her early racing was behind the wheel of an MG, a Lotus and a Maserati in sports car racing. In the early 1960s she began her involvement with the engine oil additive company STP, attempting to break records in cross-country racing and land speed attempts.

Murphy started drag racing in 1965 with a Dick Landy-prepared Oldsmobile. In 1973 she obtained her Funny Car license with the UDRA, then the NHRA, one of the first women to do so. Her stint of match racing throughout North America and Europe with a Mustang and a Barracuda was suspended solely for being a woman, even though she had driven cars in excess of 200 mph.

After racing on the NHRA, IHRA and AHRA circuits for about a year, her license (along with

Paula Murphy raced just about everything on four wheels at one time, including Indy Champ cars, NASCAR stockers, and early Funny Cars, as shown here. She was known as "Miss STP."

Californian Shirley Shahan had been racing on the west coast for several years, but in 1966 the "Drag-on-Lady" and her Plymouth won the NHRA Winternationals in Super Stock, the first woman to win any major title in drag racing.

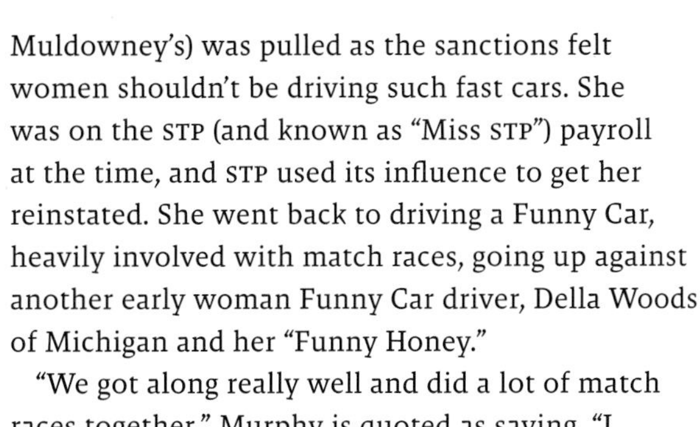

Muldowney's) was pulled as the sanctions felt women shouldn't be driving such fast cars. She was on the STP (and known as "Miss STP") payroll at the time, and STP used its influence to get her reinstated. She went back to driving a Funny Car, heavily involved with match races, going up against another early woman Funny Car driver, Della Woods of Michigan and her "Funny Honey."

"We got along really well and did a lot of match races together," Murphy is quoted as saying. "I thought if we could get a couple more girls to do it, we could have a lot of fun."

And although Murphy did not race much with Muldowney, she could be credited for helping Muldowney get into a fuel car at the time. "I suggested that Shirley get a Funny Car and then we could have match races. Then she got Connie Kalitta's car and went from there."

Shirley Shahan

While most drag racing enthusiasts are familiar with the expoits and racing career of Shirley Muldowney, there was another Shirley who literally opened the door for women competitors in major drag racing competition.

More than 10 years before Muldowney rocketed to drag racing fame in the late 1970s, California native Shirley Shahan was driving, and winning, in the NHRA's Super Stock ranks.

With husband H.L. Shahan wrenching and Shirley Shahan driving, this couple was probably drag racing's first successful husband-and-wife team.

Playing baseball as a teenager gave Shahan lots of strength for shifting gears, a mainstay of the Super Stock racing of the 1960s. The Shahans started in the late 1950s at tracks near their California home in a series of Chevrolets, and in 1965 they bought their first Chrysler. She began winning NHRA Division 7 points meets up and down the west coast with the Hemi. Late in 1965, the "Drag-On-Lady" took a couple of runner-ups, and then entered the history books as the first woman to win an NHRA National event, the Stock class at the 1966 Winternationals.

Then, highly in demand, the pair toured the country on the match-race circuit for the next two years, plus some selected national events, racing full time between 1966 and 1968. During this time she also drove a Chrysler in the Mobil Economy Runs: driving a car to obtain the best fuel mileage possible in sanctioned competition against other manufacturers, a far cry from her usual automotive activity of drag racing. In 1969, enticed by a paying opportunity with American Motors to race in the Los Angeles area, Shahan drove race-prepared AMC cars, including an AMX and Hornet Pro Stocker—in which she won her class at the 1970 Winternationals.

While she said she enjoyed the driving, by the early 1970s she was not as competitive. AMC turned down her request for a new car as it wanted to devote its time to the SCCA's Trans-Am road race series, and when her husband took a job in Denver in 1972, Shirley called it a day after 19 years. She returned to her full-time job at the Southern California Gas Company, which enabled her to spend more time with her children.

Linda Vaughn

Linda Vaughn has been to many NASCAR and IndyCar events over the years, but her role in drag racing has been the strongest.

Vaughn, the First Lady of Motorsport, has gone by many titles over her almost 50 year career. She is a true ambassador of drag racing, and when she was younger, always took center stage at major events. Sitting on the deck of a convertible during pre-race ceremonies, Vaughn would receive tremendous ovations from the fans as she smiled and waved to each crowd. Her presence was always welcome and anticipated.

Known best as "Miss Hurst Golden Shifter" and being a familiar sight at many racing venues throughout the past three decades, the Georgia native got her start in 1961 by winning the title of "Miss Atlanta International Raceway." She has continued to promote motorsports throughout her career, and with her trademark blonde hair and statuesque figure, has graced many a winner's circle, press conference and photo session.

In 1962, the former dental technician was "Miss Pontiac" in the Daytona 500, and the next year was hired by Pure Oil to be "Miss Pure Firebird" which she was known as for the next three years.

In 1966, *HOT ROD Magazine* coordinated a search across the U.S. to find a person suitable to promote George Hurst's line of transmission shifters. Vaughn was selected from about 200 applicants and became the company's premier promotional personality. And not only was Vaughn at racetracks across North America, she was a prominent sight at many automotive-related shows and aftermarket events. A legend was born.

Along with her duties as Miss Hurst, Vaughn was the spokesperson for the Detroit-based Gratiot Auto Supply in the 1970s, and then 10 years later teamed up with the Mr. Gasket Performance Group as vice president of public relations.

Aside from her work at Hurst, she has appeared in Hollywood films such as *The Gumball Rally* (1976) and *Stroker Ace* (1983). Around this time she also acquired her SCCA (Sports Car Club of America) competition license. Vaughn was also named SEMA Person of the Year in 1979, and she was inducted into the SEMA Hall of Fame in 1985.

Calling herself "just a little ol' country gal from Georgia," Linda Vaughn has been an important part of the motorsports world for decades, and has been one of the most photographed and recognized of personalities in the sport. She has posed for and signed literally thousands of photographs over the years for racing fans from just about every type of automotive competition, and continues her involvement to this day.

Now living in Southern California, and still in the public relations field, Vaughn continues to participate and promote racing-related events, and is present at such events as the Daytona 500, the Indianapolis 500, and the U.S. Nationals.

A Hurst-prepared Oldsmobile convertible, a huge replica of a Hurst shifter and Linda Vaughn in a classic setting familiar to most racing fans of the period. As "Miss Hurst Golden Shifter," Vaughn traveled across North America to racing events for many years in her unofficial role as the "First Lady of Motorsport." She is shown here at Tulsa during an AHRA meet in 1969.

HURST
INTERNATIONAL RACEWAY
TULSA OKLAHOMA
AHRA
DEPENDABLE
CHAMPION
HURST
GOODYEAR

Legends

Drag racing, like any other sport, has had competitors who have stood out from the rest, those that have excelled beyond the expectations of their peers.

But, as drag racing is a relatively young sport, many of these legendary figures are not only still alive—several are still heavily involved in the sport.

Men such as Connie Kalitta and Don Prudhomme are former top racers who have built their own teams and remain very much an integral part of team operations. Other legends include some of drag racing's pioneers, who not only helped develop the cars, but also drove them to victory; men such as Don Garlits, Bill Jenkins and George Montgomery changed the way drag racing worked while setting records.

One of the sport's true pioneers is Shirley Muldowney, who not only won multiple national championships at the top level of the sport, but had to overcome bias and intolerance on her road to success.

Most of the drivers on these pages are recognized for their winning careers, and their contributions to the sport. But drag racing, like many sports is more than competition—it's entertainment. Tommy Ivo and "Jungle Jim" Liberman understood this better than anyone else, and routinely offered fans a great show of speed, noise, and fury.

Many people have helped make drag racing what it is today, but the personalities presented here are some of the most renowned and important, providing benchmarks for others in the sport.

Don Garlits getting set to stage at Indy in 1970. This racer from Florida helped define the sport of drag racing, and is considered number one in the minds of many.

NHRA
NATIONAL
MPIONSHIP DRAG RACE
CRAGAR
DON GARLITS'
WYNNSCHARGER
TF

Joe Amato drove Alcohol Funny Cars before his step up to Top Fuelers in 1982. While not a household name yet, this Pennsylvania native was ready to expand his racing career.

Joe Amato

When it came to his early racing years, Joe Amato was not a flashy personality. He was not outspoken or controversial. His early racing career was low-key, and he was not well-known outside of the eastern U.S. But this native of Pennsylvania captured five Top Fuel championships with a structured, logical approach to racing, and became a dominant driver in the 1980s and early 1990s.

Born in 1944, Amato raced karts at a young age, and through his father's speed shop, he developed a taste for drag racing. Starting with a 1953 Ford, he moved through the ranks of faster and faster cars with Alcohol Funny Cars and dragsters. In 1982 he went Top Fuel racing.

Amato had two positives when he took up Top Fuel. After his father became ill, he looked over the speed shop business and became the boss in 1960 at age 16; eventually he and his partners developed the auto-parts-related business into Keystone Automotive Warehouses, one of the largest chains of aftermarket car parts. Not only did he have the finances to race at the top, he also had the backing, understanding and companionship of his wife, Jere, whose support was always positive.

Amato was successful right from the start, winning his first event in the NHRA's North Star Nationals at Brainerd in 1983. These were followed up with wins the same year in the Molson Grand Nationals and the Summernationals. He was runner-up at the U.S. Nationals and the Winston World Finals. He also placed second in the 1983 IHRA Top Fuel standings behind Richard Tharp. In 1984, Amato won three more NHRA national events, and his first of five NHRA Top Fuel championships.

Along with earning his first championship in 1984, Amato became the first driver to surpass the 260-mph barrier in a Fueler, with a 260.11 pass at Gainesville. Amato showed up at Gainesville with a new aerodynamic device on the back of his Fueler that was a major step in the development of the class. Sitting on struts behind the rear wheels seven feet in the air was a wide wing, designed by Eldon Rasmussen, an Indy car builder of note. This wing exerted a strong downforce on the rear of the car, increasing its speed significantly. So much so, that by the end of the year all the top teams were sporting the wing.

He was always a contender during the next two years, placing second in 1985 and fourth in 1986.

His hopes were dashed for the 1987 title when his transmission broke in the final round in the final event of the season, taking second in the points to Dick LaHaie. He won his second title in 1988, and then went on a three-season tear, winning the championship in 1990, 1991 and 1992. He was the first Top Fuel driver to win three consecutive titles.

His 1990 win was the closest and most exciting. He was deadlocked with Gary Ormsby going into the last race of the season at Pomona. Ormsby was the top qualifier for the race, so it became a must win situation for Amato if he wanted to take home the series title. In the final round, Ormsby and Amato staged their dragsters and waited for the tree. Ormsby red-lighted his start, automatically disqualifying himself. Amato had been determined not to beat himself in the all-important final, and to run a smooth race. Despite Ormsby's disqualification, the Team Valvoline, Swindahl-chassised Fueler gave Amato a ride not only to his third NHRA title, but also to a new track record, with a 4.935-second, 282.39-mph pass.

"What a finish," Amato said at the time. "I don't think a Hollywood writer could have come up with a better script. To have a championship come down to the final round of the final race on the final day of the season, and to win it with a new track record is mind-boggling."

Amato doing his burnout at the Quebec track of Sanair during the NHRA Molson Grandnationals in the early 1990s. Amato, the first to break the 260-mph mark, also won five NHRA crowns, including three in a row from 1990–92.

Amato's star did not burn as brightly in the following years. He won 18 more events from 1996 through 2000, and produced drag racing's first 4.5-second pass, in 1996, but health issues were having an affect on him.

Although he never experienced any severe crashes during his career, years of high-power quarter-mile runs took their toll on Amato's back, and although eye surgery repaired a loose retina, he was still suffering from vision problems, and decided to retire from driving in 2000.

He did go out in style, as befitting a true champ. In front of the hometown crowd at the September 2000 Keystone Nationals at the Pennsylvania track of Maple Grove, Amato won his final race. He continued to own and run a Top Fuel team for several years, and completely retired from the sport in 2005.

Garlits never stopped thinking about how to build a better race car. You can almost sense from this candid moment at Dragway 42 in West Salem, Ohio, in 1980, that he is contemplating ways of going even faster.

Don Garlits

Every sport has athletes who, through skill, determination and adversity, rise above their competitors to become icons of that sport. In football, Joe Montana, Jim Brown and Peyton Manning come to mind. Baseball greats include Babe Ruth, Hank Aaron and Mickey Mantle. In golf, it's Jack Nicklaus, and hockey has Wayne Gretzky.

Auto racing has its share of those who have become legends. Michael Schumacher. Mario Andretti. Dale Earnhardt.

And in drag racing, Don Garlits has earned the title as the sport's top player. Over his career, Garlits was an innovator, a fierce competitor and, through determination, established his reputation. In a field of greats, this legend has been the sport's ultimate drag racer.

Some of Garlits's racing benchmarks include the first dragster to run over 170 mph (1957), over 180 mph (1958), 200 mph (1964), 250 mph (1975) and 200 mph in the eighth-mile (1979). His 37-year career includes three NHRA World Championships, four IHRA World Championships, and ten AHRA World Championships. He also won the prestigious NHRA U.S. Nationals eight times. But perhaps his biggest contribution to the sport was the successful design and implementation of the rear-engined Top Fuel dragster (built and raced after Garlits suffered a serious accident in 1970).

Born in Florida in 1932, Garlits's early life was one of poverty, in a family trying to make ends meet. During his high school years, he did well, but was restless. He bought a 1940 Ford when he was 17, and became a typical hot-rodder of the era, street racing with a Mercury-powered 1940 Ford convertible before racing on the crude airport drag strips of Zephyrhills and Lake Wales.

Eventually, his semi-planned career as an accountant was dropped in favor of opening a speed shop in Tampa in 1956.

A 1936 Ford coupe was built as a race car in 1954, but that was soon replaced with a full-race Flathead Ford-powered 1927 Model T roadster in a dragster fashion with minimal body work and a long wheelbase. By 1955 he was winning at the local tracks, and knew he had to continue.

Garlits read up on the early dragster designs by pioneers such as Mickey Thompson and Calvin Rice, and emulated the popular "slingshot" design that had taken hold on the West Coast. He turned his remodeled T roadster into a winner. Garlits built a new car in 1956, inspired by the winning dragster of 1955 NHRA champ Calvin Rice. Garlits used a 1930 Chevy frame and added his favorite power, a Ford Flathead. This car was initially painted purple, but that was soon changed to black. And an engine change was not far behind.

Garlits purchased his first Chrysler Hemi engine (354 cubic inches) shortly after, but that purchase was for his tow vehicle, not the race car. He soon had to find another engine for the tow vehicle as the Hemi was put to work in the dragster.

With his new Hemi engine on his set of 1930 Chevy frame rails, along with a Crower camshaft and six Stromberg 97 carburetors, Garlits was capable of 135-mph speeds, and in 1956 he won Top Eliminator in the Florida State Championship.

He experimented with nitromethane as a fuel and attended the American Automobile Timing Association event in Illinois in 1957. Although he didn't win, he was inspired to make his car more powerful.

While Garlits was running nitro, he couldn't get more than 133 mph from his car, far from the 160-plus speeds of the leaders of the day such as Emery Cook. After Cook told the young racer to increase the amount of nitro he was blending with gasoline, suggesting he go from a percentage of 25/75 nitro-gas blend to a 95/5 nitro-gas blend, Garlits was on his way, with a car capable of well over 150 mph.

For the 1957–58 season he started using the new M&H seven-inch-wide slicks, and with an updated and larger 392-cubic-inch Chrysler Hemi, was able to run under ten seconds at 170 mph. It was also at this time that Garlits hit the road, trailering across the country to race with fellow competitors such as Setto Postoian and Pete Ogden.

With the NHRA ban on fuel-powered cars starting in 1957, Garlits raced not only in AHRA competition, but toured the match-race circuit. He did race some NHRA events with a gas-powered Swamp Rat (the name given to his line of custom dragsters that he developed), winning the first Winternationals held in Florida in 1960 and was runner-up at the U.S. Nationals in 1962, his first of 43 career final rounds in the NHRA.

Since the late 1950s, each new version of the series of Swamp Rat dragsters that came out of Garlits's Florida shop were an improved adaptation of the previous Swamp Rat. Considered an outsider to the sport by the trendy California racers who set the pace in dragster development in the early years, Garlits started to be noticed after updating and expanding on some of the West Coast innovations, such as using superchargers, experimenting with fuel mixtures and removing the car's gearbox for a direct drive setup. By 1961 the smugness of his competition turned grudgingly into acceptance as Garlits began to earn his place among the racing elite.

Come 1963, Garlits had not only several years' experience with fuel-powered, supercharged cars, but had also gained a reputation as one of the big names in the top class, and was a force to be reckoned with amongst the California teams. He won the 1963 NHRA Winternationals with the help of an innovative wing over the car's engine, which provided more downforce (traction) on the rear wheels, clocking an 8.26 time at 186 mph. In 1964, he won his first of eight U.S. Nationals titles with Swamp Rat VI at 198 mph. By 1969, Garlits had picked up six NHRA titles along with several in AHRA and U.S. Fuel and Gas Championship racing.

He also spent a lot of this time match racing with the likes of Tommy Ivo, Chris Karamesines, Connie Kalitta, and a young upstart named Don Prudhomme. His Tampa speed shop was doing well, and along with his success at racing, provided him the means to continue to race. He established a speed shop in Detroit, and had planned to move there, but instead settled in Seffner, Florida. He also had an early Funny Car operation at this time, with Emery Cook behind the wheel of a Dodge Dart bodied car.

It was in the final round of a 1970 AHRA event at Lions Drag Strip in California that the accident occurred that changed the course of Top Fuel racing forever. During Garlits's launch, the transmission in

Garlits won many NHRA and AHRA titles during his career, including this one at the 1967 NHRA U.S. Nationals. In the next several years Garlits and Wally Parks (right) would engage in an on-again, off-again feud that would eventually lead to bigger purses and increased use of nitro.

his front-engined dragster exploded, splitting the car in half between the engine and Garlits, severely injuring his lower body—Garlits almost lost a foot. While recuperating, Garlits decided he had had enough of getting beat up and injured in a car whose design had the potential for extreme danger every time out. When he went back to Florida, he started working with chassis expert Connie Swingle on a rear-engined dragster. Once the steering characteristics were straightened out on this 215-inch wheelbase 426 Dodge-engined, transmissionless car, the jokes regarding Garlits and the new Swamp Rat soon turned into admiration.

Within two years, the front-engined dragster as a competitive car was extinct. As a result, Garlits not only helped to save lives and prevent injury to drivers in a dangerous car, but he also saved the Top Fuel division, which had reached a technological standstill and was taking a beating in popularity from Funny Cars.

Throughout the 1970s, Garlits racked up the victories. He won 26 events and four titles in the IHRA, six AHRA titles, and 16 NHRA events, including a pair at Indy.

With Kendall Motor Oil sponsorship, Garlits concentrated on AHRA racing. He also did a lot of match racing, including many contests against Shirley Muldowney. The pair went back and forth for several years in the late 1970s and early 1980s as promoters matched the king and queen of drag racing. It was the black dragster of Garlits pitted against the pink Muldowney car in what has been described as the fastest battle of the sexes.

Muldowney, who had captured three NHRA Top Fuel titles, also won her share of these races, much to the chagrin of Garlits. The two racers were not only fierce competitors on the strip, they barely tolerated each other off the track, and Garlits was never happy getting beaten by a woman.

"Big Daddy" Garlits returned to NHRA racing in 1984, and won the U.S. Nationals not only that year but in 1985 and 1986 as well, becoming the event's only three-straight winner. He also put down some big numbers during this time, including the first 270-mph pass at Gainesville in 1986.

In 1986, Garlits experienced his first blowover (a term used to describe the car going backwards over the rear wheelie bar during acceleration). After a second flip-over in 1987, he retired, but came back five years later to go after the magic 300-mph barrier—only to have Kenny Bernstein beat him to it. He then left driving for several years, but returned for the 2001 U.S. Nationals, where he qualified with a borrowed car in front of a partisan crowd with a 4.720-second, 303.37-mph pass, only a few months away from his 70th birthday. He also brought his Swamp Rat 34 out of his museum a year later, tuned it up, and went to the U.S. Nationals, cranking out the best run of his long career with a 4.76-second, 318.54-mph pass.

Garlits returned to his Florida home after that, but he stayed involved in the sport in several ways, and became a television personality providing color commentary for drag racing and other auto-related productions.

The drag racing museum that Garlits had started in 1983 was expanded and enhanced, and to this day provides the most complete exhibition of the history of the sport anywhere. He has been an avid car restorer, and has a large facility next to the museum loaded with cars, trucks, gas station memorabilia, and related material, including a Flathead-powered V8 Ford automobile for each year of the engine's existence, from 1932 to 1953.

Every so often Garlits will bring out one of his old Swamp Rats for parade laps at a major drag racing show, and his presence is constantly in demand at collector car shows and nostalgia drag meets. He has published several books on his career.

His Swamp Rat 30, which he considers his best car, went into the Smithsonian Institute in 1987. This is perhaps the greatest honor that not only Garlits, but drag racing, has achieved.

Bob Glidden

Pro Stock racing in the late 1970s and throughout the latter part of the 1980s was dominated by Bob Glidden. Dominated is a strong word, but Glidden was a strong and winning individual in the division.

From an auspicious start in 1972, this former Ford dealership mechanic was unstoppable in NHRA competition, treating each round as an all-out assault on his opponent. With an unmatched work ethic, solid engine development and superior driving, Glidden achieved most of his success with a succession of Fords, which were considered by many to be lame ducks in the class.

Bob Glidden defined the Pro Stock class in the late 1970s and 1980s with his series of Ford products.

In an era when Ford was not the car of choice, Glidden made the Dearborn products work, and work well—like this Pinto in 1976. Glidden's wife, Etta, was a big part of his success as she was with him constantly; that's Etta at the rear of the Pinto keeping the car steady.

But Glidden made his Fords work, and work well, to the delight of the many Ford fans who were tired of watching their favorites get beat up by the Pontiacs, Oldsmobiles and Chevrolets that usually ruled the class.

But after a runner-up finish to Bill Jenkins in the 1972 NHRA Supernationals, Glidden started winning races in a purchased Gapp and Roush Pinto after selling his Super Stock Mustang. He won the U.S. Nationals in 1973, and took three majors in 1974, along with setting a new class benchmark with an 8.81 record.

Glidden took the Pro Stock championship in 1975 with seven wins. After a bit of a slump in the next two seasons (sixth in 1976 and second in 1977), he was back on top in 1978 with seven event wins and the NHRA Pro Stock championship, driving both the Pinto and a Ford Fairmont, a car much larger than the Plymouth Arrows or Chevy Monzas of his competitors. Perhaps Glidden thought the smaller cars had an edge in competition, for in 1979, he built and raced a Plymouth Arrow. Usually with a totally new car, it takes a while to get it sorted out, but this man from Indiana opened the 1980 season with a victory in the little Mopar. Not only did he win the Winternationals, he picked up six additional contests to capture another NHRA championship.

Back in a Ford for 1981, Glidden played catch-up with Lee Shepherd for the next few seasons, never quite catching the Chevy driver. But things changed in 1984 when Glidden and his Thunderbird started winning again, as the pair took NHRA championships in 1985 and 1986, even though he was receiving less factory backing from Ford in Dearborn than he had in the past.

In 1987, Glidden won eight events, including his 60th major victory. He also qualified for all 14 major NHRA races, a major achievement for any driver. In

1988, he won the final seven races and took home his ninth championship.

The Thunderbird was retired at this time, and he built and drove a Ford Probe with which he won his record-breaking 10th national title in 1989. With his five consecutive championships from 1985 to 1989, Glidden's winning percentage was an incredible 80.4 percent. It is no wonder the competition felt it didn't stand a chance when paired off with him at the starting line.

The winning pace began to diminish after 1989. Glidden won but six major races between 1990 and 1993, although he did post his last NHRA career victory at the 1995 Mopar Parts Nationals at Englishtown: a record setting 85th victory. This milestone stood as the benchmark across all drag racing classes for several years—until 2000 when Funny Car driver John Force won his 86th race.

Even after suffering a heart attack late in 1994, Glidden continued to race after his recovery. He retired from competition in 1997, working with Ford and its NASCAR Cup engine program.

Glidden returned briefly to the driver's seat in 1998, driving a Pro Stock Pontiac at the U.S. Nationals, but did not qualify. His failure to get into this show didn't matter to the legions of fans this racing legend had acquired. Glidden rewrote the record books during his tenure, not so much in speeds and elapsed times, but in wins, which is the most important column.

A large part of his success must be attributed to Etta Glidden, Bob's wife, who in spirit was with him on every pass, and in body was as much a part of any team as her husband and the race car. Etta Glidden was always there, not working on the car, but helping in other ways such as pouring in the fuel and loading up the car after a day's work.

Most times, the Gliddens avoided the limelight and publicity, or at least did not go looking for it. Most times, they would be toiling away in their pit. Bob and Etta Glidden had a keen work ethic, constantly involved with the car between rounds.

"It has just been our lives," Glidden has been quoted as saying. "Day and night, seven days a week. I guess we just sort of dedicated our lives to this. It's a never-ending task, I can assure you of that."

An early career in motion pictures and television gave Tommy Ivo the financial backing and promotional savvy for drag racing, especially at the touring match-race level. Here a young Ivo is shown with Charles Starrett (the Durango Kid) and Gail Davis in the 1950 film *Trail of the Rustlers*.

Tommy Ivo

Tom Ivo has been blessed with two careers in his life. The success of his first career, acting, enabled him to pursue his second career, drag racing.

Known as a showman, Ivo applied the charisma and charm from his acting to his drag racing activities, making him one of the most entertaining racers of the 1960s and '70s, and he was good, too. With the proceeds from his show business career, he provided fans across the country with new, innovative and fast cars, along with a degree of showmanship that was totally new to the sport.

His succession of dragsters, jet cars, and Funny Cars were always the best. Not only were his cars some of the best-looking to travel down a quarter-mile, they were first-rate in terms of mechanical achievements.

"It wasn't that big a change," Ivo said about his leaving movies and television to drag race. "It's all entertainment. And the drag racing had the audience right there in front of me, it wasn't just in front of a camera."

Ivo was born in Colorado in 1936. The family went west not long after, and young Tommy was a regular in the movies by 1944. By the mid-1960s he had appeared in close to 100 pictures, including *I Remember Mama*, *Sunset Boulevard* and *Blackboard Jungle*. He was also in many television shows such as *Leave It To Beaver*, *Lassie* and *Petticoat Junction*.

Already a motorhead in the late 1950s with a series of Buick-powered street rods, Ivo decided to go a step further and build a dragster.

During this time (1957–1963) the NHRA had banned fuel engines at its tracks, and racers who stayed with the NHRA, which was the biggest game around, developed cars with multiple engines in their quest for more speed. Ivo's first twin-engined car was almost too beautiful to drive. But race it he did, and as a result, Ivo was the first to reach speeds of 160,

170 and 180 mph with a gasoline powered car; more importantly, this car became the first gasoline car to break the nine-second barrier.

The fans loved the car, and Ivo and his crew, which at the time included a young Don Prudhomme, toured with the car on a professional basis, probably the first to do so.

"I was the first pro touring team," he said. "With Prudhomme we would strike out from coast to coast. I had no work except when I was doing a movie shoot or television show, and this let me be gone for long periods of time."

It has been said that Ivo wasn't quite as serious as his competition, but Ivo's perspective as a racer was different from the others, thanks to a lifestyle that allowed him to be in front of an audience, and this made him appear more laid-back than other racers.

But when it came time to race, he was serious.

"I would race at least 50 times a year with Garlits," Ivo said, "and every time I came to the line it was for blood."

The majority of Ivo's racing career was in match racing. While his talent and his cars could handily compete in regular racing, he chose the barn-storming aspect from the sport's earlier years, providing a show, the quality of which the fans had never seen.

"I was in the movies for 19 years. That background influenced me. I was aware of why people were at the track. And I put that flair into my racing, and did things as best as possible."

It has also been said that Ivo only *drove* the cars and *signed* autographs, but the reality is that from the start he always had his hands dirty. His technical savvy allowed him to build the multiple-engined cars he became famous for, including his most famous creation, the four-engined Showboat, which was on just about every car magazine cover in the early 1960s.

"Everyone thought I was the rich playboy that only did the driving," he said. "But I was it. I built, drove, tuned, and got the sponsors. And in those days we didn't fly from track to track like they do now. I drove the hauler as much as anyone."

While in television Ivo tried to keep his driving a secret. He finally got caught when he appeared in a photo with his four-engined car dressed as the character Haywood Botts who he portrayed on the show *Margie*.

"I was in the series *Margie* and they saw the four-motor car and they grounded me," Ivo said. "So Prudhomme drove the car for a while. I paid him $25 a race."

By the mid-1960s his acting career was over and he concentrated on racing, going with the trend to Hemi-powered cars running on alcohol and nitromethane. He did spend some time racing at regular sanctioned meets, but his heart was in match racing. Some years he would haul his cars over 70,000 miles to make the dates at up to 75 strips.

He built his first rear-engined dragster in 1972, and that October he ran a 5.97-second pass at Keystone Dragway in Pennsylvania—the first five-second run in the history of the sport. This new record was legitimized with a 6.03 clocking earlier that day.

In the latter half of the 1970s, Ivo campaigned a Funny Car, usually a Dodge Charger or Plymouth Arrow, which he drove to the final round of the 1978 NHRA Winternationals against his former car painter Prudhomme. He then drove a jet car, and in 1981 built a jet Funny Car, but never drove it.

It wasn't long after that Ivo seriously contemplated retiring. He had been at it more than 25 years, and with the way the sport had developed, he felt he was losing control and could no longer do as much anymore. After some exhibition runs in his original four-engined dragster, now with a Buick station wagon body, Ivo retired. A bad back injury in this car after an accident also made up his mind.

Ivo still lives in the house in Burbank he bought when he was 12 years old. The house has grown considerably, due to building and housing race cars, and is 3,000 square feet larger than its original 1,000 square foot size. He added that his present Cadillac sits in the same garage stall where he built his favorite car, Showboat.

"I would rather have done it when I did. We had fun then. Today it's too serious. When I would race with Kalitta or Shirley or Prudhomme, we'd all go out to eat after. Now the drivers don't even talk to each other."

Ivo's showmanship and promotional qualities were not just window dressing. Not only was he a fierce competitor on the track, he provided a lot of entertainment for the fans. With his glass-sided rig, he and his crew toured across North America to some of the smallest tracks, giving local fans a professional thrill.

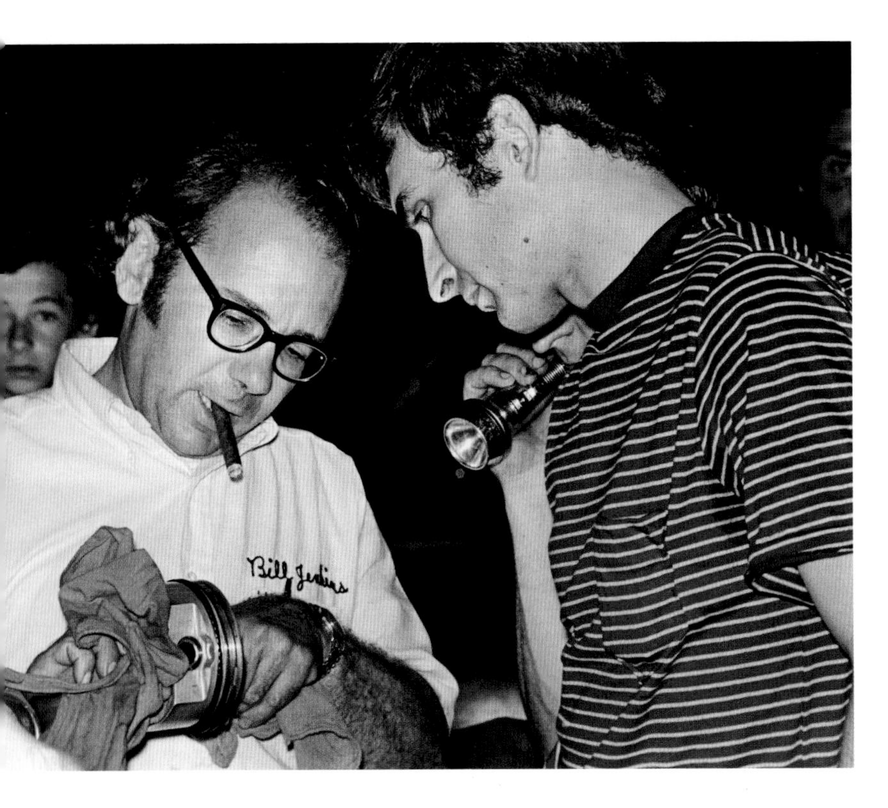

Jenkins checking a piston at night with the aid of a flashlight and his ever-present cigar. This engine guru was building small-block Chevy engines capable of 750 horsepower decades before it became the standard in NASCAR Cup racing.

Bill Jenkins

When you hear of the 750-horsepower engines in today's NASCAR Cup cars, remember Bill Jenkins was building engines with that kind of power 30 years ago. He is considered to be a master of innovation in the Super Stock and Pro Stock classes, and the best at building gasoline-burning carbureted engines. His work with the development of the small-block Chevrolet V8 has no equal.

He is also considered the driving force behind the introduction of the Pro Stock class to sanctioned racing in 1970, which continues to be one of the headliners in drag racing today.

Born in 1930, Jenkins began racing in the 1950s in his home state of Pennsylvania. His demeanor was termed gruff, rude and impatient, and as a result was given the name "Grumpy" in the mid-1960s. Jenkins raced Chevys early in his career, and teamed up with Dave Strickler to win the 1963 NHRA Nationals Little Eliminator class with an A/FX (Factory Experimental) 427-powered Chevy. And then when Chevrolet exited from auto racing due to a corporate-wide General Motors mandate banning competition, he went over to Chrysler, first with Strickler and a 1964 Dodge in A/FX, and then out on his own, driving an S/SA (Super Stock Automatic) 1965 Dodge, winning at the 1965 NHRA Winternationals.

During the heady days of auto manufacturer involvement, the high-performance years of the 1960s, car companies sponsored the best teams of the day in the hopes of selling more cars. Don Nicholson was involved with Ford and Mercury, Sox and Martin had a solid relationship with Chrysler. However, Jenkins and Chrysler could not come to terms, so for 1966 he campaigned a Chevy, without any factory support. As a result, the first in a long line of "Grumpy's Toys" hit the drag strips. This first Toy was a Chevy II with a 327-cubic-inch small-block engine of 350 horsepower. By taking advantage of class weight rules, Jenkins was able to build and compete the car successfully against the heavier 426-cubic-inch Dodge and Plymouth street Hemis of the era, clocking mid-11-second passes.

In 1967, Jenkins really got down to business with a new Camaro using the 375-horsepower 396-cubic-inch big block. With this car he won the 1967 Nationals at Indianapolis, along with the NHRA Winternationals and Gatornationals in 1968.

The late 1960s were transitory times for these high-powered doorslammers. The Stock and Super Stock classes were run as handicap events, using the Sportsman Christmas Tree setup with multiple yellow lights as opposed to the Pro tree with a single yellow light. Then there were the fledgling Funny Cars, which sort of resembled street cars but were powered with the biggest, most powerful engines and run in pure heads-up racing. As it were, there were three different types of cars all somewhat resembling stock autos that were grouped together but not raced together. The distinctions between the cars of the three classes were getting confusing and needed direction.

There were teams who wanted to continue the Funny Car route (flip-top bodies with unlimited horsepower and fuel-burning engines), and there were teams who wanted a class of stock-appearing cars with normally aspirated engines in heads-up competition. Jenkins was the main proponent of this movement, and he, along with Nicholson and Sox and Martin, lobbied for this new class.

In 1970, the NHRA introduced Pro Stock as a sanctioned series. Jenkins was successful in the new class right away, taking back-to-back wins over Ronnie Sox in the 1970 Winternationals and Gatornationals.

With the odds heavily in favor of the well-backed Chrysler entries, Jenkins hit a dry spell against the big, Hemi-engined cars. The NHRA realized it would not be good business or entertainment to see Chrysler dominate in a class that was supposed to embrace the product of the Big Three, so in 1972 the sanction modified its Pro Stock rules to provide a weight break to cars powered with small-block wedge head (Chevy) engines over big-block hemispherical head (Chrysler) engines.

After some suspension changes, Jenkins produced a killer car from his Malvern, Pennsylvania, shop. The 1972 Vega he built was a strong performer with mid-nine passes, and he captured six of eight NHRA national events in 1972.

He also won the Pro Stock class in the "National Challenge 72," a major event held by the AHRA and the Professional Racers Association at an AHRA track in Tulsa the same weekend as the NHRA's flagship event, the Nationals at Indy. Jenkins picked up $25,000 for his Tulsa victory, and along with his winnings from a heavy match-race schedule, he had the wherewithal to experiment and build upon new ideas for the class.

In 1974, Jenkins hit upon the winning combination with new features that continue to this day in the class, innovations such as the McPherson strut front suspension and dry-sump oiling.

By 1976, Jenkins had relinquished his driver's seat to spend more time on research and development. Driving for Jenkins, Larry Lombardo won the NHRA Pro Stock title in 1976, and another team driver, Ken Dondero, claimed the IHRA Pro Stock title. The Jenkins and Lombardo duo placed third in 1977 and second in 1978. But drivers such as Wally Booth, Wayne Gapp and a fellow from Indiana named Bob Glidden had started winning more races than the team from Jenkins Competition.

Jenkins broke up the act as a Pro Stock team owner in 1983. He continued to build, though, and drivers such as Joe Lepone won the 1985 Winternationals in Pro Stock with a Jenkins engine, but Jenkins was spending more time building engines for Comp class cars.

His work in the late 1990s with the GM splay-valved cylinder heads was successful in NHRA's Pro Stock Truck class, and he continued to build Pro Stock engines in 2005 and 2006 for drivers in the class such as Dave Connolly and Jim Yates.

Jenkins, who studied mechanical engineering at Cornell University, was one of the first to bring drag racing from a backyard type of endeavor to a professional level. He was inducted into the International Drag Racing Hall of Fame in 1993 and the Motorsports Hall of Fame in 1996.

An excerpt from a 1976 book entitled *The Chevrolet Racing Engine* published by S-A Design Co. provides an insight into Jenkins's philosophy:

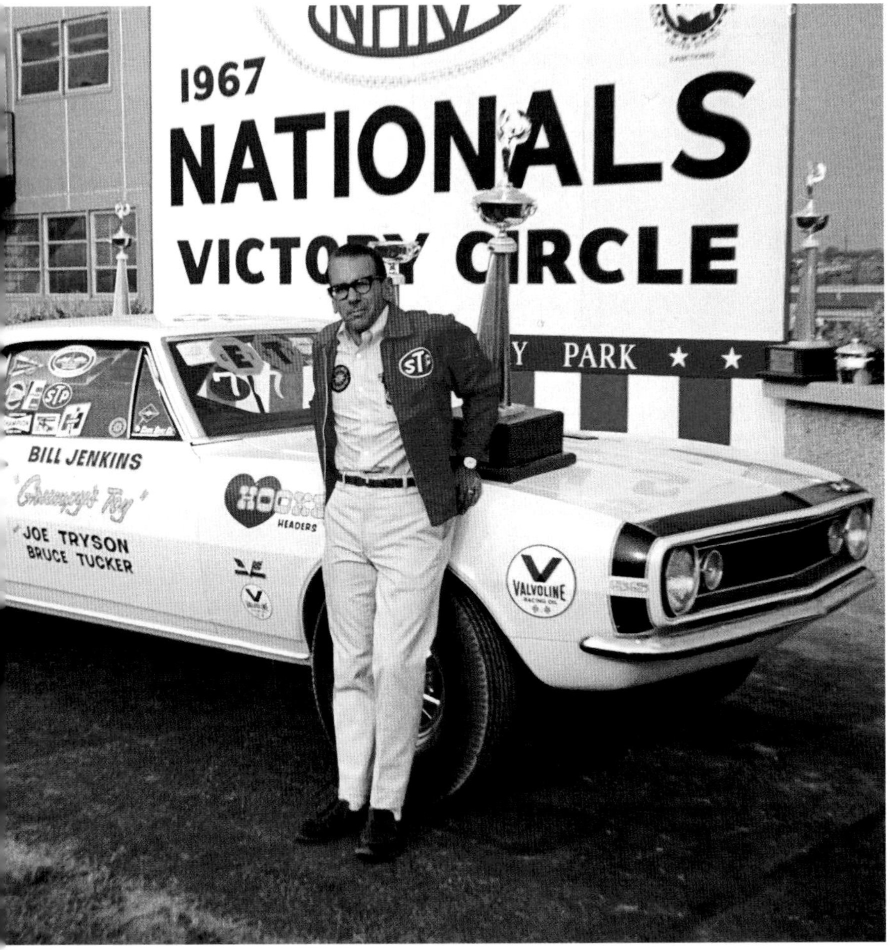

Jenkins leaning on his Super Stock Chevy Camaro with his 1967 NHRA Nationals trophy. Three years later Jenkins would become a major player when the NHRA introduced the Pro Stock class.

Known for the best burnouts in the business, like this one in 1973, "Jungle Jim" Liberman brought drag racing and showmanship to a whole new level.

"Every available resource is lavished on the all-important machines and toward creating their successors, the Grumpy's Toys that will carry the Jenkins Competition banner during the coming seasons.

"Combined with seemingly unlimited personal energy, it is the ability to foresee, predict, evaluate new approaches and develop future techniques that is the essence of his success. From any viewpoint, Bill Jenkins's impact on drag racing will be measured for years to come."

Jim Liberman

He's been dead since 1977, but the legacy of "Jungle Jim" Liberman is as strong today as when he toured the nation, dazzling fans with a degree of showmanship that has not been surpassed.

While Tommy Ivo was a showman, and provided drag race fans racing with an element of entertainment, Liberman took it to a whole new level. His exploits at the wheel of one of his famous Funny Cars are still remembered with awe for those who saw him perform in person. And there were many who saw him.

Born in Pennsylvania in 1945, Russell James Liberman got involved in drag racing in California in the mid 1960s. Starting his career behind the wheel of the Brutus GTO Funny Car in 1965, he struck out on his own with a Chevy II in 1967. With this blown altered-wheelbase car, and even without any factory backing that some of his rivals had at the time, Liberman did reasonably well, especially in the eyes of the fans who were starting to learn about this driver who laid down burnouts half the length of the track and kept the front wheels in the air for most of his passes.

The emergence of two new classes of racing came about in 1970: Pro Stock, a true extension of Super Stock, and Funny Car, an entirely new division. The classes were similar enough that before 1970 drivers of both divisions would compete against each other. When the two new heads-up racing classes formed, drivers had to make a choice. Liberman went the Funny Car route.

By 1974, when he ran Vega-bodied floppers, Liberman was an established figure on the match-race circuit. In fact, he owned the match-race circuit, as fans could not get enough of him. He also related to the fans more than to his fellow racers and those in the pits. The show for the fans was most important to him.

He was fearless on the track. Aside from wowing the throngs with his burnouts and wheelstands, he personified a rebel attitude that endeared him to the fans in that anti-establishment era.

A big part of his show, and Liberman certainly provided a show, was his constant companion Pam Hardy. Known as "Jungle Pam," this well-endowed young woman would really get the crowd going as she bounced up and down the track getting Liberman staged. The skimpier the attire on Hardy, the more the fans cheered.

Liberman's operation was based in Pennsylvania so he could be closer to the match-race circuit. It is estimated that he performed at 100 shows a year in the 1970s. His name became so prominent and sought-after by promoters that he fielded multi-car teams to keep up with the appearance schedule. Some who drove for him include Lew Arrington, who provided Liberman with the Brutus ride, Pete Williams, and Ron Attebury running a Top Fueler.

Liberman did race in regular competition also, and was no slouch when running up against "serious" drivers. He reached his first NHRA final at the 1974 Summernationals in Englishtown. A year later he won the event, his first and only major NHRA race. In 1976, he became the third driver to crack the six-second Funny Car barrier with a pair of five-second clockings at 5.96 seconds and 5.99 seconds in Texas.

But Liberman will best be remembered for his 1,000-foot burnouts, his 100-mph backups to the starting line to stage after a burnout, and going through the traps with his Vega on fire. Not unlike a rodeo clown who must know his craft well, Liberman was an excellent, charismatic driver who provided the fans with entertainment like no other racer.

A large factor in Liberman's popularity was due to Pam Hardy, who would get Liberman lined up in his lane in some very provocative attire.

Jungle Jim died at the age of 32 in a freeway collision with a bus. Liberman's star was part of the same culture as pop icons Jim Morrison and Janis Joplin: stars who captivated the population and shone brightly—be it all too briefly.

Connie Kalitta

Since he started racing in 1957 with a Chevy-powered 1951 Willys on the airstrips of Michigan, Kalitta is one of a handful of racers still involved in the sport he and others started over 50 years ago.

Connie Kalitta has always been his own person, marching to his own drummer. His determination and business acumen have provided him with an illustrious career in the sport. He fielded cars and equipment at any cost. The people he hired to work on his cars have always been the best in the business. Kalitta had one goal, and that was to win. It is still his goal.

Born in 1938, Kalitta raced locally in his early years, competing with a small-block-powered dragster when the U.S. Nationals were held in Detroit. When the NHRA lifted its fuel ban in 1963, Kalitta began touring with his fuel dragster, dicing it up with

Connie Kalitta, shown here at Las Vegas in April of 2008, is one of a handful of legends who continues to be a major player in the sport. Over the past five decades as a racer, crew chief, car owner and team owner, Kalitta has always brought a high degree of professionalism to drag racing.

drivers like Don Garlits, Chris Karamesines and Pete Robinson. In 1964, he made the first 200-mph pass at an NHRA national event.

In the mid-1960s, he replaced the traditional dragster power of the Chrysler Hemi with Ford's SOHC 427 engine, and he made this combination work successfully. He scored big in 1967, capturing the NHRA Winternationals and the AHRA Winternationals.

In 1969, Kalitta ran a 429 Ford Hemi-powered engine in his final front-engined dragster. He then drove a new rear-engined car, and after a nasty accident at the 1971 Nationals, parked the car for a while to pursue other interests.

One of those interests was in air transport. Starting with a small Cessna airplane he'd used earlier, he began to build an air freight service based in Michigan. His business grew from domestic flights to flying internationally, with a fleet of DC-8, Learjet and Boeing 747 aircraft that grew to a 100-plane operation by the time he sold the company in 1997.

After some passes with a Funny Car in the early 1970s, he sold one of his cars to Shirley Muldowney. When Muldowney went Top Fuel racing, Kalitta was her crew chief between 1973 and 1977, and the team won the NHRA Top Fuel championship in that final year.

Depending on one's point of view, and how much credence to give to the 1983 Hollywood biographical movie *Heart Like a Wheel* about Muldowney, Kalitta was either the main reason for Muldowney's success, or held back the first woman to win the title. The relationship, it has been said, was successful, but tempestuous.

Kalitta went back to driving in 1978. With solid finances due to his booming air freight business,

Kalitta had no problems in assembling a top-notch car and crew. He won the IHRA points title in 1979, took runner-up at the Grand Nationals in Quebec the same year, and was in the top 10 in NHRA points from then until 1986.

During this time, as with the rest of his driving career, the NHRA championship eluded him, although he won the IHRA title once again in 1982, and beat Muldowney in the 1982 Grand Nationals for his first NHRA win since 1967.

He continued to race in the 1980s, winning a national event in 1984 and 1986 and a pair in 1985. At the 1989 NHRA Winternationals, he became the first to break the 290-mph barrier with a 291.54-mph pass.

In 1994, well into his 50s, Kalitta beat his son Scott at Gainesville, and then went on to win the Atlanta race in Top Fuel. It was a good time for Kalitta, as son Scott earned the NHRA Top Fuel titles in both 1994 and 1995.

Today, Kalitta is heavily involved in drag racing, fielding two teams in the sport's upper echelons: nephew Doug Kalitta in the team's Top Fueler, and Jeff Arend in the Kalitta Funny Car effort.

Tragedy struck the Kalitta team in June of 2008 when Scott Kalitta, who drove the Kalitta Motorsports Funny Car entry, was killed in a horrendous crash during the NHRA Lucas Oil Supernationals at Englishtown. The younger Kalitta was a devoted and veteran drag racer who had won several NHRA Top Fuel titles before climbing into a Funny Car in 2006.

While father Connie and the rest of the team grieved over Scott's death, the team returned to its passion late in August 2008 with the signing of Jeff Arend to drive in Scott's place.

"We wanted to put someone in the car with experience and someone who would appreciate the opportunity and would fit in with our team personality-wise. We found that in Jeff," Kalitta is quoted as saying. "We had plenty of candidates for the position, but Jeff most possesses the qualities we are looking for.

"We will never be able to replace Scott, and we're not trying to. Our Funny Car will always be Scott's car, no matter who drives it. We want to get the car back out on the track to keep pursuing Scott's dream of having a successful Funny Car program for our team. Our friends at DHL and all of our sponsors have been very supportive, and we owe it to them and to Scott and our fans to keep that dream alive."

As one of the sport's major team owners, along with Kenny Bernstein, Don Prudhomme and John Force, Kalitta is also involved with the Professional Racers Association, a group of racers that liaisons with the NHRA, as a spokesperson and policy maker within the sport.

George Montgomery

One of the most memorable—and one of the most intense—times in the sport of drag racing was the Gassser wars. From the late 1950s until the advent of the Funny Car in the early 1970s, the rivalries between the supercharged, short-wheelbase, full-bodied cars had no equal.

Gassers came in several shapes and engine sizes, and while the Anglias, Willys and Austins ran in several classes depending on the engine, it was the blown cars of the AA/Gas class that really had the fans on the edge of their seats.

While the West Coast had the likes of John Mazmanian, Stone, Woods & Cook, and K.S. Pitman, it was a quiet racer from Ohio that established the standard for the AA/Gas drivers of the period. The record of George Montgomery, or "Ohio George" as he is known, in national event competition has no equal. He dominated the class at the U.S. Nationals in the late 1950s and early 1960s, taking Little Eliminator victories in 1959 and 1960. When the Nationals moved to its current home in Indianapolis in 1961, Montgomery won the title for the third straight time, driving his familiar 1933 Willys coupe.

Powered with a supercharged 414-cubic-inch Cadillac engine at first, the Willys received a 389-cubic-inch small-block Chevy engine in 1963, and Montgomery continued to win, capturing both the AA/Gas supercharged class and Middle Eliminator titles at the 1963 Nationals. He took another class win at Indy in 1964. He was consistently collecting victories with low 10-second times down the quarter-mile.

When Detroit automakers began recruiting drag racers for factory race teams, Ohio George signed on

Although better known for his early Willys Gassers, Ohio George Montgomery put together and raced some inspiring Mustang-bodied cars, including this potent twin turbo Boss 429 Mustang shown at Thompson, Ohio, in 1972.

with Ford, and put one of Ford's radical 427-cubic-inch single overhead camshaft powerplants in the Willys. This resulted in more class wins at the Nationals in 1966 and 1967.

When approached by Ford regarding the use of a more current body style (which would help fans relate to the cars they could buy at the local Ford dealership), Montgomery built a Mustang-bodied car, and was amazed at the superior handling and wind-cheating aerodynamics over the upright design of the then 30-year-old Willys body.

Running the Mustang in the early Funny Car days, Montgomery didn't miss a beat. The new car was capable of mid-eight-second clockings in excess of 160 mph.

He'd come a long way from wrenching on farm equipment at his uncle's Ford tractor dealership in Zenia, Ohio, in his early years.

Montgomery's first car, a 1934 Ford coupe, was taken and raced at Bonneville in 1951. He returned to his Ohio speedshop and engine-building facility, which he had opened in 1950, working in this fledgling business and acquiring a foundation and background for his future success at racing. And this success started soon. A Cadillac engine in another 1934 Ford coupe proved to be a quick car at the local strip in the mid 1950s, highlighted with a couple of NHRA Safari Tour wins for Top Eliminator. Montgomery was obviously pleased with the performance of the Caddy engine, as he adapted another luxury car powerplant to his Willys in the early years.

By the late 1950s, the Chrysler Hemi or Oldsmobile Rocket was the engine of choice where size and cubic inches were concerned. Chevrolet's small-block engine, introduced in 1955, could not be touched in terms of power output in relation to its size—it was in a class by itself at the time. But Montgomery was able to take the Cadillac engine and make it work for the first several years of racing the Willys.

With his new Mustang, Montgomery was routinely running the quarter-mile in nine seconds, and with the new 1,200-horsepower mount, captured the 1969 Super Eliminator titles at both the NHRA Springnationals and the Nationals.

Next was another Mustang, this one a Mach 1 variant with a hand-crafted fiberglass body. But underneath was a fallback to his roots, a 1933 Willys chassis. This car, which was capable of 1,200 horsepower in regular mode or up to 1,800 horsepower with a pair of turbochargers, did well for the next few seasons, including event wins at the Gatornationals in 1973 and 1974.

But the cars of this class were waning as the popularity of Pro Stockers and Funny Cars continued to the point of the two auto types becoming sanctioned classes. The fans liked the new classes better, relegating the Gasser-type cars to the backs of racers' shops.

Montgomery wasn't ready to retire from racing, though, and with his mechanical prowess, built a 1974 Pinto in 1976. There was no big-block in this little Ford, though. The car was powered by a turbocharged, two-liter, four-cylinder engine with about 500 horsepower, which propelled Montgomery nicely down his last few competitive runs on the drag strip. He took 14 event wins with the Pinto, and two Modifed Super Stock NHRA class records with 135-mph passes in the low 10-second range.

The shop he opened up in 1950 is still active, and along with a lot of drag racing activity, the shop strayed a bit from the straight-line work: Montgomery worked on Evel Knievel's stunt cars in the 1970s and was also involved as the builder of record for the Buick engines that went into the Indy Lights open-wheel cars.

Now a sought-after legend at nostalgia meets and drag racing reunions, Montgomery's honors for his illustrious career include inductions into the International Drag Racing Hall of Fame, a place on the NHRA's top 50 all-time personalities and an NHRA Lifetime Achievement award in 1998.

Shirley Muldowney

In 1977, drag racer Shirley Muldowney captured her first of three Top Fuel Dragster points championships in NHRA competition. The year was a big one for women in racing. While many auto fans may have heard of Muldowney's exploits, it was a woman by the name of Janet Guthrie who instead became a household name and America's racing sweetheart in 1977. Not only did this former road racer become the first woman ever to enter the Daytona 500, she was also the first woman to compete in the Indianapolis 500. In the mainstream press, Guthrie became known as a pioneer, but it should be noted that Muldowney, who had been racing steadily since the early 1960s, was the first woman to win an auto racing series championship of any kind. Guthrie finished ninth in the 1977 Indy 500.

Both Guthrie and Muldowney had to face long odds and many detractors in order to succeed. For Muldowney, her acceptance in the sport was long in coming, and with reluctance, not only from her competitors, but from track owners and sanctions who felt a woman's place was not behind the wheel of a 2,000-horsepower race car.

To show the world her 1977 championship was not a fluke, Muldowney again won NHRA Top Fuel championships in 1980 and 1982.

Born in 1940, young Shirley Roque spent her teen years in upstate New York, and married racer Jack Muldowney before she was 20. Her first trip down the strip was at the wheel of a 348-cubic-inch powered Chevy in 1958. For the next few years she ran a variety of cars, and in 1965 husband Jack built a dragster, a car she raced in the eastern U.S. for several seasons. This twin-engined car gave her some success, and the drag racing world was starting to accept her involvement.

In 1971, the Muldowneys purchased a Funny Car from Connie Kalitta, and at the wheel of this Mustang FC, Muldowney won her first major event at the IHRA Southern Nationals.

A personal and professional lifestyle change took place for Muldowney in 1972. She was divorced from Jack, moved to Michigan and teamed up with Kalitta from his Mount Clemens shop. The pair toured on the match-race circuit in Funny Cars, and they were known as the Bounty Hunter and Bounty Huntress.

While Muldowney learned her craft, early Funny Cars were not the safest of vehicles on the quarter-mile. Although the cars were very popular with fans and track promoters, the technology in driver and car safety equipment had not kept pace with the development of the class, and after four car fires, Muldowney had enough and wanted to get into the sport's premier class—Top Fuel.

After acquiring her NHRA Top Fuel license at Cayuga Dragway Park in Ontario in 1973 under the eyes of Kalitta, Don Garlits and Tommy Ivo, who all signed off on her license, Muldowney jumped into a Top Fueler, mostly in match racing, although she did compete in the 1974 U.S. Nationals, clocking a 241.28-mph pass for the second-fastest speed of the meet.

Good things happened in 1975. She was sponsored by cologne manufacturer English Leather, which gave her the money to compete at a high level in terms of a car and equipment quality. She was the first woman to record a five-second pass in the class, she went to the final round in national meets twice that year, and perhaps most importantly, she was the first woman named to the American Auto Racing Writers and Broadcasters Association All-America Team.

In 1976, Muldowney's career really started to advance. She won the NHRA Springnationals in June of that year, becoming the first woman to win an NHRA national event in a professional class. She backed up this victory with a class win at the World Finals. Her 5.77-second time and 249-mph speeds at the World Finals were also benchmarks for her season.

Winning the 1977 Springnationals was only one of her accomplishments that year. She also won the Summernationals at Englishtown and the Molson Grand Nationals in Quebec. She was the first-ever driver to win three consecutive NHRA national events. Muldowney won not only the coveted NHRA Winston World Series championship—she had won the respect of her competitors.

After a tempestuous personal life and a successful professional life with crew chief Kalitta, the pair split up, Kalitta pursuing his own driving career again behind the wheel of a dragster and Muldowny teaming up

Muldowney is checking the air pressure on her early Kalitta-team Funny Car. She was never comfortable with Floppers, and it would not be long before she was winning in Top Fuel Dragsters.

with Rahn Tobler, whom she eventually married.

She also won her second championship in 1980, winning four NHRA national events, plus she competed in the AHRA at this time, winning that sanction's 1981 Top Fuel title as well as placing fifth in the NHRA standings with wins at Gainesville and Atlanta.

Concentrating on the NHRA in 1982, Muldowney came back to record another winning season and her third Top Fuel championship, highlighted with a final-round victory over Kalitta at the U.S. Nationals. She also won at Gainesville, Columbus and Brainerd. Muldowney placed fourth in NHRA points in 1983, winning the Winternationals and the World Finals.

It was in 1983 that her biographical Hollywood movie, *Heart Like a Wheel*, was released. Movie critics at the time chastised the film for containing too much racing, but the determination of Muldowney and the obstacles she had to overcome were well documented in the film, along with her relationship with Kalitta. The movie helped to broaden the public's knowledge of drag racing, and made Muldowney the sport's major star.

By 1984, Muldowney had been through some nasty accidents in her career, but a major setback ensued during a qualifying run at the 1984 NHRA Grand Nationals. When a front wheel locked up as the tire's tube came apart at about 250 mph, her trademark pink dragster left the southern Quebec track and disintegrated. She was found about 500 feet away by rescue workers.

Muldowney was conscious, but her left foot was dangling in her lap. Her pelvis was broken, a thumb nearly severed and her right leg fractured.

For close to a year and a half, Muldowney recovered in hospital and her Detroit-area home. With several operations, therapy, bone grafts and pins in her leg, she had lots of time to think about her future while convalescing.

She was determined to return to racing. "I wasn't ready to quit," she has been quoted as saying. "I realized I've got another shot at this. I just couldn't picture doing anything other than what I do."

It took a couple of years, but Muldowney, with Tobler, was back in the chase, and by 1989 went to three NHRA finals where she won the Fallnationals in Phoenix. She also became the first woman to run a sub-five-second run, clocking a 4.974-second pass at 284 mph.

In the early 1990s, the team hit the match-race tour, traveling across North America and overseas. She also drove for team owner Larry Minor at this time.

By 1995, Muldowney was back in competition as often as finances would allow, tearing up the tracks in IHRA events, and racing in selected NHRA events.

With a lack of substantial sponsorship, Muldowney's career was waning by the turn of the century. She continued to race, and was a top draw wherever she raced, but there were fewer and fewer appearances.

In 2003, Muldowney ran her final season, running six NHRA events and registering a career-best 4.579-second, 327-mph pass in Chicago.

Many awards have been bestowed on this woman, including induction into the International Motorsports Hall of Fame. She was a recipient of the U.S. Sports Academy Babe Didriksen Zaharias Courage Award, and selected in 1998 by the New York State Senate as one of 30 "Women of Distinction" along with Eleanor Roosevelt and Susan B. Anthony.

But Muldowney, who opened the doors for women in what had been a male-dominated sport, wants to be remembered as a racer, a racer who went to the top of her profession. "I'm a driver," she has said. "I'm not a lady driver."

Perhaps long-time rival Don Garlits summed up Muldowney's prowess best: "You can't argue with what she accomplished on the race track. When you raced her, you always knew she'd do whatever she had to do to win."

Don Nicholson

"Don is a seven-day-a-week racer," Ronnie Sox said about Don Nicholson. "That's all he thinks about. He got the most out of what he had of anybody."

Later in his career, when high-dollar haulers would disgorge race cars and a team of specialists at a drag strip, Nicholson would pull up in the pits driving his own rig. He built his own engines. He experimented and tried new ideas with a natural mechanical aptitude. And although he had factory backing during stages of his long career, he did not receive the financial support his competitors had, which didn't stop him from beating them on a regular basis.

Nicholson is credited with first campaigning a car with a one-piece flip-top body shell, eventually to become the Funny Car, one of drag racing's biggest draws. He is also credited with being a dominant player in the creation of the Pro Stock class, another of the sport's biggest attractions.

Acquiring the name "Dyno Don" for his skills on an engine-data machine known as a dynamometer while working at a Chevrolet dealership, Nicholson started racing on the dry lakes of his native

Don Nicholson raced anywhere, anytime. Here he is competing in an NHRA Division 1 meet at Dragway Park in Cayuga, Ontario, in the early 1970s. Before straight-lining, Nicholson raced the California oval tracks in the late 1940s.

California and competed in oval track racing during the late 1940s. He would drag race on old airport strips, and as organized events took shape in the late 1950s, Nicholson competed in earnest and knew he had found his calling.

By 1961 when the NHRA was ready to hold its Winternationals at Pomona, Nicholson was also ready. With a 409-powered Chevy, he won Stock Eliminator, not only at Pomona, but at the U.S. Nationals that same year. He won the Nationals again in 1962.

When GM pulled out of racing the next year, he established a relationship with Lincoln-Mercury, a partnership retained for the rest of the decade.

He had moved to Atlanta before the L-M deal, as he was a big draw on the match-race circuit in the Southeast. His association with L-M came about thanks to friend Troy Ruttman, who was not only a successful Sprint and Indy Champ car driver, but he also competed in NASCAR's Grand National stock car racing, and he ran a 1948 Mercury in the Panamerican cross-country race in Mexico. A division of the Ford Motor Company, Lincoln-Mercury needed a way to get into the then-popular factory-backed drag racing teams. Ruttman introduced the racer and the automaker and the two became a great match.

In 1964 and 1965, Nicholson ran a Comet in the wide-open A/FX (Factory Experimental) class, tallying many wins with this 427 Ford-powered car complete with a fiberglass front end.

With almost no class rules, these cars started appearing at this time with altered wheelbases for better weight distribution and traction. In a no-holds barred environment, the NHRA declared these cars illegal for competition, but they were extremely popular with the fans at match races.

For the 1966 season, Nicholson debuted the Eliminator, the car credited as the sport's first true Funny Car. This car, built on a tube chassis with a one-piece, flip-top body, was a major development in drag racing, and established the Funny Car as a separate class. Nicholson was virtually unbeatable with this car, and clocked the class's first seven-second run in Michigan in 1966.

The Eliminator II appeared in 1967, and in 1968 his Cougar-based car featured a supercharger which upped the ante—and speed—from his previous fuel-injected cars.

But Nicholson was concerned with the safety aspects of the new class. Development of the cars had been heavy on speed and winning without addressing safety issues such as blower explosions, on-board fire extinguishers, and fire suits that offered little protection for the driver.

So Nicholson shifted gears, competing with others

such as Bill Jenkins and Dick Landy in heads-up match racing in carbureted, four-speed Super Stock cars. This venture proved popular, and the teams were able to convince the NHRA to form a class using this formula, so the Pro Stock class was formed in 1970.

A hastily-prepared 1970 Maverick Pro Stocker was not very successful against the Chrysler domination in the class's early years, but Nicholson and his little mid-size Ford were successful in match racing. With the help of Earl Wade and Dave McGrane in developing a 427 SOHC Ford engine, Nicholson was back in business with a class win at the 1971 NHRA Summernationals.

Throughout the 1970s, Nicholson was a strong contestant in Pro Stock. Starting with a 351 Cleveland Ford small-block Pinto in 1972, he was always in the hunt with his succession of Ford products with "Dyno Don" written on the doors.

He won both the AHRA and NHRA Winternationals with the Pinto, and the 1973 Gatornationals. There were no titles for the next couple of years, but wins at Gainesville, Columbus and Indy gave him the 1977 NHRA Pro Stock championship.

He was 50 years old when he took this title.

Nicholson carried the Ford banner through the 1980 season. He ran an Oldsmobile in 1984, but then retired from racing. Almost.

He hit the nostalgia circuit in 1988 with a re-creation of his early 1962 Chevy hardtop, running the 409-powered car up to 150 mph in races with former competitors like Arnie Beswick.

Nicholson also got his feet wet in the NHRA's Pro Stock Truck class in 1998 and 1999.

After a career spanning six decades, Nicholson died in California early in 2006. Recognition for his many contributions to the sport includes induction into the International Drag Racing Hall of Fame and the Motorsports Hall of Fame.

The evolution of the Funny Car was not the doing of one person, but Nicholson was one of the first main builders and competitors in the fledgling class. His Eliminator Cougar Funny Car was built on a tube chassis with a one-piece flip-top body. It started the trend that continues to this day.

Don Prudhomme

In a drag racing career filled with highlights, 1976 was Don Prudhomme's biggest year.

Already established with 15 years of professional racing behind him, this Californian won seven of eight NHRA Funny Car events in the U.S. Bicentennial year. This topped his 1975 season of six national event wins. In 1977, he took three Nationals, and did the same in 1978.

He won the Funny Car points title for each of those four years. No one could match Prudhomme and his nearly invincible Monza-bodied Funny Car. Every time he suited up and blasted down the quarter-mile, his runs were arrow-straight, no easy feat given that Funny Cars are known as the class hardest to keep on an even keel down the strip.

Former car painter Don Prudhomme became one of the big stars in the Funny Car division, and promoted his racing with well-known sponsors, such as Mattel (Hot Wheels) and the U.S. Army. This shot is from Dragway 42 in West Salem, Ohio, in 1971.

A consummate professional who approached his racing with 100 percent commitment, Prudhomme was one of the most gifted individuals ever to sit behind the wheel of a race car. Along with his driving capabilities, he was a master at the starting line, with one of the quickest reaction times in the business.

This drag racing legend was born in 1941, and got involved as did many others with the car craze in Southern California. He worked in an auto paint shop, built a few street rods, and was a member of the same car club as Tommy Ivo, who was established as one of the top professional drivers of the era. In 1960, Prudhomme went on the road with Ivo, paying his dues as they traveled across the country.

After a short time, Prudhomme felt he could try his hand at racing, and purchased an Ivo dragster in 1962 with Kent Fuller and Dave Zeuschel. The Buick engine in the dragster was trashed in favor of a Zeuschel-built 392 Chrysler fuel Hemi, the power of choice for the sport's top class. Driving this car, the lanky 20-year-old won a major meet at Bakersfield over almost 90 other entries.

His next ride was another team effort (Greer, Black, Prudhomme), and for the next two years their fuel dragster was totally dominant, with 230 wins to seven losses in 1963 and 1964. This success was not only due to Prudhomme's lightning-quick reflexes on the starting line (hence his nickname "The Snake") but also to Keith Black, who was to become one of the top fuel engine builders in drag racing. Not only was Black a master at engines, he was one of the first to realize it was imperative to get the power from one of these cars to the back wheels with a minimum of wheelspin, and worked diligently in clutch setups. Getting the power to the track quicker won more races, and this was proven with the G-B-P car, as other teams played catch-up with developing slipping clutches.

With this outstanding winning record, Prudhomme caught the eye of car owner Roland Leong, a well-known racer with his series of "Hawaiian" cars. Leong had a car similar to the G-B-P car built, and put Prudhomme in the driver's seat. The car was successful, winning several NHRA national events in 1965.

Wanting to be more than a driver, Prudhomme ventured out with his own car in 1966 with funding from the Bob Spar and Mort Schuman transmission-shifter company, B&M. Although his season in the

B&M Torkmaster was not as fruitful as previous campaigns, he learned a lot, both on his own and under the eye of Chris Karamesines, a dragster pioneer who took Prudhomme into his shop. Karamesines taught Prudhomme the inner workings of a race car, something he had never learnt.

Prudhomme drove for Lou Baney in 1967 with a Ford-powered dragster. With some success in NHRA events and the sanction's first six-second winner, he secured sponsorship for his own car in 1969. The timing was good for Prudhomme, as he took two consecutive Top Fuel titles in 1969 and 1970, at the NHRA's flagship event, the U.S. Nationals.

In 1970, Prudhomme got out of a dragster to compete in the up-and-coming Funny Car circuit, a new class underway that was proving to be very popular with fans. He and Tom McEwen lit up the tracks as "The Snake" and "The Mongoose" driving for the popular Mattel Hot Wheels Funny Car team. This was one of the first times financial support at this level was provided to drag racers, and it was a pioneer venture that continues to this day.

It now appeared Prudhomme was in control of his situation, and had reached the point in his career where he could concentrate on driving and not worry about the financial side of operating a high-profile professional race team. Before the Mattel funding, Prudhomme had no backup plan

Prudhomme is seen here at Indy in 1966 with his B&M Torkmaster. Notice the attempt at achieving greater aerodynamics through body styling, much like his mentor Tommy Ivo.

or financial support. He had to keep winning to earn his livelihood (an extra incentive to win as many races as possible).

When Prudhomme received more support from the U.S. Army in 1974, his security was solid. He won two NHRA national events that year and placed third in the standings.

In 1975, the NHRA received major sponsorship from Winston cigarettes for points funding. And not only did the NHRA reach a new level in respectability, Prudhomme hit his stride with his first of four Funny Car titles, dominating the class with his Vega and Plymouth Arrow-bodied floppers.

He placed second in the points race for 1979, and then started sliding a bit with a few wins but always remained in the top 10 in points. He placed fourth in the 1985 standings in a year that saw Kenny Bernstein dominate the class with six event wins. It was the first year that John Force made the NHRA top 10 in the class, a driver who would dominate the class later on as Prudhomme had done in the 1970s.

With no major funding for 1986, Prudhomme sat out and reentered the competition the next year with a Skoal Bandit Racing sponsorship. He won at the Gatornationals and finished fifth overall in the points race. He proved he was back in form for the next two years with wins at the Grand Nationals and Summernationals in 1988. He scored a big win at the 1989 U.S. Nationals along with titles at the California Nationals and the Chief Auto Parts Nationals, placing second in the 1989 standings. At this time, he became the first Funny Car driver to record a sub 5.20-second time with a 5.193-second pass.

Prudhomme returned to his dragster roots in 1990, but had some problems that year driving a rear-engined car, which was a total turnaround from his past dragster days of the standard front-engined rigs that were the norm when he last raced Top Fuel.

He finished out of the points in 1990 in Top Fuel, but returned to his usual winning ways in 1991, scoring three event wins and placing third in the NHRA class points. He took another three wins in 1992, was sixth in the standings, but placed out of the running in 1993. At over 50 years old, Prudhomme decided to relinquish his driving duties, but not before going out in style. For 1994, he won three events, recorded his best dragster time of 4.73 seconds and finished second in points before calling it a day.

Prudhomme, like many racing legends, couldn't step entirely out of the sport. Instead he began his new phase in drag racing as a car owner, and driver Larry Dixon continued to provide Prudhomme with success, placing third in the 1995 standings with four event wins.

Prudhomme then added a Funny Car to the mix with Ron Capps driving, with the two-car team benefiting from the major sponsorship of Copenhagen Tobacco and Miller Lite Beer. In 2000, a second flopper joined the team driven by Tommy Johnson Jr. The next year, this three-car fuel assault provided owner Prudhomme with 10 event wins, highlighted by Dixon's six Top Fuel victories, good for second place in the standings, 95 points behind Kenny Bernstein.

In 2002, Dixon and Prudhomme won top honors with nine event wins, and repeated this feat in 2003 with eight wins, giving Prudhomme two Top Fuel championships as a car owner. The Prudhomme team currently has interest in only one race car, Dixon's former Top Fueler, which is now driven by Spencer Massey, the 2008 IHRA Top Fuel Champion.

Throughout his career, whether it's been as a hired driver, driving his own cars or as a team owner, Prudhomme has been pure racer and one of the most charismatic figures in the sport. He always understood what it took to win, and maintained an edge over his competitors in achieving that goal. Aside from his driving prowess, he had the ability to attract and maintain major sponsorship, and was instrumental in opening the corporate doors for others in the sport. He is one of the true icons of drag racing.

Sox and Martin

The phrase Sox and Martin rolls off the tongue in an altogether natural manner. One cannot speak of Sox without Martin, and vice versa. These two men not only were masters on the drag strip, they established precedents that are continued to this day, such as team uniforms, good-looking race car haulers and a commitment to a high-level of proficiency. The accolades that have been presented to them

Caught our Strip Show yet?

It's our *Pop Stock Eliminator* contest, and it's the best thing that's hit the strip since the Clan hit 'Vegas:

In one lane, there's Ronnie Sox and Buddy Martin's race-prepared Boss Hemi-GTX, with 426 cubes, and two 4-barrels. Ronnie Sox is at the stick, and ready to let it happen.

In the other lane, there's a similarly prepared GTX, except that it packs Plymouth's wailing 440 cu. in. Wedge, which pumps out 480 lbs.-ft. of torque on a single 4-barrel. The driver is someone you know—and an amateur's amateur. A disc jockey, perhaps. Maybe a friend.

The Christmas tree blinks yellow . . . yellow . . . yellow . . . Green.

There they go! Ronnie's spotted the other guy a head start, and it's going to be close. Can an amateur actually beat the Boss? It's happened before, and it can happen again.

And that's just half the show.

The other half we call our *Supercar Clinic*.

Sox & Martin conduct it several nights prior to each contest. Together, Ronnie and Buddy give tips on racing and race-tuning; they show films; they answer questions; they hand out literature; they display the latest in Plymouth speed equipment, and even brew a mean pot of coffee. In short, it's a bull-session. With prizes, no less. And it's free to anyone who likes cars. The roof overhead is supplied by your Plymouth dealers, who happen to like cars, too. It's their way of saying Plymouth is out to win you over.

Watch for the Sox & Martin Supercar Clinic and Pop Stock Eliminator contest in your area.
Get a copy of Plymouth's wild new high-performance car catalog.
Send 25¢ to: P.O. Box 7749, Detroit, Michigan 48211

This Plymouth advertisement from 1967 is for Plymouth's "Supercar Clinic" where Super Stock all-stars Ronnie Sox and Buddy Martin gave tips and wisdom to amateur racers. The end of the clinic, featured the amateurs going a round against the legendary duo. It doesn't happen like that anymore!

With factory backing from Plymouth, Sox & Martin fielded several cars, including this Barracuda–Duster matchup. Here team driver Herb McCandless handles the driving for the Duster.

demonstrate their successes, but through their business and promotional approach to the sport, these two brought drag racing a professionalism that previously had not existed.

Ronnie Sox and Buddy Martin took the sport into the corporate consciousness, treating their quarter-mile passion as a business and offering a promotable platform for the auto companies to build upon.

Sox got his feet wet running Oldsmobiles and Fords at the local airport strip outside of Burlington, North Carolina, in the mid-1950s. After running a Pontiac in the early 1960s, he teamed up with Dave Holifield and a hot 409-equipped Chevy. Buddy Martin was also driving at this time, but was having little luck shutting down Sox, even though he was driving a nearly identical car.

Martin approached Sox about teaming up and splitting the winnings evenly. The deal was struck, and the pair went on a tear with a high-performance specially equipped 1963 Z-11 Chevy. Although they stuck close to their North Carolina base, they did wander north enough to get into lots of races and win enough for other competitors in the hot Super Stock class to take notice.

Don Nicholson, one of the biggest names in the class, was impressed enough to contract Sox and Martin to join him in a factory-backed Ford effort, racing a Mercury Comet. They made the trip to California, taking the top prize at Lions, and then got ready for the NHRA Winternationals at Pomona.

They won at Pomona, beating Nicholson in the final, and received a new Dodge as one of the Top Eliminator prizes. The car had to be sold to give them enough funds to make the trip back home.

After a successful year driving the Comet, the duo was offered a solid race car and sponsorship package from Ford in 1965. But the deal did not include a personal car for each for them. And Chrysler had been calling them, wanting to talk. When they walked out on Ford and went over to the Chrysler package (complete with personal vehicles), another famous partnership in the annals of drag racing was established.

Chrysler's long association with Sox and Martin

was very beneficial for both parties. The automaker had one of the best drag race teams promoting its product, and the team was given the sponsorship it needed to compete at this high national level.

Away from the track, Sox and Martin were becoming ambassadors, not only for their sponsor Chrysler, but for the sport of drag racing. Always presenting themselves in a professional manner, the team would tour around to Chrysler dealerships holding clinics for enthusiasts running both competition and high-performance street cars.

For the next three years, Sox drove a string of altered wheelbase Chryslers, the predecessor of what was eventually to become the Funny Car. Sox and Martin's first car was a Belvedere-bodied vehicle with the wheels obviously altered from stock, 10 inches on the front and 15 inches at the rear. Known as the "Paper Tiger," the team match-raced this car at AHRA events, and then raced a fuel-injected Barracuda with a Nicholson-inspired flip-top body.

By 1967, Chrysler was not impressed with the direction the class was going, and wanted to return to Super Stock, believing it could sell more cars when its racers were driving ones that resembled those in the showrooms.

In this first year back in Super Stock, the team won the NHRA Springnationals in a Hemi-powered Plymouth GTX, and in 1968 toured with a Hemi Barracuda, assembled by shifter giant, Hurst—a car built solely for the strip. This car won just about every race in which it was entered that year, and was a real crowd-pleaser when it left the line in high, wheelstanding fashion.

At this time, Sox was making a name for himself, not just for winning, but for the way he could shift the four-speed in his car. Throughout the late 1960s and early 1970s onlookers and fellow competitors were hard-pressed to believe anyone could shift a car that fast. Sox explained that the team, which included Jake King, did a lot of research and testing with linkages and ratios to get the best combination.

The team presented itself as a first-class, specialized operation, treating racing as a business. At the track, Sox and Martin stood out from the field of greasy jeans and shirts with their crisp team uniforms. Sox credits this to Martin, who realized he was representing his sponsors and knew how to keep the sponsors happy.

While the team was a main player in Super Stock, the duo enjoyed match racing, and competed in no-holds-barred contests in a now-famous red, white and blue Chrysler.

The NHRA introduced its Pro Stock class in 1970 after lobbying by teams such as Sox and Martin, Nicholson and Bill Jenkins for heads-up racing with the ultimate factory hot rods. For the next two seasons, the team's win record was outstanding, but the NHRA was starting to put the brakes on the team's success, making the Chrysler-powered entries add weight to the cars so the Ford and Chevrolets would stand a better chance.

Chrysler, tired of getting pushed around, along with the 1973 gas shortage and the need to produce more fuel-efficient cars, slowly dropped its factory involvement by the mid 1970s. In 1972, after claiming back-to-back to back-to-back titles—1968 NHRA Super Stock, 1969 AHRA Super Stock and NHRA Pro Stock championships in 1970 and 1971—Sox and Martin went their separate ways.

Martin went on to other business ventures, including automobile sales and leasing, while Sox continued to match race, along with taking the IHRA Pro Stock title in 1981.

In 1995 the team was reunited, running a Ford Thunderbird, which just about killed Sox when it crashed badly. He continued on though, and drove nostalgia shows in his later years and continued to amaze the fans with his lightning-quick gear shifting.

"I'm certainly glad that I was able to race at the time that I did," Sox has been quoted as saying. "Today's racing technology has diminished the role of the driver way too much. Back in the days of the four-speeds, the driver had a lot more to do with the outcome of the race, and I couldn't imagine anything being more fun than that."

Sox was always appreciative and humble for the warm reception he received at the nostalgia events he raced. He died in April 2006. Martin, now in his early 70s, got back into racing with a Pro Stock truck in the NHRA in the late 1990s, and in 2008 was involved as a consultant with a Sox & Martin-themed SS/AH Barracuda.

Schooling and the New School

Complete with registration markings on its front, an E-Type Jaguar launches at England's famous Santa Pod drag strip. Although drag racing in Europe is not a major auto sport, devoted racers compete in quarter-mile action with a wide array of vehicles.

MOTOR STORES
SST 569

Drag racing schools offer a safe, controlled environment to learn the sport, taught by racers themselves. Here school owner/ instructor, Frank Hawley, works very closely with a student during a Top Alcohol Dragster Class.

Schools and Museums

Schools

At one time, the only way to learn how to drag race was to actually compete. Racers would usually start with a slow car, learn how to read the Christmas Tree, and practice their timing off the line. Once comfortable with the speed of the car, and their rhythm, racers would purchase or build a faster car and compete at the next level, and continue up the ladder, so to speak, as their finances, or sponsorship, allowed.

As racers gained confidence in their abilities and wanted to continue, they had to obtain the blessing of the sanctioning body and, if successful, would be issued a competition license, allowing them to compete in their specified class at tracks under the sanction's umbrella.

Racers continue to follow this method, but there is help out there now in the form of drag racing schools. These facilities offer courses not only for those new to the sport, but to established racers who wish to get into a faster car and obtain the necessary skills before attempting to get their competition license.

As with racing schools for road and oval track racing, drag racing schools offer both classroom and actual hands-on situations in order to give drivers the tools necessary to compete. The schools are staffed by former racers, and provide a unique alternative in learning how to drive down the racetrack. There are entry-level courses for those who have never been behind the wheel of a drag car and on up to schooling in alcohol-powered dragsters and Funny Cars for experienced racers who wish to move up. Courses are available in most classes of cars, from full-fendered door cars to dragsters. There are also courses available for Junior Dragster drivers.

Here are some drag racing schools, and what they offer:

Frank Hawley's Drag Racing School

The Hawley school is the largest and most diversified of the drag racing schools. Started by former Funny Car driver Frank Hawley, this transplanted Canadian started his school in Florida over 20 years ago and has trained thousands over the years.

Now sanctioned by the NHRA, the Hawley school has expanded to several facilities, and offers training in Super Comp and Super Gas, Alcohol Funny Cars and Dragsters, and Pro Stock Motorcycle.

The school also allows students the opportunity to earn their NHRA license through classroom and driver training.

Some of today's biggest drag racing stars have attended the Hawley school, including Doug Kalitta, Ashley Force and Tony Schumacher.

The school also offers a chance for those who wish to try driving a dragster just for the fun of it with a series of eighth- and quarter-mile passes.

Costs vary, depending on the length of the course and car class, from around \$500 up to \$7,000.

Doug Foley's Drag Racing School

Noted Top Fuel driver Doug Foley offers a variety of racing courses from his New Jersey base with partner and Top Alcohol Dragster racer Tim Lewis.

Started after Foley and Lewis teamed up in 2002, the school offers some instruction with door cars, but its emphasis is with dragsters, right from Junior Dragsters through Super Comp and A-Fuel Dragsters to Top Fuel Dragsters. Training in the latter class is in a two-day, one-on-one setting with Foley himself, and is available only for those racers who have a Top Alcohol Dragster license and experience.

The two-day A-Fuel Dragster course is geared to take a Sportsman racer to the next level, from racing an eight-second car into a car capable of five-second runs. If successful in completing this \$8,000 course, an NHRA competition license is part of the package.

Courses in other classes are usually two days, and Junior Dragster classes are one day.

The Foley school also offers a fantasy-type dragster session for those wanting to go fast, and this half-day course starts at \$295.

Roy Hill's Drag Racing School

Based in North Carolina, former IHRA Pro Stock champ Roy Hill has shared his knowledge and expertise in his drag racing school since 1997. The emphasis is on door cars, especially Pro Stockers, but there are also training sessions in Super Comp Dragsters.

Hill's also offers courses in Bracket and Junior Dragster racing. Prices range from \$600 for the Junior course to \$6,000 for the Pro Stock sessions.

But the school offers more than just learning how to race. Hill's has courses in engine building, chassis building and classes in crew-chief management. These unique courses offer a wide range of techniques and building methods from the experts. Not everyone wants to race, and these "behind the scenes" sessions can provide the knowledge and skill set needed in a real racing environment.

Top Fuel Dragster driver Doug Foley, shown here during an NHRA meet in Virginia, operates a racing school with emphasis on dragsters, from Juniors right up to Top Fuel.

Nelson Hoyes Drag Racing School

One of the biggest names in Sport Compact racing, Nelson Hoyes, has established a school in Florida for those wishing to learn how to compete in FWD (front wheel drive), or Tuner competition.

The school was established to provide younger racers with a safe, controlled environment to learn the fundamentals of drag racing, and a solid mandate against street racing.

Hoyes, two-time NHRA PRO-FWD champ, has a variety of courses for both novice and established drivers using Chevy Cobalts and Super Comp dragsters. Course durations run between half a day to a day and a half, and consist of classroom training, safety instruction and progressively quicker runs down the quarter-mile, with prices ranging from $395 to $1,795.

NOPI (Number One Parts, Inc.) champ Lisa Kubo also provides instruction along with Hoyes. The school will provide successful students in advanced classes with their NHRA competition license.

Junior Dragsters

As with many other sports, drag racing has a solid program to get young people involved in the sport. Started in the early 1990s, Junior Dragster racing is for children and youth to race in a competitive, controlled environment. It is also an excellent way for young people to learn about drag racing, so if they wish to continue once they are too old to compete in Junior Dragsters, they have already mastered the skills associated with the sport.

Junior Dragsters are basically half-size versions of a Top Fuel dragster. Initially they were powered by five-horsepower lawnmower-type engines, but today there is a large aftermarket industry offering special race-only engines and running gear. The cars must run on gasoline or alcohol only, and the cars are started with a remote starter at the beginning of a pass.

Funny Car and roadster bodies are allowed, but the majority of cars are dragsters, using a wheelbase between 90 inches and 150 inches.

There are three class designations, based on age. All classes compete on an eighth-mile strip. Racers compete either with a handicap dial-in or a heads-up Pro-type start.

The beginner class is for children eight and nine years old, and they are not allowed to run quicker than a 12.90-second elapsed time. The intermediate class is for 10- to 17-year-olds, who are restricted to an 8.90 or slower elapsed time. The third class is for ages 12 to 17, with a time restriction of 7.90 seconds or slower, and when a racer competes in this class, he or she must have a minimum of one full year of licensed competition.

While the cars are capable of speeds approaching 85 mph, safety is paramount for the classes, both in the car and for the driver.

All cars have ignition shut-off switches within easy reach of the driver, two-wheel hydraulic braking, and deflector plates between the rear-mounted engine and the driver's compartment.

Along with SFI-approved clothing and helmet, a Junior Dragster driver is belted into the car with a five-point restraint system mounted to the car's frame. Arm restraints are mandatory, as are neck collars, full-length pants, socks, shoes and driving gloves.

Just about every drag strip has programs for Junior Dragsters, and they are recognized by major sanctioning bodies such as the NHRA and IHRA. Teams are usually comprised of a driver and his or her parents. Along with winning trophies and money, Junior Dragster drivers can win savings bonds and scholarship packages.

Museums

There are very few drag racing museums. The only two of note are the Don Garlits Museum of Drag Racing in Ocala, Florida, and the Wally Parks NHRA Motorsports Museum in Pomona, California.

The former is the history of drag racing through the personality of Don Garlits, housed in a large single-story facility opened in 1984. The building displays the cars lined up side by side, most with placards providing a short history on the vehicles.

The self-supporting Garlits museum displays quarter-mile cars only, along with documents, photos, programs, helmets and suits. Along with most of Garlits's Swamp Rat dragsters, there are many significant and historical exhibits, including cars from Jungle Jim Liberman, Mickey Thompson, Don Prudhomme and Shirley Muldowney. The first Donovan "417" aluminum fuel engine is also on display.

The Wally Parks museum in California is also a history of drag racing, but it too is a capsule of the sport through the eyes of one man: Wally Parks, founder of the NHRA. Opened in 1998, it is a 28,500-square-foot shrine to the

The Don Garlits Museum of Drag Racing in Florida offers visitors a huge variety of historically significant race cars, including this bevy of early front-engined dragsters.

sport with a definite emphasis on the NHRA and its West Coast roots. The museum houses about 80 cars, mostly drag cars, with a mixture of street rods, dry lakes and oval track cars, all assembled in a user-friendly, modern-looking environment.

Some featured drag cars include Kenny Bernstein's 300-mph record breaker, one of Tommy Ivo's four-engined cars, and Top Eliminator cars from the NHRA's early years.

There are drag cars on display at many auto racing museums and halls of fame. Some non-automotive museums will have drag cars in their sports sections. For example, Don Garlits's Swamp Rat 30 is on display in the Smithsonian Institution in Washington, D.C.

Living Museums

In the past, old drag race cars usually ended up in the back of a shop or garage, just left to collect dust. Rarely were the cars disposed of, and a much higher percentage of them remain in existence compared to stock cars which usually were so banged up they had to be scrapped.

Luckily, these dusty drag cars and hot rods began to be unearthed by enthusiasts, and now many have been restored both mechanically and cosmetically. There are several nostalgia drag racing associations, featuring every type of car from stockers to fuel cars, and a lot of classes in between. And while fans take time to check out these historic vehicles in the pits, the memories really return when the cars are fired up and driven down the strip.

If the cars, no matter what class, are to compete, or at least make exhibition runs, they are brought up to date with the latest in safety measures. Drivers also must don the latest in personal safety equipment.

Along with seeing and hearing the vintage cars, quite often the original builders and racers will be at these nostalgia events, providing a real treat for those interested in the history of drag racing.

Sport Compact Racing

The vast majority of cars used in drag racing have traditionally been based on North American vehicles—and with V8 engines. But with changes in the global economy, along with the high prices for fuel and the trend toward smaller, more fuel-efficient autos, a new breed of racing has emerged where small, four-cylinder engined cars are the ride of choice over the big-engined muscle cars of the 1960s and early 1970s.

This class of racing falls under the generic title “Sport Compact.” The autos that race in this group are compact cars that have been improved and modified by either the car owner or the manufacturer to provide a high degree of performance. This modification process is also known as “tuning.” Sport Compact cars are often called “Imports” or “Tuners.”

In a scenario similar to the introduction of the small-block Chevrolet engine in the mid and late 1950s, the import scene really got underway with groups of West Coast enthusiasts and their modified Hondas. As other Japanese cars started to appear, as well as some U.S.-made cars such as Chevy’s Cavalier, so too did an aftermarket parts industry. The movement began to spread across North America, and just as it had with the original dragsters, organized competition developed. Major sanctioning bodies were established where car owners could compete in a safe, controlled environment with their modified street cars. Classes were also established for all-out drag race cars. While this may sound similar to the way traditional drag racing has grown, import events, in addition to featuring drag racing, also include other automotive competitions, such as car shows, drifting and burnout competitions.

The racing in Sport Compact, or import events, has been a logical extension of drag racing, and the next step in the development of the sport. Classes in the Sport Compact arena have taken modern automotive technology to its limits, and this is a big part of its appeal. In the spirit of hot rodding, the builders of Sport Compact race cars have shown much ingenuity and innovation by utilizing turbocharging, nitrous oxide, and electronic engine-management controls to extract huge horsepower figures from small four-cylinder engines, as well as developing and building transmissions and final drives to handle this horsepower through a front-wheel drive setup. While the cars may look different from those in “traditional” drag racing, the premise is the same: to be the quickest competitor down the strip.

One of the first sanctions to take on Sport Compact racing was NOPI (Number One Parts Inc). This Georgia-based auto parts distributor was founded in 1996. In 1997 NOPI Motorsports was formed to produce auto events, including car shows, drifting and drag racing. From 1997–2000 NOPI operated its drag racing events under “Drag Wars,” and in 2002 NOPI created the NDRA (the NOPI Drag Race

Gary Gardella in his Chevy Cobalt Pro FWD car at the NHRA Sony Sport Compact Nationals at Las Vegas in 2007. Note the slicks positioned on the front wheels of the car as opposed to the rear wheels, the custom in traditional drag racing.

Association. In 2008 the NDRA partnered with the NHRA to deliver Sport Compact events to a wider variety of venues. Unfortunately, NOPI had to suspend operations half way through the 2008 season due to financial constraints. It is yet to be seen if NOPI will support a full 2009 effort. Sport Compact has several other sanctions throughout North America, Europe and Australia.

Classes

While Sport Compact racing does not have the number of classes that traditional drag racing does, it has encompassed just about every car and engine combination for front-drive and small-displacement cars, including dragsters. As with traditional drag racing, there are classes for both the professional and amateur (Sportsman) racers.

Pro Classes

Extreme Dragster

A rail-designed dragster-based car with a minimum 225-inch wheelbase, using a rotary, four-, six- or eight-cylinder engine that may be supercharged, turbocharged or have nitrous oxide. These cars are capable of quarter-mile times in the mid-six-second range, with speeds over 200 mph.

Pro RWD (rear-wheel drive)

Limited to a maximum engine size of 530 cubic inches, this class features rear-drive import or domestic cars with tube chassis and engine modifications similar to the Dragster class. Cars are allowed to run turbochargers, superchargers and nitrous oxide. Car bodies may be mildly customized, including lowered rooflines, but must retain stock appearance and have two functioning doors. Wings and spoilers are allowed. These cars are capable of mid six-second passes at over 200 mph.

Pro FWD (front-wheel drive)

This is perhaps the most innovative class, with most of the technology developed in only the past few years. Compared to the decades of research and development that has gone into traditional rear-drive drag racing cars, efforts to produce successful front-drive drag cars is a relatively new field. Cars of this class are built with custom tube chassis rather than the stock uni-body setup, and are powered with high-horsepower race-only four-cylinder engines. Cars may be equipped with turbochargers and run methanol for fuel. Nitrous oxide is allowed. Car bodies may be modified, including chopped (lowered) rooflines, but must retain stock-looking appearance. These cars will turn times in the mid-seven-second range at speeds approaching 200 mph.

Pro Stock

A class similar to the established Pro Stock divisions of the NHRA and IHRA in terms of rules and regulations, these are the ultimate factory-based hot rods in front- or rear-wheel drive. The engines are naturally-aspirated only (no superchargers or turbochargers), but are highly modified internally with upgraded engine components such as pistons, valves and crankshafts. Vehicles must retain stock appearance, but can use weight-saving body panels and sit on a tube chassis with a maximum wheelbase of 105 inches.

Sportsman Classes

All-Motor

In this popular class the cars are not allowed superchargers, turbochargers or nitrous oxide. Engines are limited in size (usually under four liters) to four- and six-cylinders only. Front-drive four-cylinder cars with an engine of 2.20 liters or less can weigh as little as 1,625 pounds, while cars with an engine of up to 2.6 liters can weigh as much as 1,725 pounds. Front-drive cars with a six-cylinder engine of up to 3.2 liters maximum are allowed a minimum weight of 2,200 pounds. Rear-drive cars start with an 1,800-pound minimum weight for 2.0 liters to 1,875 pounds for a 2.6 liter engine displacement. Chassis and driveline components must retain factory placement, but may be strengthened, along with the addition of some aftermarket items, such as aftermarket control arms and traction devices on the front wheels and wheelie bars. Pickup and SUV bodies are not allowed in the division, and car roofs may not be chopped. Aftermarket body panels may be used.

Street

There are several "Street" classes in Sport Compact racing, all based on engine modifications. These cars race in street-legal guise, with full interiors, body panels and mufflers. Bodies must remain stock looking, tube chassis are not allowed, and while suspension components such as lower strut braces and sway bars may be added, few modifications other than strengthening are allowed. Some of the Street classes in NDRA competition include Unlimited Street, Turbo Street and Power Street.

This photo is a vivid example of the cooperation between law enforcement agencies and the racing world. It is hoped that through events such as this "Beat the Badge" session at US 131 Motorsports Park in Martin, Michigan, that racers will compete at the track and not on the street.

Street Racing

While there are many memorable scenes in George Lucas's movie *American Graffiti*, the film's climax is the big race between the local boy in his yellow Ford coupe and the outsider in his 1955 Chevy. The race is held outside of town, on a seldom-used country road, with most of the town's youth watching, and is a classic example of street racing.

It is also a classic example of an illegal and dangerous activity.

These impromptu contests of man (or woman) and machine have been a part of automotive society since the dawn of the car. And, unfortunately, it continues to this day.

Street racing has reached an unprecedented level and has become a large underground automotive activity, which is not only illegal, it is dangerous.

Most street racing is conducted in straight-line contests, sometimes impromptu, sometimes organized. Money can be involved between the contestants, as well as a car ownership, or "racing for pinks." Racing for a "pink slip" (the car ownership) means the loser hands over his or her car.

Today's street racing is comprised mostly of younger drivers, and import, or "tuner" cars. The philosophy is to race without getting caught by police, and online chat groups offer the best places and times to race, along with updates on police activity. Here are some examples:

"[XXX] County sheriffs have received a grant from the government and now have a C5 Corvette color is yellow it is an undercover police officer that follows people to the locations to race. They also have a Kawasaki Ninja and a white Ford Bronco and the cops wear civilian clothes and will arrest you if you race.....I went to [XXX] and like it a lot and got in a few runs before a cop came."

"All of you import racers need to chill out when you go to the locations in which you will be street racing! The disorganized type of racing you do cause unnecessary attention to be drawn to yourselves! Race two cars at a time, and line up two more after those two have "finished" and returned to their parking areas! This promotes safe racing and less attention drawn to the crowd! Thank you for keeping the rest of us safe and our sport of choice enjoyable!"

"More cars than you've ever seen. More cops than you've ever seen either. But, late in the night the cops slack off and you can get some good racing in. Imports, Domestics, Turbos, Nitrous, bring it all!"

One of the earliest mandates of the NHRA back in the 1950s was to work with civic and law enforcement groups to get racing off the street and onto racetracks. It took a lot of work, but the message did get out, and for the most part, racers did compete at tracks.

Today, the NHRA, as well as other racing sanctions, continue to fight against street racing, and offer a safe, legal and viable alternative.

Most law enforcement agencies have adopted a zero-tolerance policy towards street racing. Penalties for street racers range from heavy fines to auto confiscation to jail time. And the street racers themselves are not the only ones subject to penalties. Spectators at street races can also be fined just for watching.

But the police aren't just locking racers up; law enforcement agencies have also instituted programs to help eliminate street racing with special events at racetracks. Groups such as Beat the Heat and the Los Angeles County Sheriff's Department Race Team provide positive opportunities for police groups to interact with racers, where quite often racers will be pitted against actual police vehicles on the drag strip.

There are many other anti-street organizations such as Fast Police, Keeping Kids Alive and Street Scene Revolution's Evo Street Racers, all devoted to curtailing street racing. These groups, through their websites and group meetings work with street racers, schools, community groups and law enforcement.

The Evo Street Racer organization is involved with promoting a unique event known as "Beat the Badge," where groups of racers compete against law enforcement cars at drag strips. This interaction allows street racers to compete in a proper environment in an anti-street racing campaign and hopefully promote the evolution of street racers into track racers as part of its outreach program.

As with the NHRA's Safety Safari of 50 years ago, the present-day anti-street racing groups are delivering the same message: If you want to race, take it to the track.

It's that simple.

There's a fortune in wheels alone on these cars, crushed by authorities in California after their drivers were involved in street racing. Law agencies across North America are now playing hardball with zero-tolerance policies in an effort to stem illegal racing.

Drag Racing Around the World

While the most prevalent area of drag racing is based in North America, the sport is just as alive and contested just as fiercely in many parts of the globe, including Europe, the United Kingdom (U.K.) and Australia. There is even sanctioned drag racing in the city of Dubai in the United Arab Emirates.

Perhaps the best-known drag racing facility outside of North America is the Santa Pod facility in Northamptonshire in England. The "Pod" is a former World War II airbase, which began sanctioning racing in 1966. The name is a contraction from a California strip called Santa Ana coupled with the first three letters of the nearby town of Podington.

Racing from January through November, Santa Pod is home to the European Drag Racing Championships as well as featuring 50 events a year, running classes from nitro cars to Bracket racers.

Another popular track in the U.K. is the Shakespeare County Raceway in Warwickshire, England, which lays claim to the oldest strip in the country. This former Royal Air Force station held "sprint" acceleration races in 1959. The first major event held there was in September 1973, organized by the National Drag Racing Club (NDRC) and British Top Fuel star Clive Skilton, who began his racing career in the late 1960s with an E-Type Jaguar, and then an Allard dragster. Skilton went on to race Top Fuel and Funny Car, and also raced in the U.S. in the mid-to-late 1970s.

Another pioneer of drag racing in the U.K. was Sydney Allard, best known for a series of home-built cars using U.S. V8 power.

Early on, Allard sensed that drag racing was gaining in popularity in the U.K., and in 1960 imported a Chrysler Hemi engine complete with supercharger, built a dragster chassis for it, and tried to go racing. At the

The driver of this pristine Standard Vanguard saloon (sedan) lights up the rear slicks. Originally powered by a two-liter four-cylinder engine, the Vanguard is typical of the smaller British car modified for racing.

It may be smaller than a North American car, but this Anglia, complete with painted-on grille and headlights, gets the front wheels up at a European meet. While most foreign racers use domestic car bodies from their country, engines are usually of the North American V8 variety.

time, there was no sanctioning body in Britain, so he formed the British Drag Racing Association, brought in U.S. stars of the time such as Mickey Thompson, and worked in partnership with NHRA boss Wally Parks in presenting the Drag Fest events. (Allard also had successful outings at Le Mans and the Monte Carlo Rally.)

One of the most famous racers in Britain was rocket car driver Sammy Miller. Running one of these highly novel cars in 1975, Miller ran a 348-mph pass. He built and raced a Vega Funny Car with rocket power, traveled between the U.S. and Europe, and became a fan favorite. In 1979, he ran the first over-300-mph pass in Europe with a 307.6-mph posting at Santa Pod. In 1984, he posted a 3.58-second run at Santa Pod, which is still considered the quickest elapsed time in drag racing history.

In 1997, the FIA (Fédération Internationale de l'Automobile, a world motorsport governing body) and the UEM (Union of Eurpoean Motorcycling) began its sanction of the European Drag Racing Championship, based on NHRA rules. Aside from Santa Pod, the series travels to Finland, Sweden, Norway and Germany.

While the U.K. has a host of tracks and race series, there are several European countries that feature drag racing groups and tracks. The Scandinavian countries are well-versed in quarter-mile competition and the Swedish-based European Pro Mod Association races at events across the continent with a large group of the quick door slammers. Organized drag racing takes place in Italy, Germany, France and Holland, along with Lithuania, Poland and Malta.

The majority of the professional-class cars are imported from the U.S. or Canada, as are the more powerful drag racing engines, along with bodies and running gear. But there are cars that are interesting to North Americans, and it is not unusual to see a big-block Chevy engine stuffed into a Morris Minor or Ford Cortina, or watching a pair of highly modified Volvos pairing off for an elimination run.

Australia has embraced drag racing in a large and positive way, especially over the past two decades. This large continent-country showcases the sport with over a dozen tracks of both quarter- and eighth-mile lengths. The Queensland facility of Willowbank, opened in 1985, has become the predominant track in the country, and during its 10-month season will see 130,000 people through its gates. It also hosts the country's Winternationals and Australian Nationals under the sanctioning of the ANDRA (Australian National Drag Racing Association), formed in 1973 to provide drivers and teams with sanctioned competition.

In 1975, the ANDRA established the Australian Drag Race Series (ADRS) with national points championships in a wide variety of classes. Starting with regular heads-up racing, the ANDRA introduced various handicap classes in 1981. The vehicles are now divided into Professional and Sportsman categories, the Pro classes in heads-up racing, and the Sportsman classes with indexed competition along the lines of NHRA and IHRA racing. Although the Australian drag scene is a long way from North America, the cars and teams competing would provide strong competition. In June 2008, Phillip Read of Oakville, New South Wales (NSW), set a new ANDRA time record of 4.563-seconds in Top Fuel, Aaron Hambridge, from Spring Farm in NSW set a new Top Alcohol Dragster record with a 5.572-second pass, and a 5.907-second time was recorded in Top Doorslammer (Pro Mod) by Robin Judd of Attadale, Wales. These records were recorded at the Winternationals at the Willowbrook Raceway, and are certainly consistent with performances in North America.

Glossary

Aftermarket; Aftermarket parts The replacement parts and high-performance products market. Aftermarket parts are used to replace original equipment manufacturer (OEM) parts installed on the vehicle.

Ballast A controlled amount of weight, functionally or strategically positioned, used to help cars meet class weight requirements.

Blower Slang for a supercharger.

Blueprinting The meticulous matching to factory specifications of all parts and/or components; usually associated with engine building. Components are hand-fitted to the highest degree of the manufacturer's specifications.

Burn down When both cars at the starting line intentionally hesitate before moving into the "Stage" position, thereby delaying the start of the race. Drivers seek to gain a mental advantage by trying to break an opponent's concentration.

Burnout The act of spinning rear wheels (or front wheels with front-drive cars) in water at a high engine speed to heat and clean tire rubber prior to a run in order to increase traction.

Burned piston A condition when an engine cylinder runs "lean" (too much air in the air-to-fuel mixture), causing sufficient heat to burn a hole through the piston.

Burst panel A section of the front of a Funny Car body designed to relieve pressure and minimize the effects of a supercharger explosion. This panel is in front of the supercharger, held in with nylon bolts, and will blow out if an explosion occurs in an effort to minimize body damage.

Catch can A container used to catch liquid overflow, usually from the cooling system, preventing spillage on the race track. Also known as a catch tank.

Carburetion A system used to force the fuel/air mixture into an engine. Multiple carburetors have been used on race cars for many decades.

Chassis The frame of the race car. This is the foundation of a car, and everything is bolted to it.

Christmas Tree An electronic starting device incorporating calibrated LED (light emitting diode) lights displaying a visual countdown for each driver, activated by the official starter.

Chromoly A very strong type of steel tubing used to build the frames for many race cars. Also known as Chrome Moly. Both terms are short for Chromium Molybdenum steel.

Clutch can A car's bell housing, which is shaped like a bell and encases the clutch and flywheel at the rear of an engine.

Clutch dust Carbon dust created by the wearing of the surface of the clutch discs as they slide together during the clutch lockup process.

Clutch lockup The progression of clutch disc engagement controlled by an air-timer management system.

Competition license Drivers in sanctioned events must have a competition license. To obtain a license, drivers in pro categories must be at least 18 years old or turn 18 during their first season. Drivers from the professional categories must also pass a physical examination and complete a number of licensing runs under the observation of registered drivers and officials from the sanctioning body.

Deep staged A driver deep stages when, after staging, he or she rolls a few inches farther, causing the pre-stage light to go out. In that position, the driver is closer to the finish line but dangerously close to a foul start. Also known as "double bulbing."

Dial-in Term used by a Sportsman racer when he/she establishes his/her elapsed time down the strip. This time represents the fastest the racer will be allowed to travel down the track in competition. Any faster and a "break-out" occurs, which eliminates the racer.

Diaper A blanket made from ballistic and absorbent material (often Kevlar) that surrounds the oil pan and serves as a containment device if an engine explodes.

Displacement In an engine, the total volume of air/fuel mixture an engine is theoretically capable of drawing into all cylinders during one operating cycle.

Downforce Vertical aerodynamic pressure, which aids a race car in achieving traction. Various wings, spoilers and body panels are used to create downforce.

Chute Short for parachute or dragchute, and used to assist high-speed braking.

CID Cubic inch displacement. The physical size of a cylinder in an engine, determined by the diameter of the bore (cylinder or hole) and multiplied by the stroke (the length the piston travels in the bore).

Dropped cylinder When a cylinder becomes too rich (too much fuel in the air-to-fuel mixture), preventing the engine's spark plug(s) from firing.

Dynomometer A stationary device used by engine builders that measures an engine's torque to determine horsepower.

ET; Elapsed time The total time it takes to go from starting line to finish line.

Eliminations When two cars race, the result is one winner and one loser. Only the winner continues on to race against another competitor in tournament-style competition.

Fire bottle A slang term for a fire extinguisher. This is mounted in various positions depending on the category of race car, and contains a fire retardant, which can be activated by the driver when needed. Some systems are automatic.

Flash shield A device to encompass the air inlet of a carburetor's sides, top and rear, protecting the driver in case of engine backfire.

Foul start When a car leaves the starting line before the green-light starting signal. Also known as a red light.

Fuel check A tech station at the racetrack used to chemically analyze fuels to ensure they are within the limits allowed for that particular class.

Fuel injection A system that delivers fuel under pressure into an engine's combustion chamber or air flow prior to entering the chamber. This system replaces conventional carburetion.

Gilmer belt A toothed or splined drive belt used with matching pulley. It is generally a non-slip drive belt.

Halon A special Freon-based fire extinguisher gas.

HANS device This Head and Neck Safety restraint device is positioned on a driver's shoulders, and connected to the back of his or her helmet to limit movement of the head and neck during a crash.

Headers A fine-tuned exhaust system that routes exhaust from the engine. This system replaces conventional street car exhaust manifolds.

Heads-up Term used to describe one-on-one racing with no handicaps for either driver.

Hemi An engine with a combustion chamber resembling a hemisphere or round ball cut in half. This configuration allows vastly improved movement of intake and exhaust gases through the engine's valve components.

Holeshot A starting-line advantage achieved by the quicker-reacting driver.

Horsepower Numeric value given to the amount of power produced by an engine.

Hotchkiss-type driveline An open or exposed driveshaft assembly. A type of rear suspension in which the springs absorb the rear-end torque.

Hydraulic A condition when an engine cylinder fills with too much fuel, prohibiting compression by the cylinder, causing a mechanical malfunction.

Index The elapsed time assigned by a sanction to allow various classes to race together with an equitable handicap starting system. This system allows slower and faster cars to compete together, with the slower car leaving the line before the faster car.

Inline An engine configuration that has its cylinders in a single row, or valve stems in a single row. As opposed to a "V" configured engine, which has an equal number of cylinders on each side of the engine, or "V."

Interval timers Part of a secondary timing system that records elapsed times, primarily for the racers' benefit, at 60, 330, 660, and 1,000 feet. This data is used to determine a variety of engine and drivetrain setups.

Lexan The trade name of a General Electric product of a durable thermal resistant plastic material which is used where transparent material is required (face plates, goggles, windows, etc.).

Line-loc This is a device that locks the front brakes to allow the car to do a burnout, as well as remain still on the starting line prior to the launch of a run.

Magnaflux The process of using a special electro-magnet and magnetic powder to detect cracks in iron that may be invisible to the naked eye.

Mopar Mopar is short for MOtor PARts, the service and parts division of Chrysler. Any vehicle produced in any era by Chrysler can be termed a "Mopar."

Nitromethane An organic compound used as a fuel for drag racing. It is the result of a chemical reaction between nitric acid and propane. Also known as "nitro" or "fuel."

Nomex The trade name of a DuPont product of a fire-resistant fiber used in the manufacture of fabric for protective clothing.

Onboard data recorder An electronic recording device that provides specific performance data following a run. Teams use this information to read a car's performance.

Pedaling An action where a driver lifts off the throttle, then gets back on it again in an attempt to regain traction with the rear tires.

Pilot chute A spring-loaded device that pulls the main braking parachute from its pack during the slow down of a run.

Port The opening in an engine where the valve operates and through which the air-fuel mixture or exhaust passes.

Pre-staged When a driver is approximately seven inches behind the starting line and the small yellow light atop his or her side of the Christmas Tree is illuminated. This is the first step in getting ready to race. The pre-stage light is the top light on the Christmas Tree.

Protest A complaint filed against a competitor and investigated by officials. In most cases, the racer filing the complaint must pay a pre-determined fee to the sanction for each alleged violation, which goes toward funding the investigation.

Pro Tree Used in the Top Fuel, Funny Car, Pro Stock, Pro Modified and Pro Stock Motorcycle classes that feature heads-up competition. All three amber lights on the Christmas Tree flash simultaneously, followed four-tenths of a second later by the green starting light. A perfect reaction time on a Pro Tree is .000.

RPM The measurement of engine revolutions per minute.

Reaction time The time it takes a driver to react to the green starting light on the Christmas Tree, measured in thousandths of a second. The reaction-time counter begins when the last amber light flashes on the tree and stops when the vehicle clears the staged beam. This applies to both Pro and Sportsman classes.

Redline The actual red indicator line used on an engine tachometer to warn the driver of maximum engine revolutions.

Roll cage A reinforced steel compartment that encloses the driver in the car.

Rollout The measurement of one complete revolution of a tire, measured in inches. Rollout equals 3.14 times diameter.

Seating the clutch The process of loading the clutch pack to allow the clutch discs and floaters to properly align with each other before a run.

Shoulder harness An upper-torso restraint device. Some harnesses have five straps which buckle together, some have seven straps.

Sixty-foot time The time it takes a vehicle to cover the first 60 feet of the racetrack. It is the most accurate measure of the launch from the starting line which, in most cases, determines how quick the rest of the run will be, as long as the car continues a full run.

Slider clutch A multi-disc clutch designed to slip until the car reaches a predetermined engine speed. This helps to decrease the shock load to the drive wheels.

Speed trap The final 66 feet of the track before the finish line, where top speed is recorded.

Spoiler An aerodynamic device attached directly to the vehicle's body (usually to the rear deck lid), which allows the airflow to pass only over the top of the device. A spoiler is used to create downforce, aiding in traction and stability.

Spool A one-piece ring gear carrier or housing, which allows engine power to be applied equally to both rear tires, aiding in better traction.

Staged A competitor is staged when the front wheels of the car are on the starting line and the small yellow light below the pre-staged light on his or her side of the Christmas Tree is illuminated. Once a driver is staged, the calibrated countdown of the amber lights leading to the green starting light may begin at any time (when the starter begins the sequence).

Staging lane The area of a race facility that leads to the racing surface. This is where cars are lined up and/or paired before making a run. Cars are called to the lanes from their pit areas well in advance of the actual race.

Stick A manual transmission requiring a clutch and manual gear changes. Also known as a standard transmission.

Stock As originally produced by the original equipment manufacturer (OEM). No performance modifications or enhancements may be present on the car or any component.

Street equipment Equipment generally required by law or needed for legal street operation such as license plates, windshield wipers, horns and lights.

Subframe Used in the construction of unibody vehicles when a full front-to-rear frame is not present. The body is an integral part of the car's chassis structure.

Supercharger A crank-driven air/fuel compressor situated on top of an engine. This device raises atmospheric pressure in an engine, resulting in added horsepower. It is also known as a "blower" or "huffer."

Teardown Physical inspection by sanctioning body technical staff to ensure that cars meet class specifications. Teardowns are done on a random basis during eliminations, usually after a run.

Terminal speed Maximum or top speed at the finish line.

Throttle stop A device that limits the engine speed during a burnout or a run.

Throttle travel The distance between the pedal sitting at engine idle in relation to maximum engine speed, or full throttle. The shorter the throttle travel, the quicker a car can get to full speed.

Torque The measure of the force applied to an object to produce rotational motion. It is the twisting or turning capability of an engine, the application of which is to provide power to the drive wheels.

Traction bars A device attached to the rear axle of a car to control rear-end torque and to stabilize suspension components.

Transmission blanket A flexible wrap intended to contain parts in case of transmission disintegration.

Tree See Christmas Tree.

Wedge An engine with a combustion chamber resembling a wedge in shape. It is not as efficient as a hemispherical combustion chamber (Hemi).

Weight transfer A critical step in obtaining traction in drag racing. Vehicles are set up to provide a desired weight transfer to rear wheels. When the vehicle accelerates, the front wheels lift and weight shifts to the rear wheels, making the tires less likely to spin.

Wheelie bars Used to prevent excessive front-wheel lift. A bar or bars with small wheels are attached to the car's rear.

Wing An aerodynamic device mounted in such a way that air flow passes over and under the device. It is used to create downforce. Also known as an airfoil.

Acknowledgments

This book has been a labor of love for me, and my labors have been enhanced by several people who have gone above and beyond to help make it a success.

First, I want to thank Rob Potter, who has been on this ride with me since the beginning. Rob has a vast knowledge of the sport and has few peers in this regard, along with providing invaluable insight, and photos both old and new, he has provided old programs, memorabilia and press materials.

I'd also like to thank Valerie Potter, whose illustrations are peppered throughout the book. They are a great contribution.

Others I wish to thank include Ross Martin, who allowed me to delve into his collection of old photos, and Bruce Biegler for his dramatic photography. Betsy and Fred Smith imparted insight into the sport. Bruce Mehlenbacher was instrumental in guiding me in the right direction for materials and contact information, as was Kathy Fisher, a great hot-rodder who also opened some doors for me.

A tip of the hat goes to Jim Salemi, who sat me down and talked for hours about the inner workings of the popular Pro Modified class. And thanks to Todd Paton who patiently answered my questions about Top Fuel and Funny Cars.

And to my editor, Steve Cameron, who kept me from red-lighting several times, copyeditor Sandra Manley and designer Gareth Lind, whose dynamic talents graphically brought this book to life.

Disclaimer

While researching this book it became apparent that there has been little documentation on the history of the sport. Many avenues were explored in search of the truth—if there are any discrepancies regarding factual evidence, my apologies.

You will not find any motorcycle or snowmobile drag racing in this book. While these are popular in some quarters, it was decided not to include them here. Also, the personalities profiled were chosen for their accomplishments both on and off the track, as well as their influence on the sport in general. I know I only scratched the surface...

—Tim Miller

Photo Credits

The publisher is grateful for all photographic contributions. Every effort has been made to determine the sources and give proper credit. Any oversight or error is unintentional.

Icon Spots Media
David Allio/Icon SMI 2, 6, 8, 62, 63, 73L, 81, 91, 94, 96, 97, 109, 112, 113, 114, 119, 120, 122, 124, 127, 133, 136, 139, 142, 145, 146, 147, 149, 151, 178, 198; Walter G. Arce/ASP Inc/Icon SMI 128; Jeffrey Corder/Icon SMI 61, 123, 129; David J. Griffin/Icon SMI 66, 111; Timothy L. Hale/ZUMA Press/Icon 115, 134, 144, 195; Mike McKinney/Icon SMI 64R; Sam Morris/Icon SMI 5; Doug Murray/Icon SMI 20, 98; John Pyle/Icon SMI 104, 132; Dave Smith/Icon SMI 141; Les Welch/Icon SMI 26, 121, 138, 148, 152; Chris Williams/Icon SMI 42, 64L, 70, 135, 143

Getty Images
Ralph Crane/Time Life Pictures/Getty Images 12; Efield/Getty Images 29; Jon Ferrey/Allsport 69; Allan Grant/Time Life Pictures/Getty Images 52; Ken Levine/Getty Images 68; Mike Powell/Allsport 23; RacingOne/Getty Images 55; Lara Jo Regan/Liaison 108; Hank Walker/Time Life Pictures/Getty Images 74

Additional Photographers
Associated Press/Nick Ut 201
Auto Imagery Inc./autoimagery.com 154
Bruce Biegler 79, 80, 84, 87, 107, 118, 125, 126, 137, 140
Charles Gilchrist 14, 21, 24, 36, 37, 38, 40, 166, 170, 174, 175, 176, 177, 180, 186
Ian Rae 193, 202
IHRA Print Room 131
Joe Barrett 102
Kathy Fisher 117, 156
Patrik Jacobsson 203
Rich Carlson Photo 50
Rob Potter Photography 43, 57, 165
Roger Richards Photography 82, 116
Tim Miller 86, 87, 100
William Waters 92, 95

Private Collections
Bristol Dragway 56
Dodge Division of Chrysler LLC 46, 189
Don Douglas 15
Don Garlits Museum Photos 33, 197
Donovan Engineering Corporation 45, 47
Evo Street Racers 200
Frank Hawley's Drag Racing School 194
General Motors Corp. Used with permission, GM Media Archives 30
IHRA 25, 73R, 78 130
Keith Black Racing 48
Lyndy Thompson 31
Motorsports Hall of Fame of America 169
National DRAGSTER/NHRA Publications 53
Original Photography by Ray Mann – quartermile-stones.com Archive 35, 41, 158, 161, 163, 168, 187, 190
Rob Potter 17, 22, 23, 39, 59, 164, 182, 184, 185
Ross Martin 16, 159
Tim Miller 153, 157
Tommy Ivo 11, 18, 32, 171, 172

Page 13: *Hot Rod Magazine* cover © Source Interlink Magazines, LLC

Index